The Ultimate Player's Guide to

SKYLANDERS
TRAP TEAM

Hayley Camille

que®

800 East 96th Street,
Indianapolis, Indiana 46240 USA

The Ultimate Player's Guide to Skylanders Trap Team

Copyright © 2016 by Pearson Education

ISBN-13: 978-0-7897-5546-9
ISBN-10: 0-7897-5546-7

Library of Congress Control Number: 2015947384

Printed in the United States of America

First Printing: October 2015

Trademarks

Warning and Disclaimer

Special Sales

For information about buying this title in bulk quantities, or for special sales opportunities (which may include electronic versions; custom cover designs; and content particular to your business, training goals, marketing focus, or branding interests), please contact our corporate sales department at corpsales@pearsoned.com or (800) 382-3419.

For government sales inquiries, please contact govermentsales@pearsoned.com.

For questions about sales outside the U.S., please contact international@pearsoned.com.

Editor-in-Chief
Greg Wiegand

Executive Editor
Rick Kughen

Development Editor
Todd Brakke

Managing Editor
Kristy Hart

Project Editor
Elaine Wiley

Copy Editor
Bart Reed

Indexer
Ken Johnson

Proofreader
Sarah Kearns

Technical Editor
James Floyd Kelly

Publishing Coordinator
Kristen Watterson

Book Designer
Mark Shirar

Senior Compositor
Gloria Schurick

Contents at a Glance

Table of Contents

About the Author

Hayley Camille is a dedicated writer, working from Australia. Her previous nonfiction work includes a complete published revision, as ghostwriter, of the bestselling *The Ultimate Player's Guide to Minecraft, PlayStation Edition*, by Stephen O'Brien for Que Publishing, to cater to a PlayStation gaming audience. She has also ghostwritten multiple new chapters for Que's *Advanced Minecraft Strategy Guide*.

Hayley has a strong interest in computers and gaming. Her husband is a software engineer, and together they have collaborated on numerous innovative software projects, including touchscreen and interactive games. With two young sons that are highly tech-savvy and mad about the Skylanders and Minecraft games, she is in a unique position to not only know the games well, but also to write from the different perspectives of what's important to a child gamer as the target audience, a parent-facilitator, as well as a strategy-focused teen forum-player.

Hayley's short story "Avon Calling!" was nominated for an Aurealis Award, Australia's premier speculative fiction awards, after being published in the Neo-Pulp anthology "This Mutant Life" (Kalamity Press, 2013). The feature-film screenplay has been subsequently shortlisted as a top 10% semifinalist for the International ScreenCraft Fellowship in 2014 (based in Los Angeles, California). She is currently adapting this screenplay into a novel.

Hayley holds university degrees in evolutionary biology and anthropology, including post-graduate molecular archaeology—the study of ancient residues (blood/DNA/plant) on prehistoric artifacts—which forms the underlying scientific theory behind her recently finished adult fiction novel *Human*. This is the first book in 'The Chronicles of Ivy Carter' series, which follows the adventures of an archaeologist who travels through time, uprooting human prehistory while baring the ultimate question, "How do you truly define humanity?".

Hayley is passionate about animal welfare, jazz, all things vintage, and dinosaurs, and can be found haunting social media and her blog at www.hayleycamille.com.

Dedication

This book is dedicated to Finn and Orrin, who shared their epic Skylander skills and knowledge with me and are true Skylander heroes. It is also dedicated to Eric, a little Skylander legend who got the ball rolling with his great enthusiasm and fantastic Skylander pajamas!

Acknowledgments

Writing this book was a great adventure for me—a whirlwind of late nights gaming, researching, and immersing myself in the Skylander Universe and especially, a wonderful opportunity to spend time with my little boys, Finn and Orrin, as we battled Trolls together. However, it could never have happened without the assistance of some very talented people, to whom I am truly grateful.

Firstly, to Stephen O'Brien for giving me the chance to learn from and contribute to his incredible work and for being an inspiration and friend to myself and Alex for many years. A huge thank you must go to Rick Kughen for his kind and thoughtful guidance on this project, from its inspired beginnings sharing the enthusiasm of kids for the Skylanders phenomenon, to his good humor and patience with me as it progressed to completion. The Que publishing and editorial team of Todd, Jim, Bart, Elaine, Kristen, Greg, Kristy, Mark, Gloria, Sarah, and many others have put in a great deal of time to help make this book become the best it can be, and I am truly thankful to each of you for your time, suggestions, and kind assistance.

To my family and friends who offered support, coffee, and encouragement along the way, thank you so much. Extra hugs go to Penny, Rob, Clayton, Jasmine, Kellie, Kathryn, Ben, Linda, Sian, and Teresa.

Lastly, the biggest thank you and hug goes to my husband Alex, who is a constant pillar of encouragement, wisdom, and creative genius to me, and who has never once complained that my legions of Skylander toys have taken over our home.

We Want to Hear from You!

As the reader of this book, *you* are our most important critic and commentator. We value your opinion and want to know what we're doing right, what we could do better, what areas you'd like to see us publish in, and any other words of wisdom you're willing to pass our way.

We welcome your comments. You can email or write to let us know what you did or didn't like about this book—as well as what we can do to make our books better.

Please note that we cannot help you with technical problems related to the topic of this book.

When you write, please be sure to include this book's title and author as well as your name and email address. We will carefully review your comments and share them with the author and editors who worked on the book.

Email: feedback@quepublishing.com

Mail: Que Publishing
         ATTN: Reader Feedback
         800 East 96th Street
         Indianapolis, IN 46240 USA

Reader Services

Visit our website and register this book at quepublishing.com/register for convenient access to any updates, downloads, or errata that might be available for this book.

Introduction

Are you ready to lead the Skylanders on their greatest adventure yet?

Portal Masters, Ready!

On the magical floating islands of Skylands, an epic adventure awaits you.

This is a book for fans of those funny, freaky, and fun characters known as Skylanders and their absurdly evil (and very cranky!) nemesis, Kaos.

Skylanders is one of the biggest "toys to life" games ever created and has all the family-friendly features we love. The newest edition of the game, *Skylanders Trap Team*, published by Activision, is no exception. Whether you're an old hat at the story challenges, or a newbie keen to throw yourself into the fray, this book will guide you on your journey.

Included in this guide are cheats for unlocking those tricky Lock Puzzles, a complete gameplay walkthrough, and tips on the best route to take throughout story chapters to make sure you don't miss any hidden collectibles. There are hints on what to expect in Doom Challenges and Arena Battles and advice on ways to combat even the most difficult villain attacks.

What Secrets Will You Uncover?

The first couple chapters give you some background on *Skylanders Trap Team*—what to expect of your new game, how to play, where to find important (non-console-specific) features of your game, and how to use them. The Villain Vault and Elemental Symbols are explained, and you'll find a comprehensive list of all hats and trinkets, their locations, and what they can be used for.

You'll meet all of the new Trap Team characters in Chapter 3, "Meet the Skylanders," including their biographies, attack moves, speed and strength stats, Soul Gem abilities, upgrade paths, and Wow Pows.

The introduction of trappable villains is the newest achievement in the Skylanders adventure, and an important part of the Trap Team experience. Chapter 4, "Vile Villains," brings the bad guys into focus, with some background on where they are hiding in the story chapters, how best to capture them, and what their special skills and attack moves are. Remember, once you capture a villain in a trap, they're under your complete control for the remainder of the game (bwahaha!).

Chapter 5, "Collectibles," is all about uncovering secrets—use this location guide to aid a treasure hunt of collectibles hidden within each story chapter and around Skylands Academy. Soul Gems, Story Scrolls, Legendary Treasure, Winged Sapphires, and Treasure Chests are all covered, as well as general info about trophies and achievements you can earn along the way.

Fancy a game of Skystones Smash? Chapter 6, "Learn to Play Skystones Smash," clues you in on how to beat your opponent. Then we'll take a walk through Skylands Academy in Chapter 7, "Skylander Academy," to discover the many different rooms and how to make the most of them. Get your dancing shoes on for Skaletone Showdown with Crossbones the skeleton and prepare to bounce your way through gold-filled mini-games in the Academy.

When you're ready to get your game on, Chapter 8, "Battle for Skylands!," and Chapter 9, "Expand Your Adventure," have got you covered! A complete walkthrough of each story chapter as well as the expansion packs (yes, all four!) includes how to manage in-game puzzles, where to find Villain Quests, battle tactics and hidden collectibles, as well the best path through to make sure you never miss a step.

Want to take your game further? Get the inside scoop on Kaos Doom Challenges and Brock's Arena Rumbles in Chapter 10, "Kaos Doom Challenges," and Chapter 11, "Brock's Arena Challenges," including walkthroughs on which villains will attack, battle strategies, and how to avoid traps! If you're super-stuck on a Lock Puzzle, flip to the back of the book to find cheats in the appendix (but not until you've tried to solve it yourself first!). Celebrate all of your game achievements with Chapter 12, "The Sky's the Limit!", and discover more ways to explore and enjoy Skylanders: Trap Team each time you play.

Share Your Sky-deas!

As an avid Skylander fan, I would love your feedback and ideas on ways to expand, improve, and get more out of the Skylanders games, as well as what you'd like included in future Skylander guides. Feel free to contact me any time for a chat or to share your favorite Skylander experiences.

For more Skylander fun, you can find me haunting YouTube on my Skylanders Gameplay channel **SkyPandaAus** (www.youtube.com/SkyPandaAus). Drop by to watch some gameplay walkthroughs, enter giveaways, meet Skylanders characters in unboxing vids, and find out what's new in Skylands!

If you'd like to contact me personally, send an email to SkyPanda@hayley camille.com. I can't promise that I'll be able to reply to every message, but I'll definitely read each email and try to get back to you!

Stay tuned for the next edition of this guide, *The Ultimate Guide to Skylanders: SuperChargers (Unofficial Guide)*, soon after the new game is released.

Happy Skylanding!

**Hayley Camille
(aka SkyPanda)**

Prison Breakout!

Greetings Portal Master!

A great quest is upon you if you dare to accept it! You are about to enter the magical realm of Skylands, a world of bravery and adventure bursting with bizarre creatures and incredible sights. Around every corner you'll find new places to explore, rewards to uncover, and new friends to meet—but first, there's work to do! As you can see from Figure 1.1, all is not right in this once-peaceful realm....

FIGURE 1.1 Skylands is under attack by Kaos and the evil Doom Raiders! The Skylanders are counting on you, as the new Portal Master, to save the day!

The evil Portal Master Kaos has been up to his old tricks again, causing havoc and reigning terror among the inhabitants of Skylands. He has uncovered the location of Cloudcracker Prison, the most top-secret, high-security jail in all of Skylands and home to the most infamous band of troublemakers the world had ever seen—the Doom Raiders! Planning to enlist their help to make him the most terrible ruler that Skylands has ever seen, Kaos blew apart the Traptanium crystal walls that held them secure. What a nightmare! Cloudcracker Prison was shattered into a million pieces and the evil Doom Raiders, ruled over by the cruel Golden Queen, have run free!

The brave team of heroes that protect Skylands from Darkness, the Skylanders, created the Trap Team, a special force that rushed in to save the day. But Kaos was one step ahead! He used his Dark Elemental Power to banish the Trap Team to Earth, transforming them into small toys as they fell. The splintered Traptanium shards of Cloudcracker Prison fell with them, forming crystal traps with the power to recapture the dastardly villains that broke free.

It is now your duty, as the new Portal Master, to bring the Trap Team back to life through the Traptanium Portal to serve Skylands once more! With your courage and skill, you can help them wield their Traptanium weapons to end the destruction that threatens Skylands.

It's time to prepare for the ultimate adventure—Skylands is counting on you, Portal Master!

Ready, Set, Go!

Playing *Skylanders Trap Team* can be as simple as buying a starter pack for your console or device and playing through to the end with it, or as expansive as you like by collecting all of the adventure packs, Skylander character toys, traps, and accessories (see Figure 2.1). There's a treasure trove of fun within the game itself, including mini-puzzles, arena and doom challenges, villains to capture, trinkets and achievements to collect, and new locations to explore. Let's begin by looking at how to get started and what to expect from your new *Skylanders Trap Team* game.

FIGURE 2.1 Expand your Skylanders collection or focus on your favorites—from a basic starter pack to an epic collection of character toys, traps, and gear, there's always an adventure waiting for you in Skylands!

Where You Can Play

Skylanders Trap Team is compatible with PlayStation 4, Xbox One, Wii U, and Nintendo 3DS (all developed by Beenox), as well as PlayStation 3, Xbox 360, and Wii (developed by Toys for Bob). There's even a tablet edition (developed by Vicarious Visions). The Nintendo 3DS version has different features and a unique storyline compared to the other platforms and is not covered in this book.

Two versions of the Starter Pack are compatible with most consoles: the Standard Starter Pack and the Dark Edition Starter Pack. The Standard Starter Pack for tablet devices is compatible with Android tablets, Apple iPad, and Amazon Fire devices, and a separate Starter Pack is available for the Nintendo 3DS. The following sections detail what you receive with each pack.

CONSOLE STARTER PACK (PS3/PS4, XBOX 360/XBOX ONE, WII/WII U)

- ✪ *Skylanders Trap Team* game, specific to your console
- ✪ Traptanium Portal
- ✪ Snap Shot and Food Fight Skylander figures
- ✪ Water and Life Traps
- ✪ Trap collection tray
- ✪ Two character trading cards, stickers, and toy codes
- ✪ Trap Team character poster

CONSOLE DARK EDITION STARTER PACK (PS3/PS4, XBOX 360/XBOX ONE, WII/WII U)

- *Skylanders Trap Team* game, specific to your console
- Traptanium Portal
- Dark Edition Snap Shot, Dark Edition Wildfire, and Dark Edition Food Fight Skylander Figures
- Water, Life, and the Ultimate Kaos Traps
- Dark Edition Trap collection tray
- Three character trading cards, stickers, and toy codes
- Trap Team character poster (double-sided)

TABLET STARTER PACK (APPLE IPAD, ANDROID, AMAZON FIRE DEVICES)

- *Skylanders Trap Team* game, specifically for tablets
- Wireless Traptanium Portal
- Wireless game controller
- Snap Shot and Food Fight Skylander figures
- Water and Life Traps
- Trap collection tray
- Two character trading cards, stickers, and toy codes
- Trap Team character poster

NINTENDO 3DS STARTER PACK

- ✪ *Skylanders Trap Team* game, specifically for Nintendo 3DS
- ✪ Traptanium Portal
- ✪ Wireless game controller
- ✪ Gusto and Barkley Skylander figures
- ✪ Two character trading cards, stickers, and toy codes
- ✪ Trap Team character poster

The Best Starter Pack for You

The Dark Edition Starter Pack (RRP $100), shown in Figure 2.2, contains three Special Edition Skylanders that are unavailable for individual purchase. Although the Standard Edition Food Fight and Snap Shot are also unavailable for individual purchase (Wildfire is sold separately), they are far more likely to be accessible as re-sale purchases online due to the much higher quantity of Standard Starter Packs (RRP $75) produced. The Dark Edition Starter Pack (also known as the Collector's Edition Starter Pack), is typically more limited in production, so the Dark Edition variants (Dark Snap Shot, Dark Food Fight, and bonus Dark Wildfire), will be harder to source independently.

Similarly, the Ultimate Kaos Trap is exclusive to the Dark Edition Starter Pack and features a larger and uniquely decorated form compared to the Standard Kaos trap (although both work the same).

Both the Standard and Dark Editions allow you to complete the game, so the main point of difference is in the collectability of the characters and the Ultimate Kaos Trap in the Dark Edition. Essentially, for the additional expense (an extra $25) for the Dark Edition Starter Pack, you will receive the Dark Wildfire and Ultimate Kaos Trap, valued at approximately $21. The value add in bonus toys is therefore close to the extra cost, but the exclusivity of these toys gives them a higher intrinsic value long-term.

FIGURE 2.2   The characters included in the Dark Edition Starter Pack (left-side collection) are part of a limited production run so they may be a little harder to source and more costly to buy as resale than the Standard Starter Pack characters (right-side collection). The Dark Edition Starter Pack also comes with an Ultimate Kaos Trap.

In addition to the Standard and Dark Starter Packs, some retailers also offer unique Skylander packs. The Super Bundle Pack available from Costco includes seven Skylander characters (character toys are chosen randomly and vary per pack) and three traps. Other retailers may offer bonus pre-order incentives including traps with preloaded in-game variants inside. You can find more information on current special offers and bonus packs from individual retailers.

What You Need to Play

You'll find a huge assortment of character toys, traps, and Special Edition items available to buy from retailers, so if you're a collector, you have endless opportunity to expand and enhance your game (see Figure 2.3). However, you don't need every Skylander and trap to complete the main story chapters and defeat Kaos at the end. You can actually play the game through with just the Starter Pack on its own, which is a fantastic way to get started in the Skylanders Universe.

FIGURE 2.3 With over 60 new character toys to collect, and more than 50 translucent traps for your new Traptanium Portal, it's time to hunt some villains!

However, certain areas of the game are only accessible to Trap Masters and villains. These areas may contain treasures or collectibles that, along with Villain Quests, allow you to complete 100% of the game. Elemental Gates can be found in each chapter of the story and can only be opened by a Trap Master of the same element. To access the areas and collectibles behind these gates, you'll need one Trap Master belonging to each of the ten elements, in addition to your Starter Pack.

Villain Quests are another great way to collect trinkets and treasure and to explore new areas as well as upgrade your villain to access higher stats. To trap the villains you defeat and then play as them and complete their Villain Quests or unlock a villain treasure stash, you also need an Element Trap for each of the ten elements, as well as a Kaos Trap to capture Kaos at the end of the game. With a single trap for each element, you will be able to trap all the villains in-game and hold them in the Villain Vault. Keep in mind that if you only own one trap per element, you need to plan ahead a bit more. Instead of choosing a villain for its specific skillset, you may need to transfer any required villains into them for an upcoming Villain Quest before you start each new chapter instead. Also keep in mind, if you capture a new villain in your elemental trap during the chapter, it will replace the existing trapped villain you brought along for that element.

How the Game Works

All character toys are compatible across all consoles, which opens the doors to cooperative gaming with your friends no matter what game console they have! Each character toy is embedded with an RFID (radio frequency identification) card that contains the data for that particular character. This information connects to the card reader inside the Traptanium Portal, which interprets and displays the information (your character) onscreen within the game. This RFID data constantly updates as you play, and new information (such as purchased upgrades) is resaved to the figurine as you play.

Storing the character data inside the toy means it is completely transferrable across Trap Team games—you can use your figurines on any Trap Team portal (swapping across different platforms or taking them to a friend's house to play). The character will always retain his or her level, hats and trinkets, gold coins collected, powers and upgrades, nicknames, and experience points. So you can constantly improve your Skylanders' stats, no matter where you are playing.

You can add a second player at any point in the game by putting another character toy on the portal and connecting a second controller to your game console. The Trap Team Traptanium Portal is compatible with all of the 175 previously released Skylander figures, magic toys, and location toys, which is awesome news if you already have a collection from *Giants*, *Spyro's Adventure*, or *Swap Force* (see Figure 2.4). This is a one-way journey, though—you can't use your new Trap Team character toys on an older version portal because the previous portals can't read them. However, there are a couple of exceptions to this. Firstly, re-posed Trap Team characters that originated in an earlier version of the Skylanders *are* backward-compatible (for example, the Hog Wild Fryno character toy from *Trap Team* will appear as standard Fryno in your *Swap Force* game, where the character was introduced).

FIGURE 2.4 Some characters are represented in multiple games as re-posed figures with each version. From left to right, Gill Grunt (Series 1) from Spyro's Adventure, Anchor's Away Gill Grunt (Series 3) from Swap Force, Tidal Wave Gill Grunt (Series 4) from Trap Team, and Eon's Elite Gill Grunt (far right), a Special Edition figure.

The various Gill Grunt figures will work in all four games as the character was introduced in the first game, Spyro's Adventure. The new Mini Skylander, Gill Runt, will only work in Trap Team; however, its predecessor "Sidekick Gill Runt" (not pictured) will work in all games. Eon's Elite Gill Grunt works in all Skylanders games.

Secondly, although your Trap Team Mini characters won't work in *Spyro's Adventure*, *Giants*, or *Swap Force*, their earlier counterparts (the "Sidekicks") will function in *Trap Team* in the same way the Minis do. So no need to double up on buying the little guys if you already have them (unless you're a collector!).

If you purchase second-hand characters online, you may need to remove the information stored on them from previous use. You can choose to reset the level and stats back to standard settings for a pre-loved character in the Manage settings of the Skylander info menu.

The Skylands Honor Roll

On your Skylanders journey, you're likely to meet all manner of crazy critters and monstrous minions, but none more important than the heroes (and bad guys!) listed in the following sections. Let's take some time to get to know your new friends—remember, the inhabitants of Skylands are counting on you!

MASTER EON

For a very long time, Master Eon was not only leader of the Skylanders, but the greatest Portal Master who had ever lived (see Figure 2.5). There is nothing about Skylands that Eon doesn't know. As a child working in the kitchens of Portal Master Nattybumpo, Eon once magically teleported his master away, spiraling off into the Dirt Seas! When Nattybumpo recovered from shock (and made his way home!), he realized Eon's potential and began his training as an apprentice.

FIGURE 2.5   Master Eon, the greatest Portal Master who ever lived, will oversee your journey throughout Skylands.

Over the years, as the force of Darkness grew ever stronger in Skylands, Master Eon recognized the need to gather a special team of heroes that could protect its Core of Light, an ancient machine that keeps the Darkness at bay. He has always believed in the courage and abilities of his Skylanders, many of whom he chose himself for their unique skills.

One day while patrolling with his Skylander Team, the evil Portal Master Kaos appeared, intent upon destroying the Core of Light and ruling over Skylands with Darkness as his ally. Although they fought bravely, the Skylanders were no match for the wicked Hydra that Kaos summoned to his bidding. The Core of Light was smashed into pieces and the Skylanders were banished to Earth. Master Eon himself was exiled between realms, never to appear in his true form again.

Kaos was eventually defeated, but Master Eon is now only able to appear in semi-spirit form to offer advice. He can no longer lead the Skylanders to battle, so he is passing this sacred charge on to you. As the new Portal Master, it is now your destiny to rid Skylands of the encroaching Darkness by defeating Kaos and the villainous Doom Raiders, thus saving Skylands from a terrible fate.

THE MABU CREW

The local inhabitants of Skylands are a peaceful species called the Mabu. There are many different races of them across the thousands of islands in Skylands, but you'll find most are willing to offer a helping hand on your journey. When you arrive in Skylands, you'll find Buzz, Hugo, Cali, and Flynn ready to show you around (see Figure 2.6).

FIGURE 2.6 A helping hand is never far away in Skylands! Hugo, Cali, Buzz, and Flynn (left to right) will greet you when you arrive, just in time for the grand opening of Skylanders Academy.

Hugo is Master Eon's assistant. He's an intellectual who loves reading and history, so you'll often find him buried in a book. He uses his keen intellect to help the Skylanders achieve their missions and has been with them on many of their most harrowing journeys—as long as there aren't any nasty sheep involved!

If you have a thirst for adventure, Cali is the Mabu for you. She trains young Skylanders in the art of defense and navigation. (She once mapped 4,367 islands of Skylands before she had to give up!) Although she always seems to find herself in trouble, Cali never worries. Her tough determination and awesome fighting skills always see her through.

As the Head of Security and Secret Ninja Commando Operations, Buzz is the type of guy you always want to have around in a tight spot. With his keen eye and years of experience on the ground, he'll guide you through your missions and train you in the ways of a true Skylander.

Flynn will gladly fly you around Skylands to help hunt down the dreaded Doom Raiders. After all, he is the "best pilot in Skylands"—at least, that's what *he* thinks! Although he often seems a bit silly and self-important, he has a brave and selfless heart when it matters. Just don't offer him enchiladas for dinner—he'll eat them all and leave you none!

KAOS, GLUMSHANKS, AND THE DOOM RAIDERS

Kaos is the ultimate villain—rude, obnoxious, and horribly self-important. He was scorned by his father, the King, for his ugliness as a child, and then, after he was expelled from the most expensive school of evil villainy for eating the gymnasium with his giant floating head, he was cast out of home as well. Kaos became furious and bitter.

He soon discovered he had a propensity for magic and learned all he could to become a powerful Dark Portal Master. Together, with his ever-suffering servant Glumshanks, Kaos now spends his time plotting the most devious ways to become the evil overlord of Skylands (see Figure 2.7).

This time, though, he's in over his head! Kaos has broken the villainous Doom Raiders out of Cloud Cracker Prison, but instead of helping him achieve world domination, the Doom Raiders have their own plan in mind. They're on the loose, causing havoc and terrifying the inhabitants of Skylands with their evil plans!

FIGURE 2.7   Spend some time with the bad guys during Kaos Doom Challenges—just remember to watch your back!

This nasty group of troublemakers includes Wolfgang the Werewolf, Dreamcatcher, the Chompy Mage, Luminous, the Gulper, Dr. Krankcase, Chef Pepper Jack, and Nightshade, with the cruel Golden Queen at the helm!

SKYLANDERS

In a world where dark magic threatens the peace, only the bravest team of heroes will do! Each Skylander, like those pictured in Figure 2.8, has been especially chosen for their fighting skills, bravery, and magical powers. Every fighter is unique and draws power from one of the ten elements of Skylands. These Elements are Earth, Fire, Air, Water, Life, Tech, Undead, Magic, Light, and Dark.

When Kaos destroyed Cloud Cracker Prison and released the Doom Raiders, he banished all the Skylanders to Earth. They transformed as they fell, taking the form of small toys, unable to protect Skylands any longer. It's now up to you, the new Portal Master, to open the gateway between realms and bring the Skylanders back to face the challenges that await them in Skylands.

There are different types of Skylanders in *Trap Team*, but all are recognizable by the red figurine base (you'll also find each Skylanders' element on his or her base for quick reference). Skylanders from the original *Spyro's Adventure* game have a green base, those from *Giants* have an orange base, and the character toys from *Swap Force* have a blue base (see Figure 2.9).

FIGURE 2.8 The best of the best—Skylands' team of heroes was transformed into toys and sent to Earth by evil Kaos. It's up to you as the new Portal Master to bring them back and return the Doom Raiders to prison.

FIGURE 2.9 You can identify which game your characters belong to by the color of the base plate: pictured here from left to right are Flameslinger from Spyro's Adventure (green base), Eye-Brawl from Giants (orange base), Rattle Shake from Swap Force (blue base), and Blastermind from Trap Team (red base).

Let's take a closer look at the different types of Skylanders in Trap Team.

Trap Masters

The Trap Masters are a task force of Skylanders who carry special Traptanium Crystal weapons (see Figure 2.10). These weapons can damage enemies with more power than core Skylanders and break Traptanium Crystal clusters, which unlock secret treasures. There are 18 new Trap Masters in the Trap Team, including one each for the new light and dark elements. Trap Masters have the added ability of accessing the Elemental Gates that are found in each chapter of the Trap Team story, leading to additional gameplay areas and rewards.

FIGURE 2.10 Trap Masters possess stronger fighting skills than standard Skylanders and carry Traptanium weapons, which give them access to Elemental Gates and the ability to smash Traptanium Crystals.

Minis

These tiny Skylanders were originally known as "Sidekicks" and came from an alternate reality called Skylands Miniverse (see Figure 2.11). When they heard about the fantastic adventures that their full-sized counterparts had in Skylands, they crossed realms to join in the fun. After assisting the Skylanders on many dangerous missions, the Sidekicks attended Skylander Academy where they learned everything they needed to know about defending Skylands. The 16 Minis have the same powers and upgrades available as their full-sized counterparts. If you already have Sidekick character toys from an earlier version of the game, you can use them in place of the Trap Team Mini character toy releases. They will work exactly the same, with the only noticeable difference being the color of the figurine base.

FIGURE 2.11   The Minis are the "Sidekicks" from Spyro's Adventure, Giants, and Swap Force. Sidekick character toys are also compatible with Trap Team.

Core Skylanders

There are 23 core Skylanders, some of which are re-posed characters from earlier game stories. Each Skylander begins with two unique attack moves, with additional attacks available as upgrades, which can be bought with the gold coins that your Skylander collects in-game. We'll talk about upgrades in a little more detail later in this chapter in the section titled "Power Up Your Heroes with Upgrades."

With each new version of the game, some Skylanders are reintroduced in new outfits and poses as Special Edition releases (see Figure 2.12). These are usually available in a limited release or through specific retailers. Special Edition characters are given a variation on their name and a new Wow Pow! upgrade in addition to their standard upgrades.

Each new Core Skylander begins as a Series 1 Skylander; the next variation of that same character will be a Series 2 Skylander, then Series 3, and so on. In *Trap Team*, the Series 2 Skylanders are "Sure Shot" Shroomboom and "Hog Wild" Fryno. The Series 3 characters are "Fizzy Frenzy" Pop Fizz and "Full Blast" Jet Vac. The only Series 4 Trap Team Skylander is Gill Grunt, who has appeared in *Spyro's Adventure*, *Giants*, *Swap Force* (as Anchors Away Gill Grunt), and now *Trap Team* (as Tidal Wave Gill Grunt). Each new series of a character carries a new Wow Pow! upgrade, with an attack move different from any previous version. The specific Wow Pow! upgrades are listed in Chapter 3, "Meet the Skylanders," for each re-posed character's biography.

FIGURE 2.12   The core Trap Team Skylanders include both new and re-posed characters. There are three core Skylanders for the magic, water, fire, life, and air elements; two core skylanders for the tech, earth, and undead elements; and one core Skylander each for the light and dark elements.

Dark and Legendary Skylanders

In addition to re-posed characters, some of the Trap Team also appear as Dark Skylanders (see Figure 2.13). They are released as black and silver variations of their Trap Team pose. The legend goes that Kaos experimented with Petrified Darkness made of Dark Traptanium, an evil substance that would help him dominate Skylands. Some brave Skylanders discovered Kaos's plot and attacked his lair, falling into his trap! They attacked the Petrified Darkness prison with their Traptanium weapons and it exploded into a poisonous gas. The heroes had no choice but to take the dark energy of the gas into their own bodies. Together they learned to use their Dark energy for good instead of evil, giving them an extra edge when fighting against villains. These characters come with the Dark Edition Starter Pack and include Dark Snap Shot, Dark Wildfire, and Dark Food Fight.

Legendary Skylanders are special character releases in gold and dark blue coloring. They carry higher Critical Hit and/or Armor stats than their core counterparts, with the same standard upgrades available.

In the highly competitive arenas where defensive training takes place, Skylanders have to out-do each other in a great contest of skill and strength. Only the very best fighters receive the honor of Legendary status. As a reward for his or her courage and ability, the winner gets immortalized in a golden statue that stands as guardian until such time as it is awakened by a Portal Master to defend Skylands. In *Trap Team*, there are two Legendary Trap Masters (Bushwhack and Jawbreaker) and two Legendary Core Skylanders (Blades and Déjà vu).

FIGURE 2.13 Dark Skylanders are sold exclusively with the Dark Edition Starter Pack and Legendary Skylanders are sold separately. Pictured from left to right are: Dark Wildfire, Dark Snap Shot, Dark Food Fight, Legendary Jawbreaker, Legendary Déjà vu, and Legendary Blades.

Eon's Elite Skylanders

Eon's Elite Skylanders (one for each element) lead the team into battle and can always be counted on to defend Skylands, under even the most dire of circumstances. They are available as premium character toys with a gold base in a special presentation box (see Figure 2.14). Eon's Elite characters are up to three times stronger than their standard counterparts. They're a fantastic way to smash toward your goals. The Eon's Elite character toys are Whirlwind (Air), Terrafin (Earth), Spyro (Magic), Gill Grunt (Water), Chop Chop (Undead), Stealth Elf (Life), Trigger Happy (Tech), and Eruptor (Fire).

FIGURE 2.14 Eon's Elite are the ultimate collector's character toys and are sold separately in a clear presentation box with a gold baseplate. Each character is up to three times stronger than its standard Skylander counterpart.

Elements

Each Skylander and villain draws power from one of the ten elements that make up the realms of Skylands (see Figure 2.15). They are all equally powerful, but are usually expressed in different ways through types of attack. In certain areas of the game, a Skylander of a particular element may be stronger than others. At that point, it's a good idea to interchange the Skylanders on your portal so you have the best chance of success while fighting your enemies.

FIGURE 2.15   The ten elements that make up the Skylands realms and the Core of Light (from left to right) are Magic, Water, Earth, Undead, Dark, Tech, Air, Life, Fire, and Light, plus the Kaos element (shown in the middle).

Within the Battle Arenas, each element is slightly stronger or weaker than others. You can use this knowledge for strategy when fighting to give you the best advantage:

- Magic is stronger than Life.
- Life is stronger than Water.
- Water is stronger than Fire.
- Fire is stronger than Air.
- Air is stronger than Earth.
- Earth is stronger than Tech.
- Tech is stronger than Magic.

In the Kaos Doom Challenges (visit the Kaos statue at Skylander Academy to access these, or select them from the main menu), you may also need a character of a particular element to build defensive towers. We'll have a look at these in Chapter 10, "Kaos Doom Challenges."

There is one additional element called Kaos, which is only associated with the evil Portal Master himself. This element can be used to harness the power of the other elements and use them against enemies, as well as summon Doom Sharks.

Traps and the Traptanium Portal

After Kaos blew up Cloudcracker Prison, the Traptanium shards were shattered into outer space, transforming into translucent traps made up from each of the ten elements of Skylands (see Figure 2.16). Simply place your trap into the Traptanium Portal when you fight a villain, and when they're defeated, you'll hear them being sucked away from Skylands and into your trap!

FIGURE 2.16 The shattered fragments of Cloudcracker Prison reforming into traps!

The Traptanium Portal is your gateway to the Skylands Universe! As the new Portal Master, you can place your figurines on the Portal to bring the Skylander to life inside the game. You can also use the Traptanium Portal to capture villains into a trap, then swap your traps as often as you like to alternate playable villains (see Figure 2.17).

FIGURE 2.17   Place your Traptanium Crystal Traps in the Portal to capture and play as each villain! (Image courtesy of www.dadarocks.com.)

At any time you can have up to two Skylanders on the Portal (for two-player games), as well as an adventure location or magic item, with a trap in the holding slot.

Traps, a collection of which you can see in Figure 2.18, are an awesome addition to the Trap Team experience, expanding your game significantly. You not only can play as villains, but also complete Villain Quests to upgrade them to Evolved status (see Chapter 4, "Vile Villains").

Each trap is capable of holding a single villain at a time, but you can swap one trapped villain for another by visiting the Villain Vault at Skylanders Academy between chapters. You can replace the villain inside a trap as many times as you like, but there is no way of completely emptying a trap once it has been used. While playing in story mode, simply swap between your Skylander and the trapped villain with the press of a button!

The traps will only hold a villain of a matching element inside, so to capture all the villains you will need at least one trap for each element to transport them. If you want to complete the Villain Quests as you progress through each chapter, think ahead about which villains you will need in your traps before you embark on the next level. Keep in mind, you don't need to buy any traps at all to play the game right to the end. You can actually complete the entire game without a single trap, but you won't be able to access some of the features of the game as you play through (such as Villain Quests) or play as a villain.

FIGURE 2.18 Keep your traps organized in the villain tray for quick swaps while you're playing.

As well as the elemental traps, a number of Special Edition traps have been released with special decorations. These include promotional traps such as the Easter Bunny Earth Element Trap, as well as the Legendary Traps for Flood Flask, Spectral Skull, and Spirit Sphere (see Table 2.1).

If you begin with the Skylanders Dark Edition Starter Pack, it also includes a special Ultimate Kaos Trap, which is not sold separately. This is the biggest trap and has decorative silver markings on Kaos's face, but otherwise works the same as the standard Kaos Trap.

TABLE 2.1 A Complete List of All Traptanium Traps for Storing Villains

Life		Magic	
Weed Whacker	Hammer	Axe of Illusion	Axe
Seed Serpent	Snake	Arcane Hourglass	Hourglass
Shrub Shrieker	Yawn	Biter's Bane	Log Holder
Jade Blade	Sword	Rune Rocket	Rocket
Oak Eagle	Toucan	Sorcerous Skull	Skull
Emerald Energy	Torch	Spell Slapper	Totem
Air		**Undead**	
Cloudy Cobra	Snake	Haunted Hatchet	Axe
Cyclone Sabre	Sword	Grim Gripper	Hand
Breezy Bird	Toucan	Spectral Skull	Skull
Storm Warning	Screamer	Dream Piercer	Captain's Hat
Tempest Timer	Hourglass	Spooky Snake	Snake
Draft Decanter	Jughead	Spirit Sphere	Orb

Earth		Fire	
Banded Boulder	Orb	Spark Spear	Captain's Hat
Dust of Time	Hourglass	Scorching Stopper	Screamer
Slag Hammer	Hammer	Blazing Belch	Yawn
Rubble Trouble	Handstand	Searing Spinner	Totem
Spinning	Totem	Eternal Flame	Torch
Sandstorm	Toucan	Fire Flower	Scepter
Rock Hawk	Handstand		
Easter Bunny			
Tech		**Water**	
Automatic Angel	Angel	Frost Helm	Flying Helmet
Grabbing Gadget	Hand	Wet Walter	Log Holder
Factory Flower	Scepter	Tidal Tiki	Tiki
Tech Totem	Tiki	Flood Flask	Jughead
Makers Mana	Flying Helmet	Aqua Axe	Axe
Topsy Techy	Handstand	Soaking Staff	Angel
Dark		**Light**	
Shadow Spider	Spider	Shining Ship	Rocket
Ghastly Grimace	Handstand	Heavenly Hawk	Hawk
Dark Dagger	Sword	Beam Scream	Yawn
Special Traps			
Kaos Trap		Ultimate Kaos Trap	

Trapped Variant Villains

Six additional Special Edition traps have been released (so far) with variants of villains already trapped inside them. Each trap is linked to the variant it holds, so if you change the villain inside to a different one, the variant villain transferred to your Villain Vault will become the standard version. It then transfers to other traps as standard version as well. Never fear, though, because when you reinstate the villain to the original variant villain trap it was bought in, your variant version is reinstated.

Trapped Evolved Villains

You can transfer evolved villains in and out of traps and the Villain Vault; however, just like the Variant Villains, the evolved status is linked to the original trap only. For example, if you complete a Villain Quest for Hood Sickle, then whenever he is in the trap he received his evolved status in, he will be the evolved version. In all other traps and the Villain Vault, he'll revert to standard Hood Sickle. We'll look at Villain Quests more in Chapter 4, "Vile Villains."

Study Your Stats!

As you fight your way through Skylands, you're going to be faced with some pretty tough competition. The more experience, health, and skill your Skylanders have (see Figure 2.19), the better your chances of a swift victory! In this section, we have a look at the different ways you can enhance your Skylanders to give you the greatest chance of success.

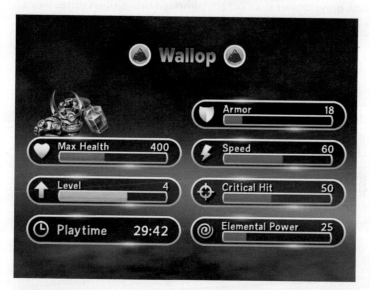

FIGURE 2.19 Every Skylander has a unique set of skills. These can be improved throughout the game via upgrades, XP points, hats, and stars.

Experience Orbs

As you defeat the villains in story mode, you'll notice they give up XP (experience) orbs. Collect these orbs to increase your Skylanders' individual experience levels (you can see how many XP orbs you have on the experience meter). When your experience (Level) meter is full, your Skylander will progress to the next level. Your Skylanders' agility and strength will increase with each level jump up to a maximum of Level 20.

Health

Each time your Level meter fills, your Max Health meter will have the potential to increase even further. This displays how much damage your Skylanders have taken when fighting—when your Max Health meter hits zero, you will need to take your Skylander off the portal and give him or her time to "rest" (until you begin the next level). You can use a different Skylander, and then another one, until you've run out of Skylanders and must begin that level again. In the case of more difficult levels, it helps to have a larger collection on hand to help fight your way through.

Speed

The Speed meter tells you how fast your Skylander can move. You'll find some Skylanders move slower than others, although this is often offset by an improvement in another stat.

Armor

Your Armor meter shows you the chance you have of deflecting an attack to your Skylander (that is, an enemy hit does no damage to your Skylander at all). Each Skylander has a specific Armor stat associated with their character. To calculate its usefulness, this stat is represented on the Armor meter as a percentage. The Armor level on the meter is calculated at a rate of 1% per six points of Armor stat. For example, a Skylander character that has 30 Armor, like Trigger Snappy, has a 5% chance to deflect an attack, which is indicated on the Armor meter. A Skylander like Bat Spin, who has an Armor stat of 12, has only a 2% chance of deflecting an attack entirely. Although the stats are initially set for each character, you can increase them in-game through buying upgrades and wearing hats, which may have an Armor boost included (we discuss hats later in this chapter).

Critical Hit

Critical hits are attack moves that create 150% of the regular damage level to an enemy—so of course, the higher the better. This stat works in a similar way to Armor. The chance for scoring a critical hit increases by 1% for every five points per Critical Hit stat that your character holds. This is represented on the Critical Hit Meter. For example, a Skylander with a Critical Hit amount of 60, like Déjà vu, has a 12% chance of scoring a critical hit against an enemy. This stat can be increased by wearing hats and buying upgrades as well.

Elemental Power

You can increase your Elemental Power meter through hats and upgrades as well. You'll find that certain areas of Skylands also give bonus damage to Skylanders of a particular element as you pass through the story chapters. This provides a great opportunity to switch up your playing characters to take advantage of additional strength against enemies. For example, if you use Ka-Boom (a fire Trap Master) with an Elemental Power stat of 39 points in a zone that favors Fire Elemental Skylanders, you will increase his power by

1% damage per point. So Ka-Boom would receive an additional 39% bonus power in these areas. The more Skylanders you collect of a particular element, the higher your overall elemental power will become.

Power Up Your Heroes with Upgrades

Every Skylander is unique, both in personality and skills. It's often for those crazy, individual attack moves that we pick favorites, and in the upgrade section, it's a smorgasbord.

Each Skylander starts with two basic attack moves. You can upgrade each character further by purchasing upgrades with the gold coins you collect during the story chapters or Kaos Doom Challenges. Remember that coins aren't transferrable—each Skylander collects his or her own coins, so you have to play with a Skylander enough to collect the coins for his or her own upgrades.

You can upgrade your Skylanders by visiting Persephone at the Skylanders Academy or wherever you find her in each chapter and also at the end of a Kaos Doom Challenge. To access the upgrades faster, you can collect Winged Sapphires throughout the chapter to earn a discount on upgrades (this covers all Skylanders). These are blue gems with wings attached that are hidden throughout each chapter. Each Winged Sapphire is worth 2%, and you can earn up to 40% off your upgrades by collecting them all.

To begin, Persephone will offer your Skylander four new upgrades. Some of these may be prerequisites to later upgrade paths. Each of the four new upgrades cost gold coins:

- Upgrade 1: 500 points
- Upgrade 2: 700 coins
- Upgrade 3: 900 coins
- Upgrade 4: 1200 coins

After you have bought the first four powers, you have a choice to take one of two further upgrade paths, consisting of three new powers each (see Figure 2.20). You must choose one path or the other to extend the capabilities of a specific attack move by the Skylander. Once you have chosen a particular attack path and bought the upgrades, you lose the ability to access the other path, unless you forgo the first path and its powers:

- Upgrade 5: 1700 points
- Upgrade 6: 2200 coins
- Upgrade 7: 3000 coins

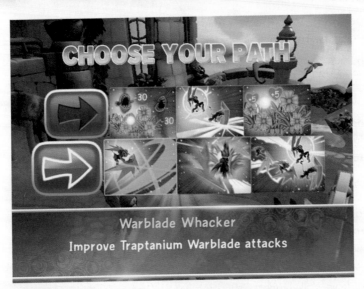

FIGURE 2.20   You can only choose one of the two upgrade paths to explore at a time.

Soul Gem Ability

Each Skylander has a Soul Gem hidden somewhere in the game. When you collect this Gem, you'll have access to another exciting attack move or ability. For those Skylanders in previous versions of the game (including re-posed characters and Mini "Sidekicks"), you can buy the upgrade without having to collect the Soul Gem first. For new Skylanders, you'll need to collect the Soul Gem before you can upgrade, at a cost of 4000 coins.

Wow Pow! Upgrades

Each re-posed character that has already appeared in *Giants*, *SwapForce*, or *Spyro's Adventure* will boast the same attack moves and upgrades as the original version. However, an additional Wow Pow! upgrade will also be available for 5000 coins, which will be different from any previous Wow Pow! upgrades the character may have had.

Portal Master Rankings

You can increase your rank as a Portal Master by earning stars throughout the game (see Table 2.2). These stars will be given in story mode, Arena Battles, and in the Kaos Doom Challenges. You'll receive a reward after you progress through each of the 40 Portal Master Ranks, such as awesome hats to make you stronger, trinkets, gems worth gold coins, and instant Level Ups.

TABLE 2.2—Earn Rewards for Your Skylander as Your Portal Mastery Grows!

Rank	Stars	Reward	Rank	Stars	Reward
1	0	No reward	21	5	Gem worth 6000
2	2	Gem worth 1000	22	5	Hat: Medieval Bard
3	2	Level Up	23	5	Trinket: Seadog Seashell
4	2	Trinket: Batterson's Bubble	24	6	Level Up
5	2	Hat: Wooden	25	6	Mongol Hat
6	2	Level Up	26	6	Trinket: T-Bone's Lucky Tie
7	3	Trinket: Teddy Clops	27	6	Gem worth 8000
8	3	Gem worth 2000	28	6	Level Up
9	3	Level Up	29	6	Mabu's Medallion
10	3	Hat: Raver	30	6	Hat: Wilikin
11	4	Level Up	31	6	Trinket: Kuckoo Kazoo
12	4	Ramses' Rune	32	6	Level Up
13	4	Gem worth 3000	33	6	Elemental Radiant
14	4	Shire Hat	34	6	Hat: Oracle
15	4	Level Up	35	6	Time Town Ticker
16	4	Trinket: Ramses' Dragon Horn	36	6	Level Up
17	4	Gem worth 4000	37	6	Hat: Sheepwrecked
18	4	Hat: Old Ruins	38	6	Cyclops's Spinner
19	5	Level Up	39	6	Gem worth 10,000
20	5	Trinket: Dark Water Daisy	40	6	Hat: Frostfest

Within each story chapter, you can collect up to three stars by searching hidden areas, picking up treasure, hats, and trinkets, capturing villains, and accessing the Elemental Gates (see Figure 2.21). Leave no area undiscovered! After you have completed the chapter (and gathered everything there is to find), you'll be offered an additional star to complete a "Difficult Dare" challenge. After you have completed all 18 story chapters, as well as the four adventure pack chapters (we'll look at these in Chapter 9, "Expand Your Adventure"), you'll be rewarded with an additional 12 stars, bringing the game total to 100.

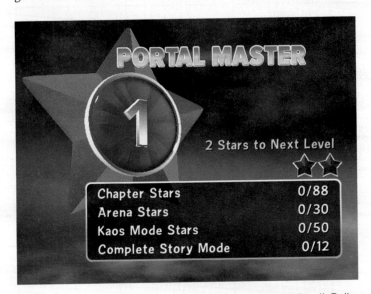

FIGURE 2.21 Take your Portal Mastery to the next level! Collect treasure and access all areas throughout the game to earn stars.

Kaos Doom Challenges reward you as you fight progressively more enemies in waves. The harder the challenge, the higher your reward! Arena challenges are another fun way to earn stars (up to five stars per challenge, plus a bonus hat!)

Accessorize!

Don't just turn up, dress up! There are literally hundreds of combinations by which you can customize your Skylanders to make them one-of-a-kind heros, as well as make them faster, stronger, and more invincible to enemies. Trinkets and hats, as shown in Figure 2.22, can be found throughout all of the story chapters, are gifted to you as rewards for your achievements, or can be bought from Skylanders Academy. Does Food Fight deserve to wear the Medal of Gallantry for his outstanding effort fighting Trolls? Would Gusto look dashing in a Pork Pie Hat? Perhaps ferocious Thunderbolt would seem a little less intimidating with a rubber glove on his head blowing bubbles from a pipe?

FIGURE 2.22 Hats don't just look great, they make your Skylander stronger and faster in battle!

Earn new accessories for your Skylanders as you play, then give them a new look that will get all the Mabu townsfolk talking. After all, that Volcano Hat is so hot right now!

Hats

Hats are an easy way to strengthen up your Skylanders—there are 99 to collect. As you can see from Table 2.3, every hat boasts a unique set of improvements to your stats (as well as looking cool, of course!). Hats are usually hidden behind Elemental Gates in a box (you'll need to get through a bit of an obstacle course to reach them). You can also earn hats by completing a Villain Quest, or you can buy them from Auric in Skylanders Academy or Hatterson's Hat Store.

TABLE 2.3—Boost Your Skylanders' Stats with a Hat!

Location	Name of Hat	Speed	Armor	Crit.	Power
Hats That Can Be Bought at Skylanders Academy after Chapter Completion					
Auric's Shop (Ch. 2)	Flight Attendant Hat			5	
Auric's Shop (Ch. 2)	Storm Hat	8		5	
Auric's Shop (Ch. 2)	Bellhop Hat				5

Location	Name of Hat	Speed	Armor	Crit.	Power
Auric's Shop (Ch. 7)	Miniature Skylands Hat	4			
Auric's Shop (Ch. 7)	Rude Boy Hat		10		
Auric's Shop (Ch. 7)	Palm Hat				10
Auric's Shop (Ch. 7)	Pork Pie Hat			10	
Auric's Shop (Ch. 13)	Weather Vane Hat		25		
Auric's Shop (Ch. 13)	Sherpa Hat				15
Auric's Shop (Ch. 13)	Toucan Hat	4	10		
Auric's Shop (Ch. 13)	Tribal Hat			15	
Auric's Shop (Ch. 13)	Croissant Hat		15		
Auric's Shop (Ch. 15)	Molekin Mountain Hat				25
Hats Gifted as Rewards for Completing a New Portal Master Rank					
Portal Master Rank 5	Wooden Hat		5	17	
Portal Master Rank 10	Raver Hat	8	5		
Portal Master Rank 14	Shire Hat	9	5		
Portal Master Rank 18	Old Ruins Hat	8		12	
Portal Master Rank 22	Medieval Bard Hat		32		
Portal Master Rank 25	Mongol Hat			32	
Portal Master Rank 30	Wilikin Hat	8		20	
Portal Master Rank 34	Oracle Hat	15			
Portal Master Rank 37	Sheepwrecked Hat			37	
Portal Master Rank 40	Frostfest Hat	20			

Location	Name of Hat	Speed	Armor	Crit.	Power
Hats to Be Collected in Arenas and Other Areas					
Arena: Brock's Rumble Clubhouse	Wizard Hat	10		10	
Arena: Drain of Sorrows	Candle Hat				25
Arena: Dreamquake	Night Cap			25	
Arena: Exhaust Junction	Planet Hat	10			
Arena: Phoenix Nest	Eggshell Hat		25		
Arena: Quicksand Coliseum	Pyramid Hat		10	20	
Beat Final Boss on Easy	Bronze Arkeyan Helm	4	15	20	
Beat Final Boss on Hard	Gold Arkeyan Helm	8	20	37	
Beat Final Boss on Medium	Silver Arkeyan Helm	6	17	30	
Beat Final Boss on Nightmare	Rainbow Hat	10	25		
Kaos Doom Challenge	Candy Cane Hat	10	20	20	
Hats to Be Collected Within Story Chapters (Including Adventure Packs)					
Ch. 1: Life Gateway	Melon Hat				5
Ch. 1: Tech Gateway	Bucket Hat		5		
Ch. 1: Water Gateway	Turtle Shell Hat		7		
Ch. 2: Dark Gateway	Skipper Hat		5		
Ch. 2: Earth Gateway	Sleuth Hat			7	
Ch. 2: Life Gateway	Hedgehog Hat	2			2

Location	Name of Hat	Speed	Armor	Crit.	Power
Ch. 3: Bruiser Cruiser	Paperboy Hat	4			
Ch. 3: Magic Gateway	Horns Be With You Hat				7
Ch. 3: Undead Gateway	Hunting Hat		2	2	
Ch. 4: Air Gateway	Ceiling Fan Hat		5	5	
Ch. 4: Buzzer Beak	Parrot Nest	7			
Ch. 4: Water Gateway	Daisy Crown	2		5	
Ch. 5: Air Gateway	Scooter Hat				10
Ch. 5: Fire Gateway	Colander Hat		10		
Ch. 5: Light Gateway	Juicer Hat	5	13		
Ch. 6: Brawlrus	Steampunk Hat		17		
Ch. 6: Earth Gateway	Imperial Hat		2		
Ch. 6: Undead Gateway	Metal Fin Hat			12	
Ch. 7: Dark Gateway	Shadow Ghost Hat		7	20	
Ch. 7: Fisticuffs	Clown Classic Hat				20
Ch. 7: Undead Gateway	Dragon Skull		10	5	
Ch. 8: Magic Gateway	Rugby Hat	3		7	
Ch. 8: Tech Gateway	Old-Time Movie Hat				15
Ch. 8: Water Gateway	Synchronized Swim Cap		10	10	
Ch. 9: Bomb Shell	Garrison Hat		20		
Ch. 9: Fire Gateway	Volcano Hat			15	

Location	Name of Hat	Speed	Armor	Crit.	Power
Ch. 9: Life Gateway	Mountie Hat		15		
Ch. 10: Fire Gateway	Trash Can Lid		10		10
Ch. 10: Pain-Yatta	Rubber Glove Hat		12	12	
Ch. 10: Water Gateway	Shower Cap	6			
Ch. 11: Magic Gateway	Lil' Elf Hat	8			
Ch. 11: Undead Gateway	Clown Bowler Hat			20	
Ch. 12: Dr. Krankcase	Skylander Bobby Hat		20		7
Ch. 12: Earth Gateway	Alarm Clock Hat	4	10		
Ch. 13: Fire Gateway	Extreme Viking Hat			15	10
Ch. 13: Light Gateway	Kokoshnik				30
Ch. 13: Wolfgang	Tin Foil Hat		10		15
Ch. 14: Bone Chompy	Nurse Hat		30		
Ch. 14: Earth Gateway	Sunday Hat			10	10
Ch. 14: Krankenstein	Kepi Hat			25	
Ch. 14: Tech Gateway	Cubano Hat	7			7
Ch. 15: Life Gateway	William Tell Hat			25	
Ch. 15: Water Gateway	Radar Dish Hat		15	5	
Ch. 16: Air Gateway	Batter Up Hat		12	15	
Ch. 16: Earth Gateway	Desert Crown				27

Location	Name of Hat	Speed	Armor	Crit.	Power
Ch. 17: Air Gateway	Classic Pot Hat		30		
Ch. 17: Bad Juju	Beetle Hat		30		
Ch. 17: Magic Gateway	Crazy Light Bulb Hat	12			
Ch. 18: Dark Gateway	Brain Hat				37
Ch. 18: Tech Gateway	Brainiac Hat	6		15	
Ch. 19: Light Gateway	Firefly Jar		30		
Ch. 19: Magic Gateway	Eye of Kaos Hat				22
Ch. 19: Nightshade	Bat Hat	4		22	
Ch. 20: Dark Gateway	Dark Helm			35	
Ch. 20: Earth Gateway	Light Bulb Hat	4		17	
Ch. 20: Luminous	Lighthouse Beacon Hat	4	23		
Ch. 21: Lob Goblin	Coconut Hat	3	21		
Ch. 21: Magic Gateway	Medic Hat		22		
Ch. 21: Tech Gateway	Outback Hat	6			
Ch. 21: Trolling Thunder	Cycling Hat	8			7
Ch. 22: Pawn Shop	Carnival Hat	4		10	
Ch. 22: Life Gateway	Cornucopia Hat	2			15
Ch. 22: Water Gateway	Gondolier Hat		5		10

Trinkets

You'll find trinkets hidden around Skylanders Academy, for sale in Auric's shop, and also given as rewards for completing Kaos Doom Challenges (see Table 2.4). They don't serve any specific function like hats—just decoration. Your Skylander can only wear one hat and one trinket at any particular time.

TABLE 2.4—Dress to Impress with Trinkets

Location	Name of Trinket
Trinkets Bought at Skylanders Academy after Chapter Completion	
Auric's Shop (Ch. 2)	Bubble Blower
Auric's Shop (Ch. 2)	Medal of Heroism
Auric's Shop (Ch. 2)	Lizard Lilly
Auric's Shop (Ch. 2)	Vote for Cyclops
Auric's Shop (Ch. 4)	Blobber's Medal of Courage
Auric's Shop (Ch. 4)	Snuckles' Sunflower
Auric's Shop (Ch. 4)	Goo Factory Gear
Auric's Shop (Ch. 4)	Medal of Gallantry
Auric's Shop (Ch. 9)	Medal of Mettle
Auric's Shop (Ch. 9)	Winged Medal of Bravery
Auric's Shop (Ch. 9)	Elemental Opal
Auric's Shop (Ch. 9)	Ullysses Uniclops
Auric's Shop (Ch. 13)	Medal of Valiance
Trinkets Gifted as Rewards for Completing a New Portal Master Rank	
Portal Master Rank 4	Batterson's Bubble
Portal Master Rank 7	Teddy Cyclops
Portal Master Rank 12	Ramses' Rune
Portal Master Rank 16	Ramses' Dragon Horn
Portal Master Rank 20	Dark Water Daisy
Portal Master Rank 23	Seadog Seashell
Portal Master Rank 26	T-Bone's Lucky Tie
Portal Master Rank 29	Mabu's Medallion
Portal Master Rank 31	Kuckoo Kazoo
Portal Master Rank 33	Elemental Radiant
Portal Master Rank 35	Time Town Ticker
Portal Master Rank 38	Cyclops Spinner

Location	Name of Trinket
Trinkets to Be Collected at Skylander Academy after Chapter Completion	
Persephone's Treehouse (Ch. 1)	Elemental Diamond
Courtyard Tower (Ch. 2)	Iris' Iris
The Great Chimney (Ch. 2)	Big Bow of Boom
Academy Defense Tower (Ch. 7)	Pirate Pinwheel
The Archives (Ch. 9)	Billy Bison
The Reading Room (Ch. 9)	Stealth Elf's Gift
Observatory* (Ch. 13)	Spyro's Shield
Crystal Caverns* (Ch. 15)	Wilikin Windmill
* Requires Legendary Treasure from same chapter	

Meet the Skylanders

What would a world be without the heroes that defend it? In this chapter, we'll meet each Skylander that forms part of Master Eon's incredible team and get to know their personalities and past achievements. Browse this section to learn about the unique skills and attack moves each character uses to protect Skylands from evil-doers, and decide ahead of time which upgrades suit your fighting style best and which paths will help you reach your Skylanders' highest potential.

All Skylanders fall into one of ten elements. They are included here in their elemental groups in the following order: Life, Magic, Air, Water, Tech, Fire, Earth, Undead, Light, and Dark. Trap Masters are featured first within each group, followed by new and re-posed series Skylanders, and lastly, the Minis. Flip through to compare powers and stats—your new favorite Skylander is waiting to be discovered!

Bushwhack: "Axe to the Max!"

Bushwhack's Stats!

Status:	Trap Master
Element:	Life
Maximum Health:	290
Speed:	60
Armor:	18
Critical Hit:	60
Elemental Power:	39

Like a mighty nature warrior, BUSHWHACK chops through enemies and LEAVES a trail of victory wherever he goes!

Arbo, the mystical and wise Tree Ent, once taught Bushwhack all the secrets of the forest. Despite Bushwhack's tiny size, Arbo knew he was brave and worthy to defend the beautiful Arcadian Timberland of his tribe. One fate-filled day, the patrolling Timberland elf rangers were overthrown by a vicious band of Lumberjack Trolls! They were bent on destroying the forest with huge tree-chopping machines! Bushwhack sprang into action! Using the enchanted axe that Arbo had given him, he fought off the evil trolls single-handedly until the Arcadian Timberland was safe once more. Bushwhack was given a Traptanium Axe and promoted to Trap Master, fulfilling his destiny as a protector of Skylands.

Attack moves:

Traptanium Axe: Press **Attack 1** to swing the Traptanium Axe. Press **Attack 1**, **Attack 1**, hold **Attack 1** for a combo attack.

Mystic Acorn: Press **Attack 2** to throw a Mystic Acorn that stuns enemies.

Soul Gem Ability: Timber! – 4000: Jump and hold **Attack 1** to plant a giant tree, which is then cut down to smash whatever's below. Find Bushwhack's Soul Gem in Chapter 3: Chompy Mountains first.

Upgrades:

Headbash – 500: Press **Attack 3** for a powerful Headbash move, damaging anything nearby.
Nut Grenade – 700: Acorns now explode on impact, doing more damage.
In a Nut Shell – 900: Get some new armor, taking reduced damage.
Thorn Trail – 1200: Traptanium Axe attack now leaves a trail of thorns that damage enemies.

Axe Avenger Path: Improve Traptanium Axe attacks.	Armor Awesomeness Path: Improve your armor for protection and attack.
An Axe to Grind – 1700 Traptanium Axe attack does extra damage.	**Bush's Shack – 1700** Hold **Attack 1** to create a leafy hut for protection and healing.
Combo Attacks – 2200 Press **Attack 1**, **Attack 1**, hold **Attack 2** for the Spin and Slash combo. Press **Attack 1**, **Attack 1**, hold **Attack 3** for Head First combo. **Go nuts! – 3000** Keep holding **Attack 2** after a Spin and Slash combo to shoot nuts in all directions.	**Primal Warrior – 2200** Get new armor, taking reduced damage and doing extra damage with the Headbash attack. **Spring Forward – 3000** Hold **Attack 3** to dash forward and perform a super Headbash attack.

Tuff Luck: "It's Your Lucky Day!"

Tuff Luck's Stats!

Status:	Trap Master
Element:	Life
Maximum Health:	310
Speed:	85
Armor:	48
Critical Hit:	80
Elemental Power:	39

If you need GOOD FORTUNE to beat the bad guys, call Tuff Luck's mean, green BLADES TO BATTLE!

Armed with razor-sharp Traptanium Warblades, Tuff Luck is a force to be reckoned with! She's renowned throughout Skylands as the luckiest charm to have around, not just because of her incredible fighting skills, but also because she once drank from the magical waters of Fortunata Springs. The magical hidden springs bring good fortune to anyone who drinks from them—which is why Kaos's minions tried to steal the water with giant sponge-tankers! Oh no! Luckily, Tuff Luck was close by patrolling. She heroically fought the minions until they fled and so earned her rightful place as a Trap Master of Skylands!

Attack moves:

Traptanium Warblades: Press **Attack 1** to swipe with Traptanium Warblades. Press **Attack 1**, **Attack 1**, **Attack 1** for a combo strike.

Pounce Mode: Press **Attack 2** to enter Pounce Mode (invisible to enemies). Then press **Attack 1** to pounce!

Soul Gem Ability: Garden of Pain! – 4000: Hold **Attack 3** and press **Attack 1** to grow spiky blades of grass that do massive damage. Prerequisite: Find Tuff Luck's Soul Gem in Chapter 16: The Golden Desert first.

Upgrades:

Warblade Stab – 500: Press Attack 3 to spring forward with a powerful Warblade Stab attack.	
Green Thumb – 700: Stay in Pounce Mode longer.	
Control Your Destiny – 900: Hold Attack 3 to control where Warblade Stab lands. Prerequisite: Warblade Stab.	
Glaive Wave – 1200: Traptanium Warblade attack now shoots an energy wave.	
Pouncy Pouncer Path: Improve Pounce Mode attacks.	**Warblade Whacker Path:** Improve Traptanium Warblade attacks.
Poison Ivy – 1700 Clover patches in Pounce Mode stun enemies.	**Wave Goodbye – 1700** Energy wave released from Traptanium Warblade attack does more damage.
Powerful Pounce – 2200 Traptanium Warblade attack from Pounce Mode does more damage.	**Lucky Spin – 2200** Press Attack 1, Attack 1, hold Attack 2 for Lucky Spin combo.
Four-Leafed Clover – 3000 Touching clover in Pounce Mode restores Health Points.	**Wingin' Warblade – 3000** Press Attack 1, Attack 1, hold Attack 3 for Wingin' Warblade combo.

Food Fight: "Eat This!"

Food Fight's Stats!

Status:	Skylander
Element:	Life
Maximum Health:	260
Speed:	60
Armor:	18
Critical Hit:	30
Elemental Power:	46

HUNGRY for action? BLAST the bad guys to the COMPOST HEAP and still be home in time for DINNER!

Don't be fooled by the size of this little green dynamo—his tomato launcher can blast a swarm of chompies into leftovers! When this artichoke-with-attitude was just a baby in the fields, the greedy troll farmers made a big mistake. They covered the soil with gunpowder in a crazy attempt to grow super-veggies that would make the trolls stronger when eaten. Worst dinner plans ever! Food Fight flourished and broke free of his stalk, then made breakfast of the bad guys! He rolled on his giant tomato, crushing the Farmers Guild Trolls that kept the garden folk imprisoned, and used his Zucchini Blaster to break down the fences. Now Food Fight travels across Skylands, using his epic veggie power to leave a nasty aftertaste in the mouth of every villain that picks on his garden-loving friends.

Attack moves:

Tomato Launcher: Press **Attack 1** to launch exploding tomatoes.

Blooms of Doom: Press **Attack 2** to plant artichoke traps, which also explode!

Soul Gem Ability: That's How I Roll! — 4000: Hold **Attack 1** to charge up a Super Tomato, release **Attack 1** to ride it and run over enemies. Prerequisite: Find Food Fight's Soul Gem in Chapter 2: Know-It-All Island.

Upgrades:

Extra Ripe Tomatoes – 500: Tomatoes do more damage.
Green Thumb – 700: Tomatoes that hit the ground grow into plants. Collect them for more powerful shots.
Zucchini Blast – 900: Press Attack 3 to deliver a Zucchini Blast. Does heavy damage over a wide area.

Blooms of Bigger Doom – 1200: Blooms of Doom make bigger explosions.	
Tomatologist Path: Improves Tomato Launcher attacks.	**Bloomer and Boomer Path:** Improves Zucchini Blast and Blooms of Doom attacks.
Heavy Harvest – 1700 Tomatoes picked up from plants are bigger and do even more damage.	**Special Squash – 1700** Hold Attack 3 to charge up the Zucchini Blast for extra damage.
HeirBOOM Tomatoes – 2200 Detonate tomato plants with a Zucchini Blast.	**Zucchini Goo – 2200** Enemies hit by the Zucchini Blast are slowed down.
Bad Aftertaste – 3000 Enemies damaged by exploding tomato plants will take damage over time. Prerequisite: HeirBOOM Tomatoes.	**Choke Chain – 3000** Blooms of Doom detonate each other.

Sure Shot Shroomboom: "He Shoots, He Spores!"

Sure Shot Shroomboom's Stats!

Status:	Skylander
Element:	Life
Maximum Health:	260
Speed:	60
Armor:	18
Critical Hit:	20
Elemental Power:	25

When you're after a PARATROOPER who can LOCK 'N' LOAD with ultimate DAMAGE, this Skylander has his EYE on the prize!

He was first discovered in *Skylanders Giants*, where his bravery and selflessness came to Master Eon's attention. Even as a tiny spore, Shroomie knew he didn't want to end up on a dinner plate—but growing in a pizza topping garden owned by Kaos meant he was fated for the main course! So this toadstool hero took a stand! He freed the other veggies by catapulting them over the fence with a homemade slingshot, then made his great escape sailing across the ocean wind on his wide-brimmed mushroom cap. What a *champignon*! These days, when trouble erupts in Skylands, you can always count on Shroomboom to parachute by and get his hands dirty. Today's weather report: Watch out for exploding mushrooms falling from the sky!

Attack moves:

Slingshot: Press **Attack 1** to shoot exploding mushrooms.

Mushroom Ring: Press **Attack 2** to spawn a ring of mushrooms that damage enemies.

Soul Gem Ability: Self Slingshot! – 4000: Hold **Attack 1** to slingshot Shroomboom towards enemies.

Wow Pow! Upgrade: High Spore! – 5000: Hold **Attack 1** to create mushroom bumpers and play pinball with enemies. Prerequisite: Self-Slingshot.

Upgrades:

Launch Paratroopers – 500: Press Attack 3 to shoot mushroom paratroopers who drop down from the sky.	
Super Shrooms – 700: Mushroom Ring gets bigger.	
Bigger Boomshrooms – 900: Hold Attack 1 to charge up a giant exploding mushroom.	
Bouncing Boomshrooms – 1200: Exploding mushrooms bounce on the ground and do increased damage.	
Barrier Boost Path: Upgrades Mushroom Ring for better protection.	**Paramushroom Promotion Path:** Provides more upgrades for the Paratrooper and Slingshot attacks.
Spore Power – 1700 Mushroom Ring creates a damaging spore cloud.	**Lock 'n' Load – 1700** Can fire exploding mushrooms faster that do increased damage.
Ultimate Ring – 2200 Mushroom Ring is the biggest it gets. **Back to the Beginning – 3000** Hold Attack 2 to remain underground, where you can move around freely.	**Fungal Infestation – 2200** Mushroom Paratroopers stick to enemies and do damage over time. **Paratrooper Invasion – 3000** Shoot three Mushroom Paratroopers at once.

High Five: "Buzz Off!"

High Five's Stats!

Status:	Skylander
Element:	Life
Maximum Health:	270
Speed:	60
Armor:	6
Critical Hit:	70
Elemental Power:	53

Hit TERMINAL VELOCITY and leave your enemies STINGING from an OVERDRIVE of BUZZ POWER!

It's hard being the youngest child—sometimes you miss out on all the fun! But High Five couldn't stand by and watch his older brother's race for glory without him, especially when he heard a buzz that the Troll Racing Team had stolen the magical Trophy of Sparx from the Royal High Flying Dragonfly racing competition! High Five dashed into the fray and set his sights on the trolls, sending them into a spin at the finish line! The crowd roared! He'd not only saved the Trophy of Sparx, but High Five had won the race! For his bravery and quick thinking, High Five scored a place in the Skylander team where he can use his super-speedy flying skills to keep the skies clear.

Attack moves:

Poison Pellets: Press **Attack 1** to shoot Poison Pellets. Hold **Attack 1** for rapid fire.

Buzz Dash: Press **Attack 2** for a speedy dash attack.

Soul Gem Ability: Organic Slam Apples! – 4000: Fly Slam Apples heal more HP. Prerequisite: Find High Five's Soul Gem in Chapter 10: The Secret of Sewers of Supreme Stink.

Upgrades:

Poison Cloud – 500: Poison Pellets attack leaves behind a poisonous cloud, damaging nearby enemies.
Fly Slam – 700: Press Attack 3 to slam down on enemies around you.
Buzz Charge – 900: Hold Attack 2 to charge up a stronger Buzz Dash.
Buzzerker Overdrive – 1200: For the cost of HP, hold Attack 3 to really power up the Fly Slam. Also move faster with lower HP. Prerequisite: Fly Slam.

Pollen Prince Path: Improve Poison Pellets attacks.	Speedy Slammer Path: Improve Buzz Dash and Fly Slam attacks.
Cloud Control – 1700 Have up to five Poison Clouds active at a time, moving faster and doing more damage. **Buzz 'em Up – 2200** Buzz Dash through Poison Clouds to power them up and extend their life. **Power Clouds – 3000** Extra big Poison Clouds do extra big damage.	**Spin Cycle – 1700** Hold Attack 3, and enemies will be sucked up into the Fly Slam zone. **Buzz Buzz Buzz – 2200** Hold Attack 2 for consecutive Buzz Dashes. **Slam Apples – 3000** Hold Attack 3 to charge up the Fly Slam attack even further and release apples that heal you.

Barkley: "Be Afraid of the Bark!"

Barkley's Stats!

Status:	Mini
Element:	Life
Maximum Health:	430
Speed:	40
Armor:	24
Critical Hit:	40
Elemental Power:	60

BRANCH OUT with your attack to SLAM the bad guys with a SERVE of GREEN POWER they'll never forget!

Barkley trained hard at Skylanders Academy so he could learn to be just as brave as his majestic role model, Tree Rex. Before he transformed into the tree-mendous protector that he is today, Tree Rex was a huge, beautiful tree growing in a forest. After the ancient Arkeyans made him mutate from the pollution of their war machine factory, he used his newfound strength to teach them some respect for nature! Like his full-sized counterpart, Barkley knows that destructive minions are a thorn in his side. He loves to charge at enemies with his mega-spikey arm and crush evil into splinters!

Attack moves:

Shockwave Slam: Press **Attack 1** to slam the ground with massive fists, causing shockwaves.

Sequoia Stampede: Press and hold **Attack 2** to charge through enemies and obstacles.

Soul Gem Ability: Woodpecker Pal! – 4000: A woodpecker buddy joins Barkley in battle.

Upgrades:

Photosynthesis Cannon – 500: Press Attack 3 to harness the power of the sun and shoot light beams.	
Big Thorn Shockwave Slam – 700: Hold Attack 1 for a bigger, more powerful Shockwave Slam.	
Super Stampede – 900: Sequoia Stampede attack does increased damage.	
Treefolk Tripleshot – 1200: Photosynthesis Cannon fires triple burst shots. Prerequisite: Photosynthesis Cannon.	
Treefolk Charger Path: Provides more upgrades for the Sequoia Stampede attacks.	**Lumbering Laserer Path:** Provides more upgrades for the Photosynthesis Cannon.
Titanic Elbow Drop – 1700 Press Attack 1 while charging to perform one serious elbow drop move. **Lightfooted – 2200** Charge longer and faster, doing more damage in the process. **Ultimate Stampede – 3000** Sequoia Stampede attack does maximum damage.	**Super-Charged Vaporizer – 1700** Hold down Attack 3 to charge up the Photosynthesis Cannon for more damage. **Sun Skewer – 2200** Photosynthesis Cannon blasts through enemies and explodes for more damage. **The Pod Maker – 3000** Vaporized enemies turn into exploding plant pods. Prerequisite: Super-Charged Vaporizer.

Whisper Elf: "Silent but Deadly!"

Whisper Elf's Stats!

Status:	Mini
Element:	Life
Maximum Health:	270
Speed:	70
Armor:	12
Critical Hit:	50
Elemental Power:	25

When GLOWING EYES haunt you in the night, don't be FRIGHTENED—this stealthy NINJA ELF has your back!

Blink and she's gone! Whisper Elf is the Miniverse counterpart of Stealth Elf, a deadly ninja fighter who knows the art of sneaking around. Her spinning daggers and poison spores prove a deadly surprise to even the most skilled villains that take her on. When trouble gets too close, Whisper Elf can leave a trail of scarecrow decoys to distract the bad guys, then sneak up to slice them unawares! Whisper's mentor Stealth Elf grew up learning the ancient skills of stealth fighting from a deep-forest creature. She's not only a fierce protector of Skylands, but she's also the Guardian Protector of the Forest. Skylands' secrets are always in safe hands with Whisper Elf.

Attack moves:

Blade Slash: Press **Attack 1** to slice enemies up with a pair of sharp blades. Press **Attack 1**, **Attack 1**, hold **Attack 1** to perform a special combo.

Stealthier Decoy: Press **Attack 2** to disappear completely but leave behind a decoy image of Whisper Elf that enemies are drawn to.

Soul Gem Ability: Sylvan Regeneration! – 4000: Regenerate health over time.

Upgrades:

Straw Pook Scarecrow – 500: A scarecrow appears in place of your decoy and distracts enemies.
Dragonfang Dagger – 700: Blade attacks do increased damage.
Sturdy Scarecrow – 900: Scarecrows last longer and take more damage to destroy. Prerequisite: Straw Pook Scarecrow.
Arboreal Acrobatics – 1200: Press Attack 3 to perform a quick acrobatic move. Hold Attack 3 and flip in any direction using the left control stick.

Pook Blade Saint Path: Further develop Whisper Elf's blade attacks.	Forest Ninja Path: Further develop Whisper Elf's Scarecrow skills.
Elf Jitsu – 1700 Press Attack 1, Attack 1, hold Attack 2 for Poison Spores. Press Attack 1, Attack 1, hold Attack 3 for Blade Flurry. **Elven Sunblade – 2200** Blade attacks deal even more increased damage. **Shadowsbane Blade Dance – 3000** Magical Blades fight alongside you.	**Scare-crio Trio – 1700** Three Scarecrows are created in place of your Whisper Elf decoy. **Scarecrow Booby Trap – 2200** Scarecrows explode and damage enemies. **Scarecrow Spin Slicer – 3000** Scarecrows have axes and do extra damage.

Enigma: "Out of Sight!"

Enigma's Stats!

Status:	Trap Master
Element:	Magic
Maximum Health:	310
Speed:	60
Armor:	30
Critical Hit:	60
Elemental Power:	32

Don't be PUZZLED in your quest for success, summon ENIGMA to unravel the MYSTERY and mend the MAGIC of Skylands!

To give up your home and lose your people forever is the bravest sacrifice of all—but when the evil Darkness threatened his homeland, Enigma didn't hesitate. When Darkness heard that a place between worlds existed behind an open gateway, he desperately wanted to conquer it for his own terrible purposes. Darkness ordered minions to attack the gate, but courageous Enigma sealed it off using his Sigil of Mystery (a magical symbol on his staff), trapping himself on the outside forever. Even the Mabu Mystic who had summoned him to Skylands was unable to help him return home. However, Enigma wasn't alone for long—Enigma was made an honorary Trap Master and now protects Skylands with his Traptanium Sigil. There's no mystery he can't unravel!

Attack moves:

Mystic Staff: Press **Attack 1** to swing the Mystic Staff. Press **Attack 1**, **Attack 1**, hold **Attack 1** for a combo.

Invisibility Mode: Press **Attack 2** to turn invisible and move around in total stealth.

Soul Gem Ability: An Eye for Several Eyes! – 4000: Hold **Attack 3** and press **Attack 1** to fire eye beams and rain down eye balls. Requires Paradox Pound. Prerequisite: Find Enigma's Soul Gem in Chapter 14: Operation: Troll Rocket Steal.

Upgrades:

Paradox Pound – 500: Press Attack 3 to slam the staff into the ground and damage all nearby enemies.	
Magic Mist – 700: Magic Mist released in Invisibility Mode damages enemies over time.	
Cloak and Dagger – 900: Invisibility Mode lasts longer and freezes enemies; cloak can do damage as well.	
Paradox Power – 1200: Paradox Pound does more damage. Prerequisite: Paradox Pound.	
Invisible Invader Path: Improve the Invisibility Mode attacks.	**Chief of Staff Path:** Improve the Mystic Staff attacks.
Ninja Style – 1700	**Eye Dash Combo – 1700**
Attacks coming out of Invisibility Mode do extra damage.	Press Attack 1, Attack 1, Attack 2 for a Cloak Dash combo.
Mindboggling – 2200	**Cloak Dash Combo – 2200**
Paradox Pound does even more damage and blasts enemies back.	Press Attack 1, Attack 1, Attack 3 for an Eye Slam combo.
Give Up the Ghost – 3000	**It's Raining Eyes – 3000**
Ghost version of yourself appears while in Invisibility Mode.	Hold Attack 3 to charge up the Paradox Pound attack and rain down magic eyeballs.

Blastermind: "Mind Over Matter!"

Blastermind's Stats!

Status:	Trap Master
Element:	Magic
Maximum Health:	240
Speed:	70
Armor:	30
Critical Hit:	50
Elemental Power:	39

When you SENSE DANGER, don't RACK YOUR BRAIN searching for clues; trust the Trap Master that OUTSMARTS THE BEST!

A powerful thought can move mountains—and that's just what Blastermind discovered when he saved his friends from a scary Ham Dragon! They'd been playing a game of "Hide and Sheep" in the Sardonic Mountains when an earthquake split the ground beneath him. Blastermind tumbled into a crystal-filled cavern, watching helplessly as the evil dragon attacked his friends up high. He was shattered! Luckily, the ancient psychic crystals surrounding him tuned into his selfless thoughts. The Psionic Power Crystals shared their magical power with Blastermind, letting him use his mind as a formidable weapon. He escaped from the cavern and saved his friends, proving himself worthy of becoming a Trap Master in the fight against evil!

Attack moves:

Brainwaves: Press **Attack 1** to blast nearby enemies with powerful Brainwaves.

Levitation: Press **Attack 2** to levitate enemies and smash them to the ground.

Soul Gem Ability: Lock Puzzle Psychic! – 4000: Hold **Attack 2** to charge up Levitation attack and shoot Lock Puzzles with it to solve them instantly. Prerequisite: Find Blastermind's Soul Gem in Chapter 15: Skyhighlands.

Upgrades:

Tasty Waves – 500: Hold Attack 1 to use the Brainwave attack for a longer duration.
Brain Freeze – 700: Press Attack 3 to create energy balls that slow enemies down.
Brain Storm – 900: Hold Attack 1 to charge up the Brainwave attack, and release for a super-powered Brain Storm. Prerequisite: Tasty Waves.

Down to Earth – 1200: Levitated enemies damage other nearby foes during the smashdown.	
Mentalist Path: Improve Brain Freeze attacks.	**Psychokinetic Path:** Improve Brainwave attacks.
Mind Control – 1700 Hold Attack 3 to create an energy ball that takes control of enemies' minds.	**Brain Blowout – 1700** Press Attack 1 near levitating enemies for a massive knockback.
The More the Merrier – 2200 Levitation Field passes through enemies and can levitate multiple foes. Prerequisite: Mind Control.	**Remote Control – 2200** Hold Attack 2 to charge up the Levitation attack and control enemies you levitate.
Mind Blown – 3000 Mind-controlled enemies damage others after going back to normal.	**Mind Mash – 3000** While levitating an enemy, press Attack 1, Attack 2, or Attack 3 to slam him or her down repeatedly. Prerequisite: Remote Control.

Déjà vu: "Did That Just Happen?"

Déjà vu's Stats!

Status:	Skylander
Element:	Magic
Maximum Health:	210
Speed:	60
Armor:	18
Critical Hit:	60
Elemental Power:	46

Don't SECOND GUESS yourself; DOUBLE THE FUN with INFINITE POWER and earn a VICTORY TO REMEMBER!

Inventive and insanely clever, Déjà vu built a machine that would let her alter the very fabric of time itself! Her aim was to boil the fastest eggs ever made, but instead of making breakfast, she cooked herself! You see, some evil, giant sea slugs were jealous that everyone could move faster than them, so they attacked Déjà vu, hoping to steal her time machine for themselves. But Déjà vu had a noble heart, and knew that power over time would be terribly dangerous in the hands of such selfish slimers. She turned the clock hands to 13 in an attempt to destroy her creation, but instead, the machine exploded into a terrifying Time Rift! Its tricky time-turning was transferred to Déjà vu! With her new powers, she sent the evil slugs sliding on a one-way slippery dip back to where they came from! With her new ability to control time, Déjà vu soon became a Legendary Champion of the Skylanders Tournament, winning a battle against Fist Bump, Fling Kong, and Trail Blazer all at once!

Attack moves:

Space-Time Shots: Press **Attack 1** to shoot a magical ball of time energy that homes in on enemies.

Past Selves: Press **Attack 2** to bring a version of your past self that explodes. Press **Attack 2** again to switch places with it.

Soul Gem Ability: Black Hole Bedlam! – 4000: Time Rifts now turn into massive black holes, releasing unstable time power. Prerequisite: Find Déjà vu's Soul Gem in Chapter 6: Rainfish Rivera.

Upgrades:

Time Rift – 500: Press Attack 3 to create a Time Rift, damaging all who touch it. Shoot the Time Rift to create a black hole.	
Long-Term Memory – 700: Past Selves last longer and replay a longer history, as well as damage anything nearby.	
Time Rifts Aplenty – 900: Have more Time Rifts active at once. Time Rifts now attract Space-Time Shots. Prerequisite: Time Rift.	
Live to Remember Path: Take a different path to improve Past Selves attacks.	**Remember to Live Path:** Improve Past Selves attacks.
Warp Field – 1700 Shoot a Past Self to create a warp field, pulling enemies toward the Past Self.	**Explosion Déjà Vu – 1700** When a Past Self explodes, the explosion is repeated two more times.
Past Self-Paralysis – 2200 Past Selves do extra damage and freeze all nearby enemies.	**Time Heals All Wounds – 2200** When a Past Self takes damage, you are healed by an equal amount.
Go Out With a Bang – 3000 When a Past Self explodes or when you switch with it, it releases Space-Time Shots.	**Space-Time Duality – 3000** Press Attack 1 to shoot two Space-Time Shots at once.
Circular Logic – 1200 Past Selves fire Space-Time Shots.	

Fizzy Frenzy Pop Fizz: "The Motion of the Potion!"

Fizzy Frenzy Pop Fizz's Stats!

Status:	Skylander
Element:	Magic
Maximum Health:	270
Speed:	60
Armor:	18
Critical Hit:	30
Elemental Power:	25

SHAKE IT UP with the MAD MIXOLOGIST to bring more BEAST to your BUBBLING BEAKER!

If you want to bring a bonanza of exploding potions and wild attack moves into your fight, call Fizzy Frenzy Pop Fizz, the crazy alchemist! Pop Fizz is always on the edge of creating catastrophe with his experiments, but he's perfectly happy to keep it that way. He throws different-colored potions at his enemies to cause acid pools, fighting mini-minions, and epic explosions. But above all, his secret weapon is his own awesome crazy spell: When he drinks his own potion, he turns totally berserk! There's nothing he loves more than chugging down on his favorite "soda"—a concoction of mysterious ingredients that transforms him into his raging, maniac alter-ego. No one is safe when Fizzy Frenzy Pop Fizz is buzzing with energy and rampaging through Skylands!

Attack moves:

Potion Lob: Press **Attack 1** to launch Pop Fizz's currently equipped potion.

Beast Form: Press **Attack 2** to drink a potion and temporarily change into a beast form.

Soul Gem Ability: Shake it! – 4000: Repeatedly press **Attack 3** to shake the potion bottle until it explodes. Prerequisite: New Concoction.

Wow Pow! Ability: Oversize Me! – 4000: Repeatedly press **Attack 2** to swallow a potion whole and become a Super Beast with overloaded attacks.

Upgrades:

New Concoction – 500: Press Attack 3 to switch to a new potion that can walk on two legs and fight by your side when thrown.
Puddle of Pain – 700: Press Attack 3 again to switch to a new potion that leaves a damaging puddle of acid when thrown. Prerequisite: New Concoction.
Raging Beast – 900: All attacks in Beast Form do additional damage.
Dexterous Delivery – 1200: Throw potions and grab new ones much faster.

Mad Scientist Path: Further develop Pop Fizz's potion attacks.	**Best of the Beast Path:** Further develop Pop Fizz's Beast Form attacks.
Master Chemist – 1700 All potions do increased damage and have improved effects.	**More Beast! – 1700** Beast Form meter drains slower and recharges faster.
Mixologist – 2200 Mix the effects of different-colored potions for brand-new effects.	**Mutant Beast – 2200** In Beast Form, press Attack 3 to perform a special attack based on which potion is active.
All In – 3000 Hold Attack 1 to pull up to three potions out and release to throw them all at once.	**Berserker Boost – 3000** In Beast Form, damaging enemies recharges the Beast Form meter.

Cobra Cadabra: "Charmed and Ready!"

Cobra Cadabra's Stats!

Status:	Skylander
Element:	Magic
Maximum Health:	290
Speed:	70
Armor:	36
Critical Hit:	40
Elemental Power:	46

SPRING AHEAD and STRIKE LUCKY with the Skylander that makes HISSSTORY of the bad guys!

This super-snake isn't just charming, he's quick to strike! Cobra Cadabra will blast enemies into dust with a bewitching song from his magic flute. If he gets really angry, villains know to run for cover or he'll make a complete basket case of them! When Cobra Cadabra was a young magician's apprentice for The Great Mabuni, he devoted all of his time to learning the art of performing magic. The audience loved him, especially when he enchanted snakes with his magic flute. But although he most longed to be accepted by the guild of Mysteriously Mad Magic Masters of Mystery and trained in the closely guarded secrets of the magic realm, the older magicians denied his request. Disappointed, Cobra Cadabra continued to learn with Mabuni and soon became an excellent enchanter—he even transfixed the magic rabbit enforcers that came to punish him for his secret lessons! The Guild of Masters eventually realized their mistake and decided to allow Cobra Cadabra to become a full magician.

Attack moves:

Magic Flute: Press **Attack 1** to musically blast enemies with your Magic Pungi Flute.

Cobra Basket: Press **Attack 2** to lob Cobra Baskets, which damage nearby enemies to the beat.

Soul Gem Ability: Big Basket Bomb! – 4000: Press **Attack 3** to launch into active Cobra Baskets to create a massive explosion. Prerequisite: Find Cobra Cadara's Soul Gem in Chapter 14: Operation: Troll Rocket Steal.

Upgrades:

Keep the Beat! – 500: Magic Flute attack does more damage when played to the beat of the music.	
Launch Cobra! – 700: Press Attack 3 to launch forward out of the basket, damaging anything in your path.	
Basket Party – 900: Can have up to ten Cobra Baskets active at once.	
Pungi Power – 1200: Magic Flute attack travels further and does more damage.	
Concerto Cobra Path: Improve Magic Flute attacks.	**Master of Baskets Path:** Improve Cobra Basket attacks.
Reverb Riff – 1700 Magic Flute music notes bounce off walls and enemies and can do extra damage. **Ultimate Flute Rock – 2200** Magic Flute attack does maximum damage. **Snake Charmer's Solo – 3000** Hold Attack 1 to play an enchanting song that charms enemies to fight for your cause.	**Basket Quintet – 1700** Throw five Cobra Baskets at once. **Call and Response – 2200** Shoot Cobra Baskets with your Magic Flute to power them up. **A Tisket, A Tasket – 3000** Hold Attack 2 to detonate all active Cobra Baskets.

Spry: "All Fired Up!"

Spry's Stats!

Status:	Mini
Element:	Magic
Maximum Health:	280
Speed:	70
Armor:	18
Critical Hit:	30
Elemental Power:	60

When ADVENTURE CALLS, BLAZE across the skies with the HORNED HERO that was BORN TO BATTLE!

Spry is a rare purple dragon and Miniverse counterpart of Spyro, which means he was destined for greatness from the moment he was born. His mentor Spyro is famous all across Skylands as its most fearless and celebrated defender. He has fought so many battles that stories of his bravery can be traced all the way back to ancient times. Just like Spyro, Spry wants to spend his life having exciting adventures and fighting for the forces of good. He was determined to be the very best fighter from his first day of school at Skylanders Academy, so he mastered flight, fire shields, and flame balls with first-class honors! Spry is now an enthusiastic and proud protector of Skylands.

Attack moves:

Flameball: Press **Attack 1** to breathe balls of fire at your enemies.

Charge: Press and hold **Attack 2** to lower your horns and charge forward, knocking over anything in your way.

Soul Gem Ability: Spry's Earth Pound! – 4000: In flight, press **Attack 1** to Dive Bomb.

Upgrades:

Long Range Raze – 500: Flameball attacks travel farther.	
Spry's Flight – 700: Press Attack 3 to fly. Increased speed and resistance while flying.	
Sprint Charge – 900: Can perform Charge attack for increased distance.	
Triple Flameballs – 1200: Shoot three Flameballs at once.	
Sheep Burner Path: Further develop Spry's Flameball attacks.	**Blitz Spry Path:** Further develop Spry's Charging attacks.

Fire Shield – 1700 A fire shield appears when using the Flameball attack. **Exploding Fireblast – 2200** Flameballs do extra damage and the middle one explodes. **The Daybringer Flame – 3000** Hold Attack 1 to charge up a Flameball attack for maximum damage.	**Stun Charge – 1700** Enemies hit by Charge attack become stunned. **Comet Dash – 2200** Charge attack does increased damage. **Ibex's Wrath Charge – 3000** Charge longer to do extra damage.

Mini Jini: "Any Last Wishes?"

Mini Jini's Stats!

Status:	Mini
Element:	Magic
Maximum Health:	410
Speed:	85
Armor:	48
Critical Hit:	80
Elemental Power:	60

Say Abra-Ca-STAB-Bra for the magical BLADES that will leave enemies WISHING for escape!

When evil gets you down, brighten your game with a magical spark of positivity! Mini Jini is the Miniverse counterpart of Ninjini, the most famous warrior of the ancient times. When an evil sorceress realized Ninjini's epic skills could bring about her undoing, she banished the magical genie into a tiny, enchanted bottle. But Ninjini refused to accept her fate and spent every day inside her tiny prison, practicing with her swords and gaining strength and skill. After many years, Ninjini finally broke free! Just like her mentor, Mini Jini's impressive powers and positive attitude fit right in with the Skylanders team. She loves blasting from her bottle when enemies least expect it and summoning her magical orbs to leave a lasting impression!

Attack moves:

Wishblades: Press **Attack 1** to swing dual swords for hacking and slashing enemies. Press **Attack 1**, **Attack 1**, hold **Attack 1** for a special combo.

Bottle Blast: Press **Attack 2** to hide inside the bottle. Press **Attack 2** again to blast out in a magical explosion.

Soul Gem Ability: Dazzling Enchantment! – 4000: While inside the bottle, hold down **Attack 3** to put enemies into a trance.

Upgrades:

Surrealistic Spheres – 500: Press Attack 3 to summon magical orbs and cast them toward the enemies.	
Abra-ca-STAB-bra – 700: Wishblades do increased damage.	
Juggling Act – 900: Hold Attack 3 to summon four magical orbs and damage multiple enemies. Prerequisite: Surrealistic Spheres.	
Bottle Rockets – 1200: While inside the bottle, press Attack 1 to launch rockets.	
Swords of Might Path: Empowers Mini-Jini's swords to wreak destruction upon her foes!	**Ancient Djinn Magic Path:** Harness ancient Djinn magic to improve Mini-Jini's bottle and Surrealistic Sphere attacks.
Wishblade Combos – 1700 Press Attack 1, Attack 1, hold Attack 2 for Fling Blade. Press Attack 1, Attack 1, hold Attack 3 for Enchanted Blade. **Wishbladesplosion – 2200** Hold the Attack 1 button to charge up the swords into an explosive blast. **Ultimate Wishblade – 3000** Wishblades do maximum damage.	**Super Surrealistic Spheres – 1700** Magical orbs do more damage and affect a greater area. **Ultimate Bottle Rockets – 2200** Bottle rockets launch faster, do more damage, and affect a greater area. **Buy a Better Bottle – 3000** Bottle is stronger and moves faster.

Gusto: "Gusts and Glory!"

Gusto's Stats!

Status:	Trap Master
Element:	Air
Maximum Health:	400
Speed:	60
Armor:	30
Critical Hit:	50
Elemental Power:	25

When the forecast calls for a COOL HEAD, this Trap Master can take the WORLD BY STORM!

He may look big and scary, but deep down Gusto is all heart. He was busy learning to be a cloud wrangler, under the guidance of the mysterious Cloud Dragon, when trouble blew his way. Some nasty Dragon Hunters came searching for the Cloud Dragon in his peaceful homeland of Thunderclap Kingdom, intent on stealing it. Bad news... until Gusto flew by to save the day! After all, he is a master of the wind! Gusto threw his boomerang right at them, again and again, chasing the evildoers away. Of course, our hero got promoted for his exceptional bravery. Gusto now carries a new Traptanium Boomerang and has a hurricane of upgrades for you to unleash!

Attack moves:

Traptanium Boomerang: Press **Attack 1** to throw a Traptanium Boomerang.

Inhaler: Press **Attack 2** to inhale enemies and press **Attack 2** again to spit them out.

Soul Gem Ability: Boomerangs 4 Breakfast! – 4000: Inhale a Traptanium Boomerang in the air for a super-powered attack. Prerequisite: Find Gusto's Soul Gem in Chapter 3: Chompy Mountain.

Upgrades:

The Breath of Life – 500: Regain HP by inhaling enemies.
Twistin' in the Wind – 700: Press Attack 3 to spin around and whack enemies with the boomerang.
Electro-Rang – 900: Hold Attack 1 to charge up the Traptanium Boomerang attack.
Lots of Lungpower – 1200: Can inhale more enemies at a time.

Air Ace Path: Improve Traptanium Boomerang attacks.	**Dizzy Destroyer Path:** Improve Twistin' in the Wind attacks.
BOOM-erang – 1700 Traptanium Boomerang and Electro-Rang do more damage. **Rang Me Like a Hurricane – 2200** Traptanium Boomerang attack creates mini hurricanes. **Boomerang Buddies – 3000** Boomerang attack releases additional 'rangs that orbit and protect Gusto.	**Spin Like the Wind – 1700** Can perform Twistin' in the Wind attack for longer and spawn mini hurricanes. **Shocking Twist – 2200** Twistin' in the Wind attack electrocutes enemies. **Lightning Ball – 3000** Hold Attack 3 to turn into an unstoppable Lightning Ball.

Thunderbolt: "A Storm Is Coming!"

Thunderbolt's Stats!

Status:	Trap Master
Element:	Air
Maximum Health:	410
Speed:	60
Armor:	48
Critical Hit:	30
Elemental Power:	25

When enemies swarm and STORM CLOUDS darken, you know that THUNDERBOLT is in CHARGE!

When Thunderbolt won a contest to let him wield the legendary Storm Sword on his homeland of Mount Cloudpierce, he was very proud. He was given the responsibility to change the seasons in Skylands—what an honor! Although a Frost Mage tried to steal the sword from him at the ceremony, Thunderbolt was quick to fight back, riding through the sky on twin bolts of lightning. What a terrifying sight to behold! Not only did Thunderbolt recover the Traptanium Storm Sword, but he now uses it to protect Skylands as one of the strongest and bravest Trap Masters.

Attack moves:

Traptanium Thundersword: Press **Attack 1** to swing the Traptanium Thundersword.

Storm Clouds: Press **Attack 2** to summon a cloud that rains pain down on enemies.

Soul Gem Ability: Lightning Rain! – 4000: Hold **Attack 1** and then press **Attack 2** to call in a lightning storm. Prerequisite: Find Thunderbolt's Soul Gem in Chapter 12: Time Town.

Upgrades:

Lightning Clouds – 500: Charge up Storm Clouds with the Thundersword, causing them to shoot lightning.	
Hurricane Pain – 700: Press Attack 3 to summon a Twister.	
More Thunder – 900: Traptanium Thundersword does more damage.	
Hurricane Pain Remains – 1200: Twister lasts longer, does more damage, and sucks in clouds. Prerequisite: Hurricane Pain.	
Power Conductor Path: Improve Traptanium Thundersword attacks.	**I of the Storm Path:** Improve Lightning attacks.
Direct Current – 1700 Press Attack 1, Attack 1, hold Attack 2 for Power Conductor combo.	**Stormier and Stormier – 1700** All lightning attacks have extra range and do increased damage.
Thunder Thrust – 2200 Press Attack 1, Attack 1, hold Attack 3 for a Thunder Thrust combo.	**Charge It Up – 2200** Charge up Storm Clouds with the Thundersword with extra power.
Just Add Lightning – 3000 Press Attack 1, Attack 1, hold Attack 1 to add some lightning power to your sword slam.	**Exploding Clouds – 3000** Storm Clouds can be overcharged with lightning and explode for maximum damage.

Blades: "Looking Sharp!"

Blades's Stats!

Status:	Skylander
Element:	Air
Maximum Health:	280
Speed:	60
Armor:	30
Critical Hit:	10
Elemental Power:	25

When you're on the CUTTING EDGE of battle, Blades is the SHARPEST SHOOTER in Skylands—NO FEAR!

Blades showed true courage from the very beginning. After facing his fears in the dungeon of Scalos Castle, he sacrificed his own freedom to save the kingdom from the terrifying Golden Fear Serpent. The serpent had awoken after 100 years asleep, and although Blades was young and dreamt of freedom and adventure more than anything in the world, he agreed to remain a captive in the dungeon forever to keep Skylands safe. Our heroic dragon had faced his ultimate fear—and so the Golden Fear Serpent disappeared, defeated forever! Although Blades can be reckless and likes to show off, he has learned the hard way (in an epic showdown with Machine Magnus!) that being part of a team is the best way to bring down the bad guys! His sharp skill has made him the youngest Skylander to ever earn Legendary status.

Attack moves:

Wing Slice: Press **Attack 1** for a Wing Slice attack. Press **Attack 1**, **Attack 1**, hold **Attack 1** for a Tail Stab combo.

Blade Shards: Press **Attack 2** to shoot Blade Shards into the ground; perform a Wing Slice to send them flying!

Soul Gem Ability: Instant Swirl Shards! – 4000: Cyclone Swirls automatically contain Blade Shards. Find Blades' Soul Gem in Chapter One: Soda Springs first.

Upgrades:

Cyclone Swirl – 500: Press Attack 3 to create a Cyclone Swirl attack, damaging anything nearby.
Sharpened Wings – 700: Wing Slice attacks do increased damage.
Shard Harder – 900: Shoot more Blade Shards and at a further distance.

Wind At Your Back – 1200: Cyclone Swirl now follows you around and does extra damage. Prerequisite: Purchase Cyclone Swirl.	
Wind Wielder Path: Improve Cyclone Swirl attacks.	**Shard Shooter Path:** Improve Blade Shard attacks.
Follow Like the Wind – 1700 Cyclone Swirl follows you more closely and spins Blade Shards faster.	**Slice Shards – 1700** Wing Slice attacks occasionally shoot Blade Shards.
Crushing Cyclones – 2200 Enemies inside the Cyclone Swirl take increased damage from other attacks.	**Cutting Edge – 2200** Blade Shards do increased damage.
Shielding Swirl – 3000 Cyclone Swirl is bigger and can deflect enemy projectiles.	**Shard Shrapnel – 3000** Blade Shards stick to enemies, causing more damage over time.

Full Blast Jet-Vac: "Hawk and Awe!"

Full Blast Jet-Vac's Stats!

Status:	Skylander
Element:	Air
Maximum Health:	240
Speed:	70
Armor:	30
Critical Hit:	30
Elemental Power:	25

Pull the THROTTLE and TAKE TO THE SKIES with the hero that fights BEAK and CLAW!

Full Blast Jet-Vac is the famous Sky Baron and bravest flyer in Windham. When Jet-Vac showed true honor by sacrificing his magical wings to help a mother save her children in a terrifying raid, Master Eon was very impressed. As a reward for his bravery and loss, Jet-Vac now flies using a super-charged vacuum jet-pack strapped to his body, protecting Skylands and blasting enemies out of the sky! Full Blast Jet-Vac has the same powers as his Mini Sidekick Pet-Vac as well as an extra upgrade called Double Barrel. The Double Barrel upgrade gives Jet-Vac two super-blasting guns to shoot at enemies, instead of his standard Vac Blaster. Make sure you stop and cool down, though—if your guns overheat, Jet-Vac tailspins out of action!

Attack moves:

Vac-Blaster: Press **Attack 1** to shoot enemies with a powerful blast of air.

Suction Gun: Hold **Attack 2** to suck enemies into the spinning fan blades.

Soul Gem Ability: Eagle-Air Battle Gear! – 4000: Jet-Vac gets enhanced resistances and a pretty sweet visor.

Wow Pow! Ability: Double Barrel – 5000: While flying, swap the Vac Blaster for two super-powered guns and hold **Attack 1** to fire continuously until they overheat. Prerequisite: Jet-Vac Jet Pack.

Upgrades:

Feistier Fan – 500: Bigger spinning fan blades on the Suction Gun do increased damage to enemies.	
Jet-Vac Jet Pack – 700: Press Attack 3 to fly and perform new attacks in the air.	
Vac-Blaster 9000 – 900: Vac-Blaster does increased damage.	
Turbine Suction Fan – 1200: Suction Gun attacks do even more increased damage. Prerequisite: Feistier Fan.	
Bird Blaster Path: Further develop Jet-Vac's Vac-Blaster attacks.	**Vac-Packeteer Path:** Further develop Jet-Vac's Suction and Flight attacks.
Piercing Winds – 1700 Vac-Blaster does even more increased damage and pierces multiple enemies.	**Tank Reserves – 1700** Can remain in flight longer and recharge faster.
Vac Master-Blaster 20X – 2200 Vac-Blaster does maximum damage.	**The Mulcher – 2200** Suction Gun attacks do maximum damage.
Super Suction Air Blaster – 3000 Suck up enemies with the Suction Gun, and it gives the Vac-Blaster a super shot.	**Flying Corkscrew – 3000** While flying, press Attack 2 to blast forward and perform a powerful corkscrew attack.

Fling Kong: "Monkey See, Monkey Doom!"

Fling Kong's Stats!

Status:	Skylander
Element:	Air
Maximum Health:	240
Speed:	70
Armor:	12
Critical Hit:	70
Elemental Power:	25

Don't HANG AROUND waiting for a hero; let FLING KONG put an end to the MONKEY BUSINESS!

Master Eon couldn't help but be impressed by the incredible air-fighting skills of Fling Kong, especially after he defeated the greedy General Snot and his band of terrible-smelling Gorilla-Goos! General Snot tried to the steal the solid gold idol of Kubla-Wa—but Fling Kong wouldn't take that kind of monkey business! True to his honor as a royal protector of the statue, Fling Kong swept through the troublemakers on his flying rug, flinging cortex discs to take out the thieves. Using the epic fighting skills of Monk-Ru that he'd learned, Fling Kong sent the evil Gorilla-Goos barreling into defeat. The temple was saved and the idol returned! Fling Kong's brave and noble instincts now carry him high above Skylands, fighting to protect the innocent like it's a breeze!

Attack moves:

Power Discs: Press **Attack 1** to fling Power Discs.

Magic Carpet Dash: Press **Attack 2** to dash forward and smash into enemies.

Soul Gem Ability: Make it Rain! – 4000: Hold **Attack 2** even longer and then release to fly up into the air, unleashing a rain of Power Discs from above. Prerequisite: Find Fling Kong's Soul Gem during Chapter 11: Wilikin Workshop.

Upgrades:

Spiked! – 500: Power Discs with spikes do more damage.	
Cymbal Crash – 700: Press Attack 3 to smash Power Discs together and create sound waves to damage nearby enemies.	
Mad Dash – 900: Hold Attack 2 to charge up the Magic Carpet Dash to do more damage and last longer.	
The Kong Klang – 1200: Hold Attack 3 for a more powerful Cymbal Crash that also stuns enemies. Prerequisite: Cymbal Crash.	
Disc Jockey Path: Improve Power Discs attacks.	**Carpet Captain Path:** Improve Magic Carpet Dash attacks.
Trick Shot – 1700 Power Discs can go through enemies and bounce off walls.	**Smash 'n' Dash – 1700** Hitting an enemy with a Magic Carpet Dash makes the dash last longer.
Smash Hit – 2200 Do a Cymbal Crash toward the end of a Magic Carpet Dash for a super-smash combo.	**Double Whammy – 2200** Throw a Power Disc toward the end of a Magic Carpet Dash for a double-disc combo.
A Toss-Up – 3000 Hold Attack 1 to charge up Power Discs for a massive overhead throw.	**Shock Treatment – 3000** Leave a trail of electricity after a Magic Carpet Dash that damages enemies.

Breeze: "Twists of Fury!"

Breeze's Stats!

Status:	Mini
Element:	Air
Maximum Health:	270
Speed:	70
Armor:	18
Critical Hit:	50
Elemental Power:	25

THROW CAUTION TO THE WIND and paint a RAINBOW of DOOM in the fight against evil!

Breeze is a unicorn/dragon hybrid and a proud mini Skylander. She is the Miniverse counterpart of Whirlwind, the beautiful and brave hybrid that fought back trolls single-handedly to save her ancestral species from attack. When Whirlwind needed a sidekick to help fight the evil minions of Kaos, Breeze was first in line! Don't let her size fool you, though—this little firework has the strength of a fully fledged dragon warrior with a unicorn's courage and heart! She commands the wind and clouds to do her bidding and has been known to create the deadliest black holes in all of Skylands.

Attack moves:

Rainbow of Doom: Press **Attack 1** to fire an arced blast of rainbow energy.

Tempest Cloud: Press **Attack 2** to send forth clouds that electrocute enemies. Hold **Attack 2** to make Tempest Clouds travel farther.

Soul Gem Ability: Rainbow of Healing! – 4000: Rainbows heal your allies!

Upgrades:

Rainbow Chain – 500: Rainbows do extra damage—shoot a Tempest Cloud with a Rainbow of Doom and a second rainbow chains off of it.	
Triple Tempest – 700: Have three Tempest Clouds active at once. Tempest Clouds do extra damage.	
Dragon Flight – 900: Press Attack 3 to fly. Speed and armor are increased while flying.	
Dual Rainbows – 1200: Hit a Tempest Cloud with a Rainbow of Doom, and two rainbows will chain off of it. Prerequisite: Rainbow Chain.	
Ultimate Rainbower Path: Further develop Breeze's Rainbow of Doom attack.	**Tempest Dragon Path:** Further develop Breeze's Tempest Cloud attack.
Double Dose of Rainbow – 1700 Shoot two Rainbows of Doom at once. **Atomic Rainbow – 2200** Rainbow of Doom attack does increased damage. **Rainbow Singularity – 3000** Hold Attack 1 to charge up a super-powerful Rainbow of Doom black hole.	**Triple Rainbow, It's Full On – 1700** Hit a Tempest Cloud with a Rainbow of Doom, and three rainbows will chain off of it. **Tempest Tantrum – 2200** Bigger Tempest Cloud does increased damage with increased range. **Tempest Matrix – 3000** Electricity forms between Tempest Clouds that hurts enemies.

Pet Vac: "Hawk 'N' AWE!"

Pet Vac's Stats!

Status:	Mini
Element:	Air
Maximum Health:	240
Speed:	70
Armor:	12
Critical Hit:	20
Elemental Power:	25

He may be MINI, but this courageous flying-soldier PACKS A POWERFUL PUNCH!

Pet Vac is the Miniverse counterpart of the famous Sky Baron Jet-Vac, the bravest flyer in Windham. When Jet-Vac showed true honor by sacrificing his magical wings to help a mother save her children in a terrible raid, Master Eon was mightily impressed. As a reward for his bravery and loss, Jet-Vac now flies using a super-charged vacuum jet-pack strapped to his body, protecting Skylands and blasting enemies out of the sky! Pet Vac may be pint-sized, but just like his full-sized hero, he swoops and soars in daring battles—like a true Skylander champion!

Attack moves:

Vac-Blaster: Press **Attack 1** to shoot enemies with a powerful blast of air.

Suction Gun: Hold **Attack 2** to suck enemies into the spinning fan blades.

Soul Gem Ability: Eagle-Air Battle Gear! – 4000: Enhanced armor and a pretty sweet visor.

Upgrades:

Feistier Fan – 500: Bigger spinning fan blades on the Suction Gun do increased damage to enemies.
Jet-Vac Jet Pack – 700: Press Attack 3 to fly and perform new attacks in the air.
Vac Blaster 9000 – 900: Vac-Blaster does increased damage.
Turbine Suction Fan – 1200: Suction Gun attacks do even more increased damage. Prerequisite: Feistier Fan.

Bird Blaster Path: Further develop Pet Vac's Vac-Blaster attacks.	Vac-Packeteer Path: Further develop Pet Vac's Suction and Flight attacks.
Piercing Winds – 1700 Vac-Blaster does even more increased damage and pierces multiple enemies.	**Tank Reserves – 1700** Can remain in flight longer and recharge faster.
Vac Master-Blaster 20X – 2200 Vac-Blaster does maximum damage.	**The Mulcher – 2200** Suction Gun attacks do maximum damage.
Super Suction Air Blaster – 3000 Suck up enemies with the Suction Gun, and it gives the Vac-Blaster a super shot.	**Flying Corkscrew – 3000** While flying, press Attack 2 to blast forward and perform a powerful corkscrew attack.

Snap Shot: "Croc and Roll!"

Snap Shot's Stats!

Status:	Trap Master
Element:	Water
Maximum Health:	290
Speed:	70
Armor:	24
Critical Hit:	30
Elemental Power:	46

TURN THE TIDES of every battle with a SMASH HIT of CROC POWER!

Snap Shot is the sharpest hero in Skylands. He leads the Trap Team into battle every time evil Kaos and his minions threaten the peace. During the infamous battle against the Doom Raiders, Snap Shot used his skills as a world-famous monster hunter to round up all the villains and lock them away in Cloud Cracker Prison—until Kaos set them free again! Now Snap Shot is determined to track the Doom Raiders down and imprison them once more, with the help of the Trap Team. This Crocogator is a no-nonsense veteran of protecting Skylands. His epic archery skills (elf-taught) and hunting skills (he learned to track monsters with the wild wolves!) make Snap Shot a true hero. He once brought down Wolfgang the Werewolf with the simple snap of his Traptanium Arrow—but he still prefers hunting chompies in remote Swamplands for fun.

Attack moves:

Traptanium Arrow: Press **Attack 1** to fire Traptanium arrows.

Crystal Slam: Press **Attack 2** to perform a Crystal Slam.

Soul Gem Ability: A Shard Act to Follow! – 4000: Crystal Slam in the air creates a new Traptanium attack. Prerequisite: Find Snap Shot's Soul Gem in Chapter 4: Phoenix Psanctuary.

Upgrades:

Sure Shot Croc – 500: Hold Attack 1 to charge up a Traptanium Arrow attack.	
Torrential Tidepool – 700: Hold Attack 3 to create a controllable Torrential Tidepool.	
Super Slam – 900: Hold Attack 2 to charge up an extra powerful Crystal Slam.	
Amazing Arrow – 1200: Improved Traptanium Arrow does extra damage.	
Crackshot Croc Path: Improve Traptanium Arrow attacks.	**Tide Turner Path:** Improve Tide Turner attacks.
Arrowsplosion – 1700 Traptanium Arrows now explode on impact.	**Big Wave Torrent – 1700** Torrential Tidepool is bigger and does more damage.
Traptanium Flechette – 2200 Shards of Traptanium splinter off arrows doing additional damage.	**Water Trap – 2200** Enemies caught in Torrential Tidepool become trapped.
Hydro Arrow – 3000 Hold Attack 1 to charge up a Water Element–infused Traptanium Arrow.	**What's Kraken? – 3000** Torrential Tidepool now calls forth the power of the Kraken!

Lob-Star: "Star Bright, Star Fight!"

Lob-Star's Stats!

Status:	Trap Master
Element:	Water
Maximum Health:	240
Speed:	60
Armor:	30
Critical Hit:	40
Elemental Power:	46

If there's SOMETHING FISHY on the tides of Skylands and you're getting steamed by the bad guys, get BACK IN THE ACTION with LOB-STAR!

When you're dishing out trouble to bad guys, make sure you have Lob-Star on the side! Following his passion for all things food, Lob-Star opened his own top-notch restaurant. He served only the very best delicacies and grew quite famous! Soon his reputation brought the impressive King Fish to his table—but that brought trouble! A hungry Leviathan (a terribly huge monster fish with lots of sharp teeth) tried to eat the guests and kidnap King Fish! Oh Snap! Luckily, Lob-Star was secretly trained in a mysterious fighting style and managed to send the Leviathan to the packing house! Sadly, Lob-Star's secret identity was blown. In honor of his hard work and dedication to the art of fighting, he was given Traptanium Throwing Stars and declared to be one of Skylands' finest Trap Masters!

Attack moves:

Starshooter: Press **Attack 1** to shoot Traptanium Stars. Shoot faster when "Boiled."

Boiling Temper: Press **Attack 2** to release a steam blast. Hold **Attack 2** to boil up with rage, increasing speed and power.

Soul Gem Ability: The Boiler! – 4000: Improve Boiling Temper attacks. Prerequisite: Find Lob-Star's Soul Gem in Chapter 6: Rainfish Riviera.

Upgrades:

Lob-Star Roll – 500: Press Attack 3 to dash and evade attacks. Go faster and further while Boiled.
Sharp Shot – 700: New Traptanium Stars do increased damage.
Boiling Over – 900: Release steam while boiling to repel enemies. Tap Attack 2 to let off more steam.

Lob-Star Express – 1200: Lob-Star Roll is faster and knocks away enemies. If Boiled, releases a steam blast afterward. Prerequisite: Lob-Star Roll.	
Shooting Star Path: Improve Starshooter attacks.	**Hard Boiled Path:** Fully charge up the Boiling Temper attack to release the ultimate steam blast.
Super Stars – 1700 While Lob-Star is Boiled, Traptanium Stars do increased damage and cut through enemies.	**Getting Steamed! – 1700** After getting hit by enemies, automatically release steam to damage them right back.
Twice the Starpower – 2200 Hold Attack 1 and release to shoot two Traptanium Stars at once.	**Self E-Steam – 2200** All steam abilities get stronger and consume less Boiling Power.
Star Defense – 3000 Hold Attack 1 longer to create more Traptanium Stars for protection. Prerequisite: Twice the Starpower.	**Full Steam Ahead – 3000** Leave a trail of damaging steam behind. Prerequisite: Self E-Steam.

Tidal Wave Gill Grunt: "Fear the Fish!"

Tidal Wave Gill Grunt's Stats!

Status:	Skylander
Element:	Water
Maximum Health:	270
Speed:	50
Armor:	6
Critical Hit:	50
Elemental Power:	25

If you need a FIN FOR THE WIN, make a SPLASH with the GILLMAN that NEVER GIVES UP!

Forever searching for his lost mermaid love, Gill Grunt is a romantic at heart. He practices singing love ballads (terribly!) while he travels around Skylands, courageously defending against the evil Doom Raiders. Once he traveled to Deep Water Wasteland to search for a missing fragment of the Mask of Power before evil Kaos could use it to cast Skylands into a world of Darkness. After a crazy bar brawl with a Cloud Kraken and the pirate crew of the Fearsome Fang, Gill Grunt followed a city of entranced merpeople to the cavern of Captain Grimslobber, where he fought for their freedom and recovered the missing water fragment. What a hero! You can be sure that whenever Kaos rears his ugly head, Tidal Wave Gill Grunt will always be ready for him!

Attack moves:

Harpoon Gun: Press **Attack 1** to shoot high-velocity harpoons at your enemies.

Power Hose: Press and hold **Attack 2** to spray water at your enemies to knock them back.

Soul Gem Ability: Anchor Cannon! – 4000: Hold **Attack 1** to charge Anchor Cannon.

Wow Pow! Ability – Ride the Leviathan! – 5000: In Jet Pack Mode, press **Attack 2** to ride a giant Leviathan, taking out anything in its path. Prerequisite: Water Jetpack.

Upgrades:

Barbed Harpoons – 500: Harpoons do increased damage.	
High Pressure Hose – 700: Power Hose attack does extra damage and knocks enemies back further.	
Harpoon Repeater – 900: Harpoons reload faster.	
Water Jetpack – 1200: Press Attack 3 to fly until the Water Jetpack runs out. Increased speed and armor while flying.	
Harpooner Path: Further Develop Gill Grunt's Harpoon attacks.	**Water Weaver Path:** Further Develop Gill Grunt's Power Hose and Jetpack skills.
Quadent Harpoons – 1700 Harpoons do even more increased damage.	**Reserve Water Tank – 1700** The Power Hose and Water Jetpack never run out of water.
Piercing Harpoons – 2200 Harpoons travel straight through enemies and hit new targets.	**Boiling Water Hose – 2200** Power Hose attack does even more increased damage.
Tripleshot Harpoon – 3000 Shoot three Harpoons at once.	**Neptune Gun – 3000** When using the Power Hose, press Attack 1 to launch exploding creatures.

Echo: "Let's Make Some Noise!"

Echo's Stats!

Status:	Skylander
Element:	Water
Maximum Health:	270
Speed:	50
Armor:	42
Critical Hit:	20
Elemental Power:	46

Summon the SUBSONIC SIREN if you're sinking fast in a fight—she'll BURST THE BUBBLE of trouble every time!

Living in a bubble of silence isn't fun at all, especially for a little Water Dragon with a big voice. Echo lived near the magical Pearl of Wisdom in a kingdom on the bottom of the ocean. Showing off her subsonic singing talent was her favorite pastime, but it always got her in trouble. The Water Dragons were only allowed to whisper in case they offended the visitors that came to seek the Pearl's wisdom each day. But Echo quickly found her voice when a greedy band of seahorses tried to steal the Pearl and keep it for themselves! Echo let out a sonar blast, shattering the unbreakable bubble the Aqua Jocks had cast around it! They fled, terrified of the thundering sound waves that chased them home. Echo returned the Pearl of Wisdom to its rightful throne in a huge oyster shell and all of the Water Dragons nearby cheered (very quietly—they hadn't used their voices for so long they had almost disappeared!). Her explosive sonic screams now blast away bad guys all over Skylands.

Attack moves:

Siren Scream: Hold **Attack 1** for a Siren Scream, damaging enemies.

Bubble Bombs: Press **Attack 2** to create explosive bubbles that move to the beat.

Soul Gem Ability: Call of the Siren! – 4000: Use Siren Scream on a Bubble Bomb to put enemies in a painful trance. Prerequisite: Find Echo's Soul Gem in Chapter 10: The Secret Sewers of Supreme Stink.

Upgrades:

Sonic Slam – 500: Press Attack 3 to create a sonic slam, damaging enemies on the ground.
Pitch Control – 700: Can hold the Siren Scream notes for longer, doing more damage.
Four-Beat – 900: Deploy up to four Bubble Bombs at any one time, which now do extra damage.
Subsonic – 1200: Sonic Slam now creates an aftershock that deals extra damage. Prerequisite: Sonic Slam.

Bubble Up Path: Improve Bubble Bomb attacks.	**Singalong Path:** Improve Siren Scream attacks.
Bubble Shield – 1700 Hold Attack 2 to protect yourself in a bubble that absorbs damage until it pops.	**Ultimate Pitch Control – 1700** Hold Attack 1 indefinitely for a never-ending Siren Scream.
Power Pop – 2200 All Bubble Bombs do maximum damage at an increased range.	**Scream Out – 2200** Quickly press Attack 1 again after a Siren Scream to deliver a powerful shout attack.
Burst My Bubble – 3000 While in a Bubble Shield, press Attack 3 to make it explode and damage nearby enemies. Prerequisite: Bubble Shield.	**Ultrasound – 3000** Hold Attack 3 to charge the Sonic Slam attack and unleash another, more powerful burst.

Flip Wreck: "Making Waves!"

Flip Wreck's Stats!

Status:	Skylander
Element:	Water
Maximum Health:	300
Speed:	60
Armor:	30
Critical Hit:	30
Elemental Power:	39

Don't BOTTLE up your troubles—call the SEA SLAMMER that FLIPS evil on its head!

Some Skylanders are born heroes—and Flip Wreck is no exception. When his homeland of Bottlenose Bay needed a shield against evil, this courageous dolphin swam in flipper first! He had been exploring shipwrecks near his underwater village when a hidden army of Ice Vikings attacked. As the other dolphins tried helplessly to escape, Flip Wreck scoured the graveyard of ship-wrecks for a weapon and shield, then fought every last Ice Viking until their bravery melted to puddles and they jumped ship and disappeared forever. Victorious, Flip Wreck decided to make even more of a splash in Skylands, so he joined the Skylanders to battle Kaos and his evil minions as well!

Attack moves:

Sea Saw: Press **Attack 1** to swing the saw sword.

Wheeling and Dealing: Press **Attack 2** to hop on the wheel shield, damaging anything in your path.

Soul Gem Ability: Sea Slammer! – 4000: While riding the wheel shield, press **Attack 1**, **Attack 1**, **Attack 1** to slam down on the ground. Prerequisite: Find Flip Wreck's Soul Gem in Chapter 9: Mystic Mill.

Upgrades:

Wheel Shield Bash – 500: Press Attack 3 to bash enemies with the wheel shield.	
Splash Damage – 700: Hold Attack 1 to blast enemies with your blowhole.	
Super Sea Saw – 900: Sea Saw does increased damage.	
Shield Mode – 1200: Hold Attack 3 to enter Shield Mode, invulnerable to enemy attacks.	
Fish Commander Path: Improve Wheeling & Dealing attacks.	**Sword Specialist Path:** Improve Sea Saw attacks.
Fish?!? – 1700 Press Attack 3 to release fish projectiles while riding the Wheel Shield.	**Sword Swells – 1700** Press Attack 1, Attack 1, Attack 1 to gush forward a damaging water swell.
Homing Fish – 2200 Press Attack 3 to release a fish projectile that hops toward enemies.	**Sea Saw Combos – 2200** Press Attack 1, Attack 1, hold Attack 2 for Whirlpool combo. Press Attack 1, Attack 1, hold Attack 3 for an Undersea Ambush combo.
Endless Fish – 3000 While riding the wheel shield, hold Attack 3 to shoot unlimited fish projectiles.	**Blowhole Blaster – 3000** Splash Damage attack has more range and does increased damage.

Thumpling: "Hail to the Whale!"

Thumpling's Stats!

Status:	Mini
Element:	Water
Maximum Health:	460
Speed:	40
Armor:	30
Critical Hit:	50
Elemental Power:	25

MAKE WAVES with a WHIRLPOOL of damage and hear your enemies WHALE with pain!

When you love to fish as much as Thumpling does, you'll dive in to any fight to turn the tide on evil, just to get a well-deserved fishing break afterward! Thumpling is a loyal and brave hero who is always around when his friends need help. He's the Miniverse counterpart of the monstrous whale-beast Thumpback. Thumpback was once a pirate on the dreaded ship *The Phantom Tide*. Rather than pillaging and causing havoc across Skylands like his crewmates, Thumpback preferred to relax on deck for a spot of deep-sky fishing. This was all well and good until the day a Leviathan Cloud Crab pulled him overboard and took him for a ride! Giving up pirating for the heroic life of a Skylander was the best decision Thumpback ever made—because now Thumpling has the ultimate mentor combo—a fighting and fishing partner!

Attack moves:

Anchor Assault: Press **Attack 1** to swing Thumpling's anchor at enemies. Press **Attack 1**, **Attack 1**, hold **Attack 1** for a special combo!

Belly Flop: Press **Attack 2** to dive into a belly flop, damaging enemies.

Soul Gem Ability: Blowhard! – 4000: While belly sliding, press **Attack 1** to spray water and starfish.

Upgrades:

A Whale of a Chomp – 500: Press Attack 3 for a big, whale-sized chomp.
Slippery Belly – 700: Slide longer after a Belly Flop and do increased damage.
The Whalest Chomp – 900: Bigger, most powerful Whale Chomp attack.
Now There's an Anchor! – 1200: Increases Anchor Assault's damage.

Anchor's A-Yay! Path: Provides more upgrades for the Anchor attacks.	Up Close and Personal Path: Provides more upgrades for the Belly Flop and Chomp attacks.
Thumpling Combos – 1700 Press Attack 1, Attack 1, and hold Attack 2 for Power Swing. Press Attack 1, Attack 1, and hold Attack 3 for Whirlpool Ripper. **Bermuda Triangle – 2200** Increase the power of the Whirlpool Ripper combo attack. Prerequisite: Thumpling Combos. **Ultimate Anchor – 3000** Best anchor you can find! Does maximum damage.	**Breakfast in Bed – 1700** While belly sliding, press Attack 3 to chomp enemies. **Armor of the Sea – 2200** Seashells make for better armor. **Bad Sushi – 3000** Hold the Attack 3 button to release a stream of projectile water vomit, damaging enemies.

Gill Runt: "Fear the Fish!"

Gill Runt's Stats!

Status:	Mini
Element:	Water
Maximum Health:	270
Speed:	50
Armor:	6
Critical Hit:	50
Elemental Power:	25

When you're after a POWER HO(U)SE of FURY, call the FLYING FISH that NEVER GIVES UP!

Gill Runt is the best kind of fish to have around in a tight spot—he's brave and loyal and loves to make a splash! Just like his full-sized counterpart, Gill Grunt, this Mini Skylander is at his best in a water fight. His harpoon gun is always locked and loaded, and he thrills to blast enemies with his high-pressure power hose and exploding starfish. Every day, Gill Runt travels alongside his mentor in an endless quest to protect Skylands from evil and to search for Gill Grunts' one true love—an enchanting mermaid from the misty lagoons who was kidnapped by cruel pirates.

Attack moves:

Harpoon Gun: Press **Attack 1** to shoot high-velocity harpoons at your enemies.

Power Hose: Press and hold **Attack 2** to spray water at your enemies to knock them back.

Soul Gem Ability: Anchor Cannon! – 4000: Hold **Attack 1** to charge Anchor Cannon.

Upgrades:

Barbed Harpoons – 500: Harpoons do increased damage.	
High-Pressure Hose – 700: Power Hose attack does extra damage and knocks enemies back further.	
Harpoon Repeater – 900: Harpoons reload faster.	
Water Jetpack – 1200: Press Attack 3 to fly until the water jetpack runs out. Increased speed and armor while flying.	
Harpooner Path: Further Develop Gill Runt's Harpoon attacks.	**Water Weaver Path:** Further Develop Gill Runt's Power Hose and Jetpack skills.
Quadent Harpoons – 1700 Harpoons do even more increased damage.	**Reserve Water Tank – 1700** The Power Hose and Water Jetpack never run out of water.
Piercing Harpoons – 2200 Harpoons travel straight through enemies and hit new targets.	**Boiling Water Hose – 2200** Power Hose attack does even more increased damage.
Tripleshot Harpoon – 3000 Shoot three Harpoons at once.	**Neptune Gun – 3000** When using the Power Hose, press Attack 1 to launch exploding creatures.

Jawbreaker: "Down For the Count!"

Jawbreaker's Stats!

Status:	Trap Master
Element:	Tech
Maximum Health:	340
Speed:	50
Armor:	12
Critical Hit:	70
Elemental Power:	25

If you've GOT A SCORE TO SETTLE, bring more POWER TO THE PUNCH with JAWBREAKER! He's a KNOCKOUT!

Jawbreaker isn't just a robot—he's a punchy hero that knows how to stand out from the crowd. When a massive army of Gear Trolls broke into the underground machines running the Sky Train intent on taking over, Jawbreaker knocked aside his old life of following rules and plundered the bad guys into submission. They surrendered and ran away—leaving the Sky Train all set to get back on schedule. In honor of his individuality and courage, Jawbreaker was made into an honorary Trap Master. Now, his magnetic personality shines as brightly as his Traptanium Fists!

Attack moves:

Traptanium Punch: Press **Attack 1** to throw a powerful punch with big, Traptanium fists.

Robo Rage Mode: Press **Attack 3** to enter Robo Rage Mode, moving faster, punching harder, and doing more damage.

Soul Gem Ability: Hypercharged Haymaker! – 4000: Hold **Attack 3** to charge up a powerful, electromagnetic punch. Prerequisite: Find Jawbreaker's Soul Gem in Chapter 1: Soda Springs.

Upgrades:

Ragin' Robo Rage – 500: Robo Rage Mode lasts even longer.
Spark Shock – 700: Press Attack 3 to punch the ground and release a wave of electric sparks.
Alternating Current – 900: Punching in Robo Rage Mode shocks enemies, doing extra damage over time.
Heavy Hands – 1200: Traptanium Punches do more damage.

High Voltage Path: Improve Spark Shock attacks.	Out-RAGE-ous Path: Improve Robo Rage Mode attacks.
Static Cling – 1700	**Jolting Jab – 1700**
Spark Shock attack sticks to enemies, doing damage over time.	Punching in Robo Rage Mode creates static bursts, which damage other enemies.
Hands Off – 2200	
Getting hit by an enemy automatically releases a wave of electric sparks.	**Defense Firmware Update – 2200**
	Take less damage while in Robo Rage Mode.
Sparking Interest – 3000	
Constantly release electric sparks in Robo Rage Mode.	**Punch for Power – 3000**
	Stay in Robo Rage Mode longer by landing punches.

Gearshift: "All Geared Up!"

Gearshift's Stats!

Status:	Trap Master
Element:	Tech
Maximum Health:	300
Speed:	70
Armor:	24
Critical Hit:	40
Elemental Power:	39

Kick your game into OVERLOAD and send enemies SPINNING with a supercharged attack made from all the right GEAR!

When Gearshift was created, she seemed to be the perfect successor to King Mercurus, the royal monarch of Metallana. But although he loved her like a daughter, Gearshift's wild spirit couldn't be kept tamed. Far under the kingdom of the robot island, Gearshift spent her days engineering the great machines that kept the city turning. One day, an army of Undead Stormriders laid siege upon the city, intent on taking her father as a prisoner! Although the king was angry to learn his daughter had not been performing her royal duties, soon he was prouder than ever. She saved her father by escaping with him underground—to the very place she had spent so many years working. She encouraged her subjects that they were strong enough to fight back by arming herself with their royal symbol—The Great Gear—and, of course, led them to victory!

Attack moves:

Traptanium Gear: Press **Attack 1** to perform a Traptanium Gear attack, depending on which mode you are in.

Mode Toggle: Press **Attack 2** to toggle between Hoop Mode, Dual Mode, and Fragment Mode, all with different attacks.

Soul Gem Ability: Swing Shift! – 4000: Traptanium Gear is more powerful and can switch modes much faster. Prerequisite: Find Gearshift's Soul Gem in Chapter 13: The Future of Skylands.

Upgrades:

Gear Grind – 500: Press Attack 3 to cartwheel forward, damaging anything in your path.	
Gear Saw – 700: Press Attack 2 to switch modes and release a Gear Saw. Gear Grind into it to make it spin again.	
Many Mini-Gears – 900: Press Attack 3 to Gear Grind and release a bunch of dangerous Mini-Gears. Prerequisite: Gear Grind.	
Mini-Gear Distribution – 1200: After Mini-Gears are released, press Attack 1 in Hoop Mode to knock Mini-Gears into enemies. Prerequisite: Many Mini-Gears.	
Dual Mode Duelist Path: Improve attacks in Dual Mode.	**Fragment Mode Freak Path:** Improve attacks in Fragment Mode.
Spare Parts – 1700 In Dual Mode, press Attack 1, Attack 1, Attack 1 to release a Gear Saw.	**Enhanced Fragmentation – 1700** In Fragment Mode, press Attack 1 to fire more fragments out.
Keep 'em Spinning – 2200 In Dual Mode, press Attack 1 to hit a Gear Saw and make it spin longer.	**Kick It Into High Gear – 2200** In Fragment Mode, press Attack 1 to also release Mini-Gears.
Geared Up – 3000 Gear Saws are larger and occasionally release Mini-Gears.	**Hardware Overload – 3000** In Fragment Mode, repeatedly press Attack 1 to lob out a ton of Mini-Gears.

Chopper: "Dino Might!"

Chopper's Stats!

Status:	Skylander
Element:	Tech
Maximum Health:	250
Speed:	60
Armor:	6
Critical Hit:	50
Elemental Power:	25

Do DINO-SIZED damage to have a ROARING good time with Skylands' BLAST FROM THE PAST!

Chopper may be a little T-Rex, but he's sure leaving a mighty footprint on Skylands! In his custom-built Gyro-Dino-Exo-Suit, there's no escape once Chopper sets his homing missiles and blasts evil out of sight with a ferocious roar! He's not all scare, though; Chopper once saved his whole village by flying each dino to safety when they became trapped by an erupting volcano during a ceremonial hunt. Later, he bravely flew in to save Flynn after an attack by Kaos on the Dread-Yacht. Together, they hijacked an old Arkeyan Copter to return to Skylander Academy and help thwart evil Kaos's plans. Never underestimate the Dino Destructive Power of Chopper when he's on a mission!

Attack moves:

Raptor Rockets: Press **Attack 1** to shoot Raptor Rockets.

Chopper Blades: Press **Attack 2** to fly into enemies with Chopper Blades.

Soul Gem Ability: Ultimate Dino Destruction! – 4000: Press **Jump** twice to enter Flight Mode, then press **Attack 3** to release a rocket strike of epic proportions. Prerequisite: Find Chopper's Soul Gem in Chapter 5: Chef Zeppelin.

Upgrades:

Roar! – 500: Press Attack 3 to unleash a powerful roar attack.	
Rev'd Up Rockets – 700: Raptor Rockets do extra damage.	
Homing Missiles – 900: Raptor Rockets seek out enemies for a sure hit.	
Better Blades – 1200: Chopper Blades do extra damage.	
Roar Like Never Before Path: Improve Roar attacks.	**Blaster from the Past Path:** Improve Raptor Rocket and Chopper Blades attacks.

Call of the Wild – 1700	The Bigger the Boom – 1700
Roar attack does extra damage and travels further.	Raptor Rockets create bigger explosions, doing extra damage.
R.O.A.R. Missiles – 2200	**Props to You – 2200**
Hold Attack 1 to charge up Raptor Rockets to release super Rage of All Raptor Missiles.	Chopper Blades do maximum damage.
	More Missile – 3000
King of the Jurassic Jungle – 3000	Hold Attack 1 to charge up Raptor Rockets to release bigger missiles doing more damage.
Roar attack does maximum damage, with maximum range. Prerequisite: Call of the Wild.	

Tread Head: "Tread and Shred!"

Tread Head's Stats!

Status:	Skylander
Element:	Tech
Maximum Health:	270
Speed:	85
Armor:	18
Critical Hit:	20
Elemental Power:	25

Make your enemies EAT DUST when this SUPER-CHARGED RACER hits HIGH GEAR!

Tread Head is a Skylander who knows that winning isn't everything—bravery and kindness make the true champions shine! Before becoming a Skylander, Tread Head desperately wanted to win the super-fast road race at Dizzying Dunes. But even after building a supersonic racing pod all by himself, he still gave up first place to fight away a horde of nasty goblin troops that threatened to block the other contestants. His wheelies and backfires are famous for blasting away villains when he's in a tight spot!

Attack moves:

Wheelie: Press **Attack 1** to speed up and pop a wheelie right through enemies.

Backfire Blast: Press **Attack 2** to shoot enemies behind you with backfire from your cycle.

Soul Gem Ability: Rocket Boost! – 4000: Once you hit maximum speed in Wheelie Mode, press **Attack 3** to rocket boost off of a ramp. Prerequisite: Find Tread Head's Soul Gem in Chapter 9: Mystic Mill.

Upgrades:

Pedal to the Metal – 500: Perform the Wheelie attack for longer.	
Spin Out! – 700: Press Attack 3 for a spin attack—any damage you take while spinning is cut in half.	
Tread Heavily – 900: Bigger treads equal bigger damage from the Wheelie attack.	
Kick Up Some Dust – 1200: Spin Out! attack does extra damage around a larger area. Prerequisite: Spin Out!	
Drag Racer Path: Improve Wheelie attacks.	**Pavement Peeler Path:** Improve Spin Out! attacks.
Spike a Wheelie – 1700	**Eat My Dust** – 1700
Spiked wheels make the Wheelie attack do extra damage.	Enemies hit by the Spin Out! attack are slowed down by a dust cloud.
Go Out With a Bang – 2200	**Spray It, Don't Say It** – 2200
Shoot out a massive backfire during the last stage of a Wheelie.	In Wheelie Mode, make tight turns to spray enemies with dirt and rocks.
Burning Rubber – 3000	**Fire Spin** – 3000
Leave a fire trail during the last stages of a Wheelie.	The Spin Out! attack goes so fast that it sets the ground on fire.

Drobit: "Blink and Destroy!"

Drobit's Stats!

Status:	Mini
Element:	Tech
Maximum Health:	290
Speed:	60
Armor:	24
Critical Hit:	20
Elemental Power:	25

For TACTICAL skill, summon the DRAGON with unparalleled BRAIN-POWER to CUT the COMPETITION!

Drobit is a clever mini-dragon with awesome fighting skills and a heart of gold. Every battle is a chance to out-smart the enemy, and with his laser-gun eyes and robotic flying suit, Drobit sure does it in style! He is the Miniverse Sidekick of Drobot, a genius dragon who never quite fit in with his friends. When Drobot had the misfortune of crashing onto a deserted island, it turned out to be his lucky day—the island was a treasure trove of abandoned technology. Drobot used the parts to build himself an unbeatable fighting suit and proudly offered his skills to Master Eon. Just like his mentor, Drobit loves nothing more than using his dizzying intellect to crunch enemies and numbers in the battle against evil for Skylands.

Attack moves:

Mega Blasters: Press **Attack 1** to shoot rapid-fire laser blasts out of your eyes.

Tactical Bladegears: Press **Attack 2** to deploy Bladegears that ricochet off of walls and pummel enemies.

Soul Gem Ability: Afterburners! – 4000: Fly faster, and afterburners damage enemies.

Upgrades:

Thruster Flight – 500: Hold Attack 3 to have Drobit fly. Drobit gets increased speed and armor while flying.	
Galvanized Bladegear – 700: Bladegears do increased damage.	
Axon Focus Crystals – 900: Eye Blasters do increased damage.	
Hover Mode – 1200: Hold Attack 3 to have Drobit hover. Prerequisite: Thruster Flight.	
Master Blaster Path: Further develop Drobit's Blaster attacks.	**Clockwork Dragon Path:** Further develop Drobit's Bladegear attacks.
Dendrite Focus Crystals – 1700 Eye Blasters do even more increased damage.	**Depleted Uranium Bladegears – 1700** Bladegears do even more increased damage.
Antimatter Changes – 2200 Eye Blaster beams explode on contact, doing damage to enemies.	**Explosive Bladegears – 2200** Bladegears explode on contact, doing damage to nearby enemies.
Quadratic Blasters – 3000 Press Attack 1 to shoot lasers out of your wings as well.	**Tri-spread Bladegears – 3000** Press Attack 2 to shoot three Bladegears at once.

Trigger Snappy: "No Gold, No Glory!"

Trigger Snappy's Stats!

Status:	Mini
Element:	Tech
Maximum Health:	200
Speed:	70
Armor:	30
Critical Hit:	50
Elemental Power:	25

Let the GUN-SLINGING GREMLIN with the GOLDEN TOUCH super-charge your PISTOLS!

This crazy mini-gremlin is all tongue-lolling tricks and fun, especially when there are villains to chase out of town! He's a crack shot too! He shoots oodles of coins from his handcrafted golden weapons with giddy laughter and hopping feet; he just can't keep still! His guns can shoot golden beams of light to bring down the bad guys; in fact, this Miniverse Skylander is unstoppable! One thing is for certain—he always leaves the townsfolk cheering as they gather the treasures he happily leaves behind! With guns a-blazing and a wacky grin on his face, this is one Mini Skylander that won't be left out of a fight!

Attack moves:

Golden Pistols: Press **Attack 1** to shoot rapid-fire coins out of both Golden Pistols.

Lob Goblin Safe: Press **Attack 2** to lob golden safes at your enemies.

Soul Gem Ability: Infinite Ammo! – 4000: Golden Machine Gun has unlimited Ammo.

Upgrades:

Golden Super Charge – 500: Hold Attack 1 to charge up your Golden Pistols, then release to fire a bullet that does extra damage.
Pot 'o Gold – 700: Throw a Pot of Gold, which deals increased damage.
Golden Mega Charge – 900: Charge up your Golden Pistols longer to do even more damage.
Golden Machine Gun – 1200: Hold Attack 3 to activate Golden Machine Gun and swivel its aim using the left control stick.

Golden Frenzy Path: Further develop Trigger Snappy's Golden Gun attacks.	Golden Money Bags Path: Further develop Trigger Snappy's throwing skills.
Happiness is a Golden Gun – 1700 Golden Pistols deal increased damage. **Bouncing Bullets – 2200** Golden Pistols' bullets bounce off walls. **Golden Yomato Blast – 3000** Charge up your Golden Pistols even longer to do maximum damage. Prerequisite: Happiness is a Golden Gun.	**Just Throwing Money Away – 1700** Lob attacks have longer range. **Coinsplosion – 2200** Lob attacks explode in a shower of damaging coins. **Heads or Tails – 3000** Toss a giant coin that deals extra damage. If it lands on heads, it turns into a mine, damaging enemies that touch it.

Wildfire: "Bringing the Heat!"

Wildfire's Stats!

Status:	Trap Master
Element:	Fire
Maximum Health:	330
Speed:	60
Armor:	30
Critical Hit:	30
Elemental Power:	25

FUEL THE FIRE of your fight with a LION'S SHARE of fury!

There's no taming the flames of Wildfire's fury when he throws himself into a fight! This golden lion began as an initiate in the Rite of Infernos for the Fire Claw Clan, a special test of courage and skill for all young lions. In the dark night of the dangerous fire plains, Wildfire set out to prove his bravery and worth, determined not to be excluded because he was different. Little did he know he would return that night a hero! When he discovered the other initiates being attacked by a giant flame scorpion, Wildfire burst into the fray! He hid them beneath his enchanted shield and took its powers into his golden body, morphing into a warrior to be feared above all others. His reputation has been known to send the Troll Bombers scuttling to their ships with only a warning!

Attack moves:

Traptanium Shield Bash: Press **Attack 1** for a single Shield Bash attack. Press **Attack 1**, **Attack 1** and **Attack 1**, **Attack 1**, **Attack 1** for Shield Bash combos.

Chains of Fire: Press **Attack 2** to summon the Chains of Fire, which not only burn enemies but pull them closer.

Soul Gem Ability: Lion Form! – 4000: Hold **Attack 1** to enter Heatshield Mode, then press **Attack 1** again to transform into a wild Fire Lion. Prerequisite: Find Wildfire's Soul Gem in Chapter 8: Telescope Towers.

Upgrades:

Heat Shield – 500: Hold Attack 1 to use the Heat Shield for protection and damage to nearby enemies.	
Extra Chains – 700: Chains of Fire can now pull four enemies at once.	
Fire Roar – 900: Press **Attack 3** to unleash a Fire Roar attack.	
Hotter Heat Shield – 1200: Heat Shield now burns brighter and does extra damage. Prerequisite: Heat Shield.	
Shield Slasher Path: Improve Traptanium Shield Bash attacks.	**Chain Champion Path:** Improve Chains of Fire attacks.
Burning Bash – 1700	**Lots of Chains – 1700**
Press Attack 1, Attack 1, hold Attack 2 for a Heat Wave combo.	Chains of Fire can now pull five enemies at once.
Fire Spin – 2200	**Blazing Breath – 2200**
Press Attack 1, Attack 1, hold Attack 3 for a Fire Spin combo.	Fire Roar has longer range and does extra damage.
Searing Slam – 3000	**No Escape! – 5000**
Press Attack 1 in the air for a Searing Slam attack.	Chains of Fire have a wider area of effect and can pull five enemies at once. Prerequisite: Lots of Chains.

Ka-Boom: "Boom Time!"

Ka-Boom's Stats!

Status:	Trap Master
Element:	Fire
Maximum Health:	250
Speed:	60
Armor:	12
Critical Hit:	80
Elemental Power:	39

BURN UP the bad guys with the MASTER BLASTER of FIRE POWER!

There's no escaping the deadly aim and firepower of Ka-Boom's epic machinery creations—he's an inventor with an iron fist! When evil Captain Ironbeard and his fleet of greedy pirates threatened to invade the Munitions Forge where he worked, Ka-Boom got really fired-up! He forged a weapon that would make cannon-fodder of even the most deadly pirates, and soon they were on the run. His Traptanium Cannonballs and jumping fire explosions blast a hole through the ranks of evil every time!

Attack moves:

Traptanium Cannonballs: Press **Attack 1** to shoot Traptanium Cannonballs.

Cannon Jump: Press **Attack 2** to blast the ground and leap toward an enemy, leaving a big explosion.

Soul Gem Ability: Missile Rain! – 4000: Mortar Strike attack now rains down fiery Traptanium Missiles. Prerequisite: Find Ka-Boom's Soul Gem in Chapter 18: The Ultimate Weapon.

Upgrades:

Jumpquake – 500: Cannon Jump now creates an earthquake that damages nearby enemies over time.	
Mortar Strike – 700: Press Attack 3 to fire exploding cannonballs into the air. Hold Attack 3 to aim your shot.	
The Long Ranger – 900: Increases the range of the Mortar Strike attack.	
Cannon Charge – 1200: Hold Attack 1 to charge up the cannon and release to fire a more powerful Traptanium Cannonball.	
Cannonball Runner Path: Improve Traptanium Cannonball attacks.	**Jumping Juggernaut Path:** Improve Cannon Jump attacks.

Bouncing Balls – 1700	Fire Fly – 1700
Traptanium Cannonballs ricochet off of walls.	Scorch all enemies in the path of Ka-Boom's Cannon Jump.
Super Bouncing Balls – 2200	**Big Air – 2200**
Traptanium Cannonballs bounce between enemies.	Cannon Jump has a greater area of effect and stuns enemies.
Triple Shot – 3000	**Triple Jump – 3000**
Shoot three Traptanium Cannonballs at once.	Can do three Cannon Jump attacks in a row without having to rest.

Torch: "Fire It Up!"

Torch's Stats!

Status:	Skylander
Element:	Fire
Maximum Health:	230
Speed:	60
Armor:	12
Critical Hit:	40
Elemental Power:	25

BRING THE HEAT on evil with a fearless fighter who has ENERGY TO BURN!

Dragons are a girl's best friend—unless they're the evil kind! Torch loved spending sweltering days in the dragon stables, helping her grandfather tend the kind guard dragons of her village. But one day she was caught out in the cold—the terrifying Snow Dragon attacked her village and breathed an enormous ice glacier across the land, freezing all the other villagers inside! Torch was hopping mad—but one step ahead! She grabbed her Firespout Flamethrower and set off to battle the cruel dragon on her own terms. With a blaze of glory and a flaming whip of her fiery hair, Flame defeated the Snow Dragon and the villagers melted back to safety. All but one—her grandfather was missing! Now, Torch carries his lucky flaming horseshoe to fire up villains and bring them down to size as she searches fearlessly for him across Skylands.

Attack moves:

Blazing Bellows: Press and hold **Attack 1** to roast enemies with a flame-thrower attack.

Flaming Horseshoes: Press **Attack 2** to pitch Flaming Horseshoes that stick to enemies.

Soul Gem Ability: The Incinerator! – 4000: Press **Attack 1** rapidly to create the ultimate flamethrower. Prerequisite: Find Torch's Soul Gem in Chapter 9: Mystic Mill.

Upgrades:

Heating Up – 500: Blazing Bellows attack shoots farther and does extra damage.	
Flaming Hair Whip – 700: Press Attack 3 to whip flaming hair around and knock back nearby enemies.	
Pyro Pendant – 900: Enemies with Flaming Horseshoes stuck to them take extra damage from fire.	
Blue Flame – 1200: Hold Attack 1 for a little longer, and flames turn blue, doing extra damage and going through enemies.	
Forged in Flames Path: Improve Blazing Bellows and Flaming Hair attacks.	**Maid of Metal Path:** Improve Flaming Horseshoe attacks.
Scorched Earth Policy – 1700 Blazing Bellows attack now sets the ground on fire, damaging anyone who touches it.	**Extra Hot Shoes – 1700** Flaming Horseshoes stuck to enemies do additional damage to them over time.
Hair's Getting Long – 2200 Flaming Hair Whip has increased range and does extra damage.	**Fireworks Display – 2200** Flaming Horseshoes will explode upon wearing off.
Double Barrel Bellows – 3000 Bigger Blazing Bellows flames.	**Hopping Mad Horseshoes – 3000** Use a fire attack on a Flaming Horseshoe and it comes to life, attacking enemies.

Trail Blazer: "The Mane Event!"

Trail Blazer's Stats!

Status:	Skylander
Element:	Fire
Maximum Health:	270
Speed:	85
Armor:	18
Critical Hit:	30
Elemental Power:	25

With a BLAZING HORN and STAMPEDE of FIREBALL FURY, this Skylander is just getting WARMED UP!

Trail Blazer is a noble unicorn who always fights for justice. If he sees a fellow Skylander in a situation that seems unfair, he'll stampede in to help settle the score. When a mystical unicorn (a rare creature that sprinkles enchanted cinnamon from its Churro Horn!) was caught in a trap, Trail Blazer did the only thing he knew was right—he used his horn to cut it from the twisted net. As it turns out, freeing the unicorn was a stroke of good luck—it sprinkled cinnamon all over Trail Blazer as it tried to escape, setting his elemental fire alight! Well, that sure got him all fired up! After chasing away the cruel hunters in a blasting flame of fury, Trail Blazer decided to put his fire power to good use by joining the Skylanders' quest.

Attack moves:

Fireball: Press **Attack 1** to shoot Fireballs.

Roundhouse Kick: Press **Attack 2** to deliver a Roundhouse Kick.

Soul Gem Ability: Heat Wave! – 4000: Hold **Attack 1** to charge up the Fireball attack, then release for a wave of fire. Prerequisite: Find Trail Blazer's Soul Gem in Chapter 13: The Future of Skylands.

Upgrades:

Bring the Heat – 500: Fireball attack does extra damage.
Stampede – 700: Press Attack 3 for a charge attack, shooting fire out of your horn.
Bucking Bronco – 900: Hold Attack 2 to go into Bucking Bronco Mode, kicking in every direction.
Fuel to Fire – 1200: All attacks do extra damage.

Equine Excellence Path: Improve Stampede attacks.	**Fireballer Path:** Improve Fireball attacks.
Flaming Forms – 1700	**Kick it Up a Notch – 1700**
Two flaming forms accompany you during the Stampede attack.	Roundhouse Kick and Bucking Bronco attacks have increased power and duration.
Firewalker – 2200	**Bouncing Fireballs – 2200**
Stampede attack leaves behind a trail of fiery footprints that damage enemies.	Fireballs now bounce along the ground and travel further.
Triple Fireballs – 3000	**Not His 1st Rodeo – 3000**
Shoot three Fireballs at a time.	Hold Attack 2 to stay in Bucking Bronco Mode for longer and kick up extra flame dust.

Hog Wild Fryno: "Crash and Burn!"

Hog Wild Fryno's Stats!

Status:	Skylander
Element:	Fire
Maximum Health:	330
Speed:	60
Armor:	6
Critical Hit:	20
Elemental Power:	25

Don't PLAY WITH FIRE when you're in the HOT SEAT; summon the HORN WITH SCORN to smash enemies with a single PUNCH!

Don't ever let Hog Wild Fryno catch you out telling a fib! This hot-tempered rhino is a stickler for the truth. When he found out that his gang of biker friends, the Blazing Biker Brigade, had been up to no good stealing from the villagers of Skylands, he was raging mad. When Fryno confronted them, the bikers refused to return the stolen possessions, or even to say sorry—big mistake! Wild Hog Fryno decided to teach them a red-hot lesson. He flew into a rage, fighting every biker until they were running scared. Hog Wild Fryno then set upon the task of making up for all the wrong they had done in Skylands. Before long, the Skylanders decided that Hog Wild Fryno, because of his integrity and bravery, had the makings of a great protector of Skylands. Now he and his new friends are the hottest gang in town!

Attack moves:

Brawl: Press **Attack 1** to punch nearby enemies. The speed and damage of punches are increased depending on heat.

Heated: Press **Attack 2** repeatedly to smash the ground and increase the heat level.

Soul Gem Ability: Madness Maxed! – 4000: Press **Attack 2** rapidly to make Fryno even more heated. So angry!

Wow Pow! Ability: Burning Rubber – 5000: While riding the motorcycle, hold **Attack 2** to go into a power drift, blasting enemies with molten rocks.

Upgrades:

The Horn and The Hog – 500: Press Attack 3 to dash forward, dealing damage to enemies in the way. When heated, Fryno jumps on a motorcycle to deal damage to nearby enemies.	
Built Tough – 700: Health is increased (probably from punching the ground so much).	
Fired Up! – 900: Press Attack 2 repeatedly to throw a tantrum and become heated. Tantrums now have increased range and damage.	
Molten Fury – 1200: All attacks do increased damage when Fryno is heated.	
Brawler Path: Improve punching attacks.	**Hot Shop Path:** Improve motorcycle attacks.
Hot Hands – 1700 Hold Attack 1 to rapidly punch nearby enemies and release heat.	**Born to Ride – 1700** The Horn and The Hog will always summon a molten motorcycle.
Spiked Up – 2200 New metal gloves cause Hot Hands to do increased damage. Prerequisite: Hot Hands.	**Hot Rod – 2200** All attacks with the motorcycle do increased damage.
Temperature Tantrum – 3000 Nearby enemies take damage while Fryno is heated.	**Crash and Burn – 3000** Fryno throws the motorcycle at the end of a dash, causing a massive explosion that damages nearby enemies. (Who's paying for that?)

Weeruptor: "Born to Burn!"

Weeruptor's Stats!

Status:	Mini
Element:	Fire
Maximum Health:	290
Speed:	50
Armor:	18
Critical Hit:	30
Elemental Power:	25

BURN UP the bad guys with a LAVA-LAUNCHING HOT HEAD for a VICTORY of VOLCANIC proportions!

Weeruptor never means to lose his temper, but when villains start causing trouble in his part of town, he burns up inside. As a brand-new student on his way to Skylander Academy, Weeruptor became the unfortunate victim of an evil scheme by Kaos—he was pushed overboard onto a life raft and left floating in the sea! Weeruptor's fiery body soon burnt through the raft and he almost fell into the wet sea—disaster! He grabbed a branch and was rescued by Cali, Tessa, and Whiskers right as the branch began to snap! Just like his full-sized counterpart Eruptor, Weeruptor throws molten fireballs and spews an avalanche of lava all around to damage enemies.

Attack moves:

Lava Lob: Press **Attack 1** to lob blobs of lava at your enemies.

Eruption: Press **Attack 2** to erupt into a pool of lava, damaging enemies all around you.

Soul Gem Ability: Mega Magma Balls! – 4000: Shoot up to three Magma Balls at a time that do extra damage.

Upgrades:

Big Blob Lava Throw – 500: Lava Blob attack gets bigger and does increased damage.
Fiery Remains – 700: Lava Blobs leave behind pools of flame when they hit the ground.
Eruption-Flying Tephra – 900: Lava balls shoot out during the Eruption attack.
Magma Ball – 1200: Press Attack 3 to spit out Magma Balls.

Magmantor Path: Further develop Weeruptor's Lava Blobs and Magma Balls.	Volcanor Path: Further develop Weeruptor's Eruption attacks.
Heavy Duty Plasma – 1700 Lava Blobs bounce and travel further. **Lava Blob Bomb – 2200** Lava Blobs explode and damage nearby enemies. **Beast of Conflagration – 3000** Lava Blobs do increased damage in the form of a fiery beast.	**Quick Eruption – 1700** It takes much less time to perform an Eruption attack. **Pyroxysmal Super Eruption – 2200** Eruption attack does increased damage. **Revenge of Prometheus – 3000** Eruption causes small volcanoes to form, doing extra damage. Prerequisite: Pyroxysmal Super Eruption.

Small Fry: "Crash and Burn!"

Small Fry's Stats!

Status:	Mini
Element:	Fire
Maximum Health:	330
Speed:	60
Armor:	6
Critical Hit:	20
Elemental Power:	25

You can't CAGE THE RAGE of the RED HOT REV-HEAD who CHARGES THROUGH evil!

Small Fry is a tiny rhino with a big temper! Just like his full-sized mentor Fryno, this hot-headed Skylander is a stickler for the truth. When Fryno found out that his own gang of biker friends, the Blazing Biker Brigade, had been stealing things, he was raging mad. But Fryno returned all the stolen possessions to the villagers of Skylands and then taught those bad bikers a lesson they wouldn't forget by chasing them right out of town. These days, nothing gets by the rhino team. Whenever evil rears its head in Skylands, you can always count on Small Fry to ride into the fight beside Fryno, burning rubber on his motorcycle and revving up the bad guys!

Attack moves:

Brawl: Press **Attack 1** to punch nearby enemies. The speed and damage of punches are increased depending on heat.

Heated: Press **Attack 2** repeatedly to smash the ground and increase the heat level.

Soul Gem Ability: Madness Maxed! – 4000: Press **Attack 2** rapidly to make Small Fry even more heated. So angry!

Upgrades:

The Horn and The Hog – 500: Press Attack 3 to dash forward, dealing damage to enemies in the way. When heated, Small Fry jumps on a motorcycle to deal damage to nearby enemies.	
Built Tough – 700: Health is increased (probably from punching the ground so much).	
Fired Up! – 900: Press Attack 2 repeatedly to throw a tantrum and become heated. Tantrums now have increased range and damage.	
Molten Fury – 1200: All attacks do increased damage when heated.	
Brawler Path: Improve punching attacks.	**Hot Shop Path:** Improve motorcycle attacks.
Hot Hands – 1700 Hold Attack 1 to rapidly punch nearby enemies and release heat.	**Born to Ride – 1700** The Horn and The Hog will always summon a molten motorcycle.
Spiked Up – 2200 New metal gloves cause Hot Hands to do increased damage. Prerequisite: Hot Hands.	**Hot Rod – 2200** All attacks with the motorcycle do increased damage.
Temperature Tantrum – 3000 Nearby enemies take damage while Small Fry is heated.	**Crash and Burn – 3000** Small Fry throws the motorcycle at the end of a dash, causing a massive explosion that damages nearby enemies. (Who's paying for that?)

Head Rush: "Taking Charge!"

Head Rush's Stats!

Status:	Trap Master
Element:	Earth
Maximum Health:	340
Speed:	60
Armor:	48
Critical Hit:	10
Elemental Power:	25

SHATTER the bad guys with a BATTLECRY that grips destiny BY THE HORNS!

Sometimes all it takes to defeat evil is to find your voice. Head Rush lived on a quiet farming island that she dearly loved. For years it was ruled by an evil Harvest Sphinx who turned the villagers into slaves. One day, Head Rush refused to let her family and friends succumb to his tyranny anymore, so she gathered all her courage and lifted her horns high and proud. She bolted through the village toward the evil Sphinx, yodeling a cry of freedom! The villagers realized that together they were far more powerful than any one person alone. They followed Head Rush into battle against the Sphinx until he was banished forever. This courageous Trap Master now uses her Traptanium horns to defend and inspire the villagers of Skylands every day!

Attack moves:

Traptanium Horns: Press **Attack 1** to head bash enemies; hold **Attack 1** to charge ahead.

Stomp!: Press **Attack 2** to stomp the ground so hard that anything nearby takes damage.

Soul Gem Ability: Horns Aplenty! – 4000: New Traptanium Horns do ultimate damage. Prerequisite: Find Head Rush's Soul Gem in Chapter 11: Wilikin Workshop.

Upgrades:

Mega Stomp – 500: Press Attack 2, Attack 2, Attack 2 for a Mega Stomp combo.
Yodel – 700: Press Attack 3 to perform a powerful yodel attack, damaging all enemies within earshot.
Stomping on Air – 900: While in the air, press Attack 2 to stomp down with more power.

Charge Control – 1200: Can turn while performing a charge attack, which also does extra damage.	
Lungs of Steel Path: Improve Yodel attacks.	**Stomp Harder Path:** Improve Stomp attacks.
High Note – 1700 Yodel attack does extra damage.	**A Stomp to Remember – 1700** Stomp attack does extra damage.
Modulate Yodel – 2200 Yodel attack does even more damage, and you can control the pitch.	**Power Steering – 2200** Turning during a charge attack makes it do additional extra damage with each turn.
Forget Breaking Glass – 3000 Yodel attack is so loud, it destroys the ground beneath you.	**Omega Stomp – 3000** Stomp attack does extra damage and destroys the ground beneath you.

Wallop: "Hammer It Home!"

Wallop's Stats!

Status:	Trap Master
Element:	Earth
Maximum Health:	300
Speed:	60
Armor:	18
Critical Hit:	50
Elemental Power:	25

When you're HOT under the collar fighting MINIONS and machines, SMASH through with the master of MELTDOWN POWER!

Wallop's hard-hitting Traptanium Hammers come in handy when you're in a tight spot. Once, he helped the Skylanders defeat the evil musical genius Wolfgang the Werewolf and his Troll minions, locking them safely back in Cloudcracker Prison. Before he became a Trap Master, Wallop spent his days learning to forge weapons in his homeland of Mount Scorch. With strength and unrelenting effort, he shaped hot metal into hammers and swords in the boiling lava pits of the volcano. But Wallop wasn't the only creature to call the grumbling volcano home. An enormous fire viper who had been hibernating in the coals awoke to the sounds of his hammers and—STRIKE!—attacked the peaceful tribe of Mount Scorch! Wallop leapt in action, thrashing and slamming his hammers at the beast until it fled from the volcano, never to be seen again!

Attack moves:

Traptanium Hammer: Press **Attack 1** to swing the mighty Traptanium Hammers.

Hammer Toss: Press **Attack 2** to toss Traptanium Hammers, which smash down with mighty force.

Soul Gem Ability: Now That's a Hammer! – 4000: Hold **Attack 2** to charge up the Hammer Toss and make super hammers. Prerequisite: Find Wallop's Soul Gem in Chapter 3: Chompy Mountains.

Upgrades:

Tantrum Mode – 500: Rapidly press Attack 1 to enter Tantrum Mode.	
Hammer Slammer – 700: Hammer Toss attack does extra damage.	
When Hammers Collide – 900: Press Attack 3 to spin both hammers into the battlefield, which then smash together.	
Cutting Edge – 1200: New Traptanium Hammers do extra damage.	
Tantrum Thrower Path: Improve Tantrum Mode attacks.	Hammer Handler Path: Improve Hammer Toss attacks.
Instant Tantrum – 1700 Hold Attack 1 to instantly enter Tantrum Mode.	Better with Shrapnel – 1700 Tossed Hammers shoot out Traptanium shrapnel on impact.
Total Meltdown – 2200 Hold Attack 1 to remain in Tantrum Mode for longer and do extra damage.	What a Collision! – 2200 The When Hammers Collide attack creates a bigger explosion that does extra damage.
Aftershock Wave – 3000 Release a powerful wave of Earth energy after coming out of Tantrum Mode.	Traptanium Splinters – 3000 Traptanium shrapnel from Hammer Toss sticks to enemies and does damage over time.

Fist Bump: "Knock, Knock...Too Late!"

Fist Bump's Stats!

Status:	Skylander
Element:	Earth
Maximum Health:	280
Speed:	60
Armor:	30
Critical Hit:	20
Elemental Power:	25

Get your HANDS DIRTY in every fight with the GROUND-BREAKING skills of a ROCK STAR!

Fist Bump may look like a hard case, but he's a party animal at heart! His break-dancing moves are always the talk of the town. (When he gets too excited, he tends to break the dance floor!) Before he became a Skylander, this rock panda had been in hibernation for many years. The Bubbling Bamboo Forest was peaceful—perfect for a good, long nap—until the day the evil Greebles came! The Greebles decided it was the perfect place to set up camp. They tore down trees and ripped up the earth to prepare for building. What a mess! Fist Bump woke as they began smashing rocks with their huge machines of destruction. He flew into a rage at the sight of them and smashed the ground with his fists of stone until it shattered beneath their feet. The rock-crunching machines broke into little pieces, and the evil Greebles ran for their lives! With the forest peaceful once more, Fist Bump set off to crush the plans of evildoers everywhere as part of the Skylander team.

Attack moves:

Panda Pound: Press **Attack 1** to smash the ground and also activate Fault Lines.

Fault Line Slam: Press **Attack 2** to slam the ground so hard, it creates Fault Lines.

Soul Gem Ability: Riding the Rails! – 4000: Walking creates Fault Lines and mini fault cracks. Prerequisite: Find Fist Bump's Soul Gem in Chapter 7: Monster Marsh.

Upgrades:

Seismic Slide – 500: Press **Attack 3** to slide across the ground and ram into enemies.

Panquake – 700: Panda Pound attack creates mini fault cracks, and performing it in the air creates Fault Lines.

Hold The Line – 900: Fault Lines travel further.

Don't Bump Fist Bump – 1200: All Fault Lines are automatically activated when you take damage.

Rowdy Richter Path: Improve Fault Line attacks.	Bamboo Bonanza Path: Grow Bamboo from your Fault Lines.
Fault Lines in Glass Houses – 1700 When Fault Lines are activated, some of them shoot stones at enemies. **Quake 'n' Bake – 2200** Activated Fault Lines are more powerful and do extra damage. **A Bolder Boulder – 3000** When Fault Lines are activated, some shoot spikey boulders at enemies.	**Healing Bamboo – 1700** When Fault Lines are activated, some of them spawn bamboo. Slide into them to regain HP. **Bamboo Harvest – 2200** Perform a Panda Pound in the air, and bamboo plants explode, damaging enemies. **Jump for It – 3000** Can perform a Panda Pound in the air much quicker and create an extra Fault Line.

Rocky Roll: "Roll with It!"

Rocky Roll's Stats!

Status:	Skylander
Element:	Earth
Maximum Health:	270
Speed:	60
Armor:	30
Critical Hit:	40
Elemental Power:	25

When you're stuck between a ROCK and a HARD PLACE, ROLL with the duo that make RUBBLE of the rebels!

This dynamic duo are best friends with a common goal—traveling through Skylands to help make it a better place for everyone! Both knew there was a greater adventure out there waiting for them after mining school. Rocky graduated as a first-class rock digger, and Roll impressed the whole school with his final Boulder Dash performance, but soon they went their separate ways. As fate would have it after years apart, Roll and Rocky ended up on the same journey to achieve their childhood dream of visiting Peek's Peak, a mystical place where true destinies are foretold. There they discovered that they were an unbeatable team! Together, they set off to explore and protect Skylands, turning every day into an epic adventure.

Attack moves:

Spit Ball: Press **Attack 1** to have Roll spit out a bouncing rock projectile.

Boulder Dash: Press **Attack 2** to perform a Boulder Dash charge attack.

Soul Gem Ability: Boulder Posse! – 4000: Press **Attack 3** to increase the amount of boulders in the Boulder Barrier, all the way up to nine. Prerequisite: Find Rocky Roll's Soul Gem in Chapter 12: Time Town.

Upgrades:

Boulder Barrier – 500: Press Attack 3 to form a protective Boulder Barrier; then press Attack 3 again to launch the boulders out.	
Rock On – 700: Spit Ball and Boulder Barrier attacks do more damage.	
Bouncy Attack Mode – 900: Press Attack 3 to create Boulder Barriers; then hold Attack 2 to enter Bouncy Attack Mode.	
Moh Boulders – 1200: Press Attack 3 to increase the number of boulders in the Boulder Barrier from three to six. Prerequisite: Boulder Barrier.	
Geological Grandmaster Path: Improve Spit Ball attacks.	Rolling Rumbler Path: Improve Roll attacks.
Super Spit Ball – 1700	Let's Roll – 1700
Hold Attack 1 to charge up your Spit Ball attack into a giant boulder projectile.	Rapidly press Attack 2 to rev up the Boulder Dash for more damage and speed.
Rock Hardest – 2200	Roll with the Punches – 2200
Spit Ball and Boulder Barrier attacks do maximum damage.	In Bouncy Attack Mode, press Attack 1 to perform a spinning fist attack.
Triple Spit Balls – 3000	Rocky Boxing – 3000
Shoot three Spit Balls at once that ricochet into smaller boulders.	In Bouncy Attack Mode, press Attack 2 to throw a dashing punch attack.

Bop: "Rock and Roll!"

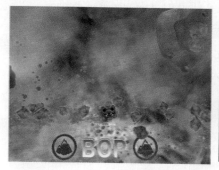

Bop's Stats!

Status:	Mini
Element:	Earth
Maximum Health:	310
Speed:	50
Armor:	12
Critical Hit:	20
Elemental Power:	25

CRUSH evil by a LANDSLIDE with the IRON TAIL of DRAGON DESTRUCTION!

Growing up as a dragon in Miniverse Skylands is a challenge, especially if you can't fly. But Bop has never been one to give up when the going gets tough—he just gets tougher! Just like his mentor Bash, this Miniverse Skylander has a very thick skin. He uses it to his best advantage by rolling into a ball and powering through enemies, knocking them flat with his spiky spines. When the villains close in, Bop calls on the rocky earth to smash upward, breaking through evil in one swift blow. Although he'll never fly, Bop found a better way to use his talents: to tear through obstacles that threaten Skylands—the true mark of a hero!

Attack moves:

Tail Swipe: Press **Attack 1** to swing your tail around to attack 360 degrees of enemies.

Rock and Roll: Hold **Attack 2** to roll into a ball and then over your enemies.

Soul Gem Ability: Triceratops Honor Guard! – 4000: New armor makes you harder to hit.

Upgrades:

Tennis Tail – 500: Deflect incoming objects with your Tail Swipe.	
Iron Tail – 700: Tail Swipe does increased damage.	
Summoning Stone Projection – 900: Hold Attack 3 to summon a rock wall; hit it with your Tail Swipe to launch rocks.	
Double Roll – 1200: Use the Roll attack for twice as long.	
Granite Dragon Path: Further develop Tail Swipe & Summoning attacks.	Pulver Dragon Path: Further develop Roll attack.

Mace of Destruction – 1700 Tail Swipe does more increased damage. **Summoning: Stone Uppercut – 2200** Stone Projection does increased damage. **Gaia Hammer – 3000** Hold Attack 1 to charge up the Tail Swipe and do extra damage. Prerequisite: Mace of Destruction.	**Pulver Roll – 1700** Roll attack does increased damage. **Earthen Force Roll – 2200** Roll does more damage and can roll right through enemy attacks. **Continental Boulder – 3000** Become a giant ball while rolling—roll faster and do even more damage. Prerequisite: Pulver Roll.

Terrabite: "It's Beatin' Time!"

Terrabite's Stats!

Status:	Mini
Element:	Earth
Maximum Health:	310
Speed:	50
Armor:	18
Critical Hit:	30
Elemental Power:	25

Unleash the KING OF THE RING to slam evil UNDERGROUND!

There's no stopping Terrabite when this shark gets his fins dirty! He loves a good fight and always plays to win, especially if there's money involved! Terrabite transforms the earth around him, smashing down mountains and burrowing underground, ready to spring up and attack his enemies when they least expect it. With his school of dirt-sharks in multi-attack mode, Terrabite does extra damage, leaving the villains quaking in fear! He's a skilled boxer and loves to hear his mentor Terrafin recount stories of when he battled Kaos and the Cyclops Choppers to protect the Core of Light.

Attack moves:

Punch: Press **Attack 1** to punch the enemy. Press **Attack 1**, **Attack 1**, hold **Attack 1** to perform a combo.

Earth Swim: Press **Attack 2** to burrow underground, and press **Attack 1** to perform a belly flop.

Soul Gem Ability: Surface Feeder! – 4000: Collect power-ups while burrowed.

Upgrades:

Brass Knuckles – 500: Punch attacks do increased damage.
Mega Bellyflop – 700: Belly flop does increased damage and affects a larger area.
Feeding Frenzy – 900: Press Attack 3 to spawn mini-sharks that burrow and latch onto enemies.
Multi Target Punches – 1200: Punch attack hits multiple enemies.

Sand Hog Path: Further develop burrowing abilities.	Brawler Path: Further develop punching abilities.
Master Earth Swimmer – 1700 Increased speed while burrowing. **Homing Frenzy – 2200** Mini-sharks home in on enemies and do extra damage. **Razorfin – 3000** While burrowed, your dorsal fin does damage to enemies.	**Pugilist – 1700** Press Attack 1, Attack 1, hold Attack 2 for Body Slam. Press Attack 1, Attack 1, hold Attack 3 for Uppercut. **Spiked Knuckles – 2200** All punch attacks do even more damage! **Frenzy Shield – 3000** You launch mini-sharks at enemies who damage you.

Krypt King: "I've Got the Edge!"

Krypt King's Stats!

Status:	Trap Master
Element:	Undead
Maximum Health:	300
Speed:	60
Armor:	24
Critical Hit:	40
Elemental Power:	32

When EVIL creeps under darkness, summon the KING from the KRYPT to champion your fight in true ARKEYAN style!

It was a sad and lonely life for the ghost of a noble knight as he wandered from town to town in Skylands. He had nobody (literally, no body!) at all, so one day, when he found an empty suit of armor in an ancient Arkeyan weapon vault, he tried it on. Terrible idea! The armor was booby trapped! A battalion of evil machines smashed out of a secret chamber and launched an attack on the poor spirit. In defiance, he took up the great sword of his new armor and bravely fought back. As he fought, the ancient power of the Arkeyans filled his spirit. The Krypt King summoned a swarm of insects to aid his attack and battled the machines with his broadsword until he defeated every one of them. His honor led him to the Skylanders, to whom he offered his undying service in haunting evil wherever it lurks.

Attack moves:

Traptanium Broadsword: Press **Attack 1** to swing the Traptanium Broadsword. Press **Attack 1**, **Attack 1**, **Attack 1** for a combo attack.

The Swarm: Press **Attack 2** to release a swarm of Undead insects that seek out enemies.

Soul Gem Ability: Unlimited Traptanium Works! – 4000: Landing a critical hit causes swords to rain down upon Krypt King's enemies. Prerequisite: Find Krypt King's Soul Gem in Chapter 7: Monster Marsh.

Upgrades:

Haunted Sword – 500: Press Attack 3 to release the Traptanium Broadsword and steer it toward enemies.	
Spectral Slowdown – 700: Haunted Sword slows down all enemies it touches.	
The Broader the Broadsword – 900: Traptanium Broadsword attack does extra damage with greater reach.	
Super Swarm – 1200: Hold Attack 2 to charge up the Swarm attack to unleash a larger swarm.	
Lord of the Sword Path: Improve Traptanium Broadsword attacks.	**Swarm Summoner Path:** Improved Swarm attacks.
Enchanted Armor – 1700 Armor is increased upon defeating an enemy. **The Rich Get Richer – 2200** Attacks do increased damage after defeating an enemy. **Combo Attacks – 3000** Press Attack 1, Attack 1, Attack 2 for Sabre Spin Combo. Press Attack 1, Attack 1, Attack 3 for Nether Blast Combo.	**Stunning Sting – 1700** Swarm attack now stuns enemies. **Stir Up the Swarm – 2200** Hit the Swarm with your Traptanium Broadsword to power it up. **Parasitic Power – 3000** Get healed by the Swarm after it dies.

Short Cut: "Cut to the Chase!"

Short Cut's Stats!

Status:	Trap Master
Element:	Undead
Maximum Health:	280
Speed:	70
Armor:	18
Critical Hit:	80
Elemental Power:	39

Trust Traptanium SHEARS to CUT evil down to size and leave the bad guys ALL SEWN UP!

Short Cut was famous for his flair with fashion, but before he became one of Eon's finest, the Skeleton Pirates had him all stitched up! They kidnapped him onto a flying sailing ship and forced him to sew a magic hat made of stolen golden yarn. Short Cut knew the hat would be used to foretell the future of the people of Skylands—and in the mean hands of the Skeleton leader, that meant disaster! While the members of the crew were snoring in their bunks, Short Cut swiftly sewed their clothes together and left them in a tangle! With his giant shears, he slit the sails and hemmed the pirate prisoners inside. Now, that's a fancy way to cut down the bad guys!

Attack moves:

Traptanium Scissors: Press **Attack 1** to snip away with Traptanium Scissors.

Phantom Puppets: Press **Attack 2** to summon puppet minions who attack enemies.

Soul Gem Ability: Scissor Stilts! – 4000: Hold **Attack 1** and press **Attack 2** to walk on the Traptanium Scissors like stilts, damaging anything in your path. Prerequisite: Find Short Cut's Soul Gem in Chapter 17: Lair of the Golden Queen.

Upgrades:

Cutting Frenzy – 500: Rapidly press Attack 1 to go into a cutting frenzy.
Nether Needle – 700: Press Attack 3 to shoot a Nether Needle and pull enemies you hit in closer.
No Strings Attached – 900: Cut a Puppet's string with Traptanium Scissors to make it faster and more powerful.

Cut Through Worlds – 1200: Hold Attack 1 and release to cut open a rift into another dimension.	
Scary Seamster Path: Upgrade Traptanium Scissor attacks.	**Puppet Master Path:** Upgrade Phantom Puppet attacks.
Treacherous Tangle – 1700 Enemies reeled in by the Nether Needle are tangled up in thread.	**Go Out with a Bang – 1700** Phantom Puppets explode before disappearing, damaging anything around them.
Super Snips – 2200 Enemies tangled up in thread take extra damage from Scissor attacks.	**Puppet Population – 2200** Can summon more Phantom Puppets at a time, and all do extra damage.
Threadsplosion – 3000 After an enemy becomes untangled, an explosion occurs, doing extra damage.	**Paging Dr. Puppets – 3000** Phantom Puppets can heal you after damaging an enemy.

Funny Bone: "I Have a Bone to Pick!"

Funny Bone's Stats!

Status:	Skylander
Element:	Undead
Maximum Health:	270
Speed:	70
Armor:	24
Critical Hit:	20
Elemental Power:	46

When there's GRAVE DANGER AHEAD, you'd better get the TOP DOG in town to UNLEASH some damage!

He may look frightening, but this playful puppy loves to fetch a bone and flings phantom Frisbees while he nips at the heels of evil minions. He's always up to mischief—like the time he buried his neighbor's birthday cake near the Eternal Chuckling Trees. The trees are the most popular spot in Punch Line Island for picnics because of their magical ability to make everybody laugh. On this particular day, Funny Bone's mischief came to good use when he spotted the nasty minions of Count Money Bone trying to chop down the Chuckling Trees. He dropped his doggy treat and attacked the minions instead, foiling their evil plans to overpower Skylands by creating a devastating "Funny Bomb" from the magic wood. Funny Bone digs up skeletal Bone Paws to attack enemies in a tight spot, and his spinning Bone Saw attack cuts through enemy lines with ease, making him all bark and all bite in a fight!

Attack moves:

Bone Saw: Press **Attack 1** to dash forward and slice enemies.

Flying Bone Disc: Press **Attack 2** to shoot a Flying Bone Disc.

Soul Gem Ability: Healing Paws! – 4000: Bone Paws pet Funny Bone to heal him. Prerequisite: Find Funny Bone's Soul Gem in Chapter 4: The Phoenix Psanctuary.

Upgrades:

Bone Paws – 500: Press Attack 3 to raise Bone Paws from the ground, which attack enemies.	
Disc Demon – 700: Flying Bone Disc does extra damage.	
Ferocious Fetch – 900: Press and hold Attack 2 to chase after the Flying Bone Disc and release to fetch it.	
Bump Up the Blades – 1200: Press and hold Attack 1 to charge the Bone Saw.	
Tail Wagger Path: Improve Bone Saw attacks.	**Bone Zoner Path:** Improve Flying Bone Disc attacks.
Supercharged Saw – 1700 Press and hold Attack 3 to supercharge the Bone Saw.	**Flying Bone Boom – 1700** Flying Bone Discs now explode and do additional damage.
Bone Paw Power – 2200 Dash toward a Bone Paw to supercharge the Bone Saw.	**Ultimate FBD – 2200** Flying Bone Disc Slam affects a larger area.
Head Case – 3000 Press and hold Attack 3 during the Bone Saw attack to summon a ghostly skull to devour enemies.	**Play Catch – 3000** Hit a Bone Paw with a Flying Bone Disc to play catch with other paws.

Bat Spin: "No Rest for the Wicked!"

Bat Spin's Stats!

Status:	Skylander
Element:	Undead
Maximum Health:	240
Speed:	85
Armor:	12
Critical Hit:	50
Elemental Power:	46

When evil SWARMS in Skylands, sound your BAT-TLE CRY loud and clear for a BAT ATTACK that will send Kaos SCREECHING in fear!

Bat Spin was an underworld orphaned vampire who had wandered lost and lonely for a very long time when she finally stumbled across a colony of magical bats. Although she was scared and sad, the bat family took her in and cared for her, teaching Bat Spin everything they knew about the magical sonar powers they possessed. One day, the bat cave was attacked by a cruel horde of undead trolls, bent on stealing the bats' magic to build an evil sonar weapon. Bat Spin flew into attack, summoning magic pet bats to protect her family. She transformed herself into an enormous screeching bat, attacking the trolls. They fled in terror, never to return! Her bat colony was safe once again, so Bat Spin began her new adventure with the Skylanders, searching out the lurking forces of evil and sending them into a spin.

Attack moves:

Bat Attack: Press **Attack 1** to shoot bitey pet bats out at enemies.

Bat Swarm: Press **Attack 2** to summon a maelstrom of bat damage.

Soul Gem Ability: Great Balls of Bats! – 4000: Hold **Attack 1** to launch a giant ball of bats! Prerequisite: Find Bat Spin's Soul Gem in Chapter 8: Telescope Towers.

Upgrades:

Healing Bite – 500: Collect pet bats after they have bitten enemies to regain HP.
Brawny Bats – 700: Pet bats last longer, do more damage, and are more aggressive.
Go Batty! – 900: Press Attack 3 to transform into a Giant Bat! In Bat Form, press Attack 1 to bite and Attack 2 to screech.

A Colony of Bats – 1200: Increase the maximum number of pet bats.	
Pet Purveyor Path: Improve abilities to summon bats.	**Bat Betterment Path:** Improve Bat Form abilities.
Mr. Dizzy – 1700 A new pet bat, Mr. Dizzy, stuns and confuses enemies.	**Bat-tle Cry – 1700** In Bat Form, the screech attack does extra damage and powers up pet bats.
Mr. Blocky – 2200 A new pet bat, Mr. Blocky, protects you by deflecting projectiles.	**Ultimate Bat Squad – 2200** More pet bats fly with you and have additional powers.
Mr. Bitey – 3000 A new pet bat, Mr. Bitey, does extra biting damage.	**Chiropteran Call – 3000** In Bat Form, the bite attack shoots out three additional pet bats.

Eye-Small: "I've Got My Eye on You!"

Eye-Small's Stats!

Status:	Mini
Element:	Undead
Maximum Health:	430
Speed:	50
Armor:	30
Critical Hit:	50
Elemental Power:	53

Keep your EYE ON THE PRIZE with the LASER GLARE fighter that punches evil OUT OF SIGHT!

What do you get when you cross a headless giant with an enormous flying eyeball? Seriously, it's no joke! You get an epic fist-smashing hero with an eye out for trouble (literally!). There's nowhere to hide when Eye-Small comes looking! This Mini Skylander is ruthless in a fight and demands an eye for an eye, just like his full-sized mentor, Eye Brawl. It took over a century of fighting for Eye Brawl to become the respected Skylander he is today! What originally began as a friendly staring contest between a giant and an eyeball turned bad, and soon became an epic battle for the history books—until they both realized they were actually a fantastic crime-fighting team when they could learn to cooperate! These days, when Eye-Small follows Eye Brawl into battle with reckless abandon, he never misses a trick!

Attack moves:

Haymaker: Press **Attack 1** to throw some heavy punches. Press **Attack 1**, **Attack 1**, hold **Attack 1** for a special combo.

Eye Fly: Press the **Attack 2** button to detach the eyeball and fly around. While flying, press **Attack 1** to shoot eye lasers.

Soul Gem Ability: You'll Shoot Your Eye Out! – 4000: Hold **Attack 1** to charge up Eye-Small's eye and then release to pop it off the body, smashing directly ahead.

Upgrades:

An Eye in Team – 500: Press Attack 3 to summon more eyeballs from the earth to attack enemies.	
Awesome Occu-Blast – 700: Eye laser has a faster rate of fire.	
The Pummeler – 900: Punch attacks do increased damage.	
Headless, Not Helpless – 1200: While flying the eyeball, his headless body punches continuously.	
Eye Brawler Path: Further develop Eye Small's melee combat skills.	**Eye for an Eye Path:** Further develop Flying Eyeball abilities.
Eye-Small Combos – 1700 Press Attack 1, Attack 1, hold Attack 2 for Eye Ball Spin. Press Attack 1, Attack 1, hold Attack 3 for 360 Spin.	**Asserting Independence – 1700** Eyeball can now fly faster and for a longer duration. **Eye-Crawlers – 2200**
Ultimate Pummeler – 2200 Melee attacks do additional damage.	When enemies are hit with eye lasers, eyes form around the point of impact.
Beats an Eye Patch – 3000 New armor provides additional protection.	**Bouncy Bouncy! – 3000** While flying the eyeball, press Attack 3 to bounce the eye on the ground.

Hijinx: "Fear the Dark!"

Hijinx's Stats!

Status:	Mini
Element:	Undead
Maximum Health:	270
Speed:	60
Armor:	18
Critical Hit:	30
Elemental Power:	60

Take a WALK ON THE DARK SIDE with the Undead Elf that puts every villain to REST IN PEACE.

With a swish of her black gown and a death stare to terrify the most hardened villains, Hijinx is a force to be reckoned with! Although the other Skylanders think she's a little too serious for her own good, this Miniverse fighter is too busy being awesome to care! Her full-sized counterpart, Hex, was once a great elven sorceress who hunted the evil Dragon King Malefor into his Undead lair to defeat him. It was only upon returning home that Hex discovered that the veil of the Undead had fallen upon her as she entered the Underworld—forever changing her into a specter of fear. Just like Hex, Hijinx has an affinity for skulls and bones, drowning her enemies in skeletal rain and imprisoning them in a wall of bones!

Attack moves:

Conjure Phantom Orb: Press **Attack 1** to launch magic orbs of spectral energy that track Hijinx's foes.

Rain of Skulls: Hold **Attack 2** to begin casting this spell. Release when the attack is fully charged, and ghostly skulls rain down on Hijinx's enemies.

Soul Gem Ability: Skull Shield! – 4000: Skull Rain knocks away enemies and attacks.

Upgrades:

Wall of Bones – 500: Press Attack 3 to create a Wall of Bones to protect Hijinx.
Storm of Skulls – 700: Conjure up to four skulls with your Skull Rain attack.
Bone Fortress – 900: The Wall of Bones is larger and takes more damage to destroy. Prerequisite: Wall of Bones.

Twice the Orbage – 1200: Press Attack 1 to shoot two Phantom Orbs at once.	
Shade Master Path: Further develop Hijinx's Phantom Orb attack.	**Bone Crafter Path:** Further develop Hijinx's Skull Rain and Wall of Bones abilities.
Long Distance Orbs – 1700 Hold Attack 1 to increase the range of your Phantom Orbs.	**Compound Fracture – 1700** Wall of Bones damages any enemy that touches it.
Caustic Phantom Orbs – 2200 Phantom Orbs do increased damage.	**Master Caster – 2200** Takes much less time to cast Skull Rain and Wall of Bones.
Unstable Phantom Orbs – 3000 Phantom Orbs explode, damaging nearby enemies.	**Troll Skulls – 3000** Skull Rain does increased damage.

Knight Light: "See the Light!"

Knight Light's Stats!

Status:	Trap Master
Element:	Light
Maximum Health:	430
Speed:	70
Armor:	12
Critical Hit:	70
Elemental Power:	35

BANISH villains at the SPEED OF LIGHT with this SHINING STAR'S SPINNING SCIMITAR!

Knight Light is no stranger to battle. In years past, he fought the evil reign of Luminous, the greedy villain who desired to steal Starlight from under Knight Light's noble protection. The Starlight wasn't just a beacon of brightness and energy for the inhabitants of Radiant City—it represented all that was good and wise in their world. Without it, the city would plunge into darkness and despair! Knight Light fought Luminous unrelentingly, until the evil creature was banished to Sunscraper Spire forever. With Radiant City safe once more, Knight Light now protects all of Skylands, channeling the elemental power of Light to aid him in his quest.

Attack moves:

Traptanium Scimitar: Press **Attack 1** to swing the Traptanium Scimitar. Press **Attack 1**, **Attack 1**, hold **Attack 1** for a combo attack.

Prismatic Pounce: Press **Attack 2** for a Scimitar slash attack and create a Light Aura, where Scimitar attacks do more damage.

Soul Gem Ability: Brilliant Blade! – **4000:** Traptanium Scimitar is upgraded to its ultimate form and does maximum damage. Prerequisite: Find Knight Light's Soul Gem in Sunscraper Spire Adventure Pack.

Upgrades:

Hallowed Ground – 500: Enemies in Light Auras move slower and do reduced damage.	
Light Up– 700: Hold Attack 3 to create a circle of light; release to levitate and damage anything near the circle.	
Lasting Light – 900: Light Auras last longer.	
Scharper Scimitar – 1200: Traptanium Scimitar does more damage. Improve Traptanium Scimitar attacks.	
Scimitar Slasher Path: Improve Traptanium Scimitar attacks.	**Luminary of Light Path:** Improve Prismatic Pounce attacks.
Ascending Strike – 1700 Traptanium Scimitar knocks enemies into the air.	**Radiant Radius – 1700** Prismatic Pounce hits a larger area, and Light Auras are larger as well.
Speed of Light – 2200 While holding Attack 3, press Attack 2 to teleport to the Light Up target and perform an upward strike.	**Illumination Detonation – 2200** Light Auras explode before disappearing, damaging anything nearby.
Spinning Slash – 3000 Hold Attack 1 to charge up the Traptanium Scimitar and release for a 360-degree attack.	**Flash Dash – 3000** Press Attack 2, Attack 2 for a more powerful Prismatic Pounce attack and invulnerability while flickering.

Spotlight: "Time to Shine!"

Spotlight's Stats!

Status:	Skylander
Element:	Light
Maximum Health:	270
Speed:	60
Armor:	36
Critical Hit:	20
Elemental Power:	35

Be mesmerised by the HALO EFFECT that glows BRIGHTER with each STRIKE!

Spotlight is a one-of-a-kind pure white dragon of the Light Element, who magically appeared to Master Eon when he touched the Crystal Orb of Light in the Prismatic Palace. Both Spotlight and Eon immediately recognized the wisdom and power that the other was imbued with. Master Eon knew the dragon was important, so he decided Spotlight should be the Skylander Protector of the Core of Light. Her intense laser beam eyes and blinding aura always kept enemies at bay, until the day evil Kaos and his four-headed dragon attacked! Kaos smashed the Core of Light, scattering the Skylanders to Earth to await a new Portal Master that could return them. In the greatest mystery of all, Spotlight disappeared, never to be seen since.

Attack moves:

Eye Beams: Press **Attack 1** to fire concentrated beams of light.

Halo Rings: Press **Attack 2** to release Halo Rings, which damage enemies and refract Eye Beams.

Soul Gem Ability: Light Dragons! – 4000: Shoot a Heavenly Aura with Eye Beams to create Light Dragons who attack enemies. Prerequisite: Find Spotlight's Soul Gem in Chapter 1: Soda Springs.

Upgrades:

Bright Eyes – 500: Eye Beams do more damage.
Heavenly Aura – 700: Press Attack 3 to create a Heavenly Aura, damaging enemies inside.
The Halo Effect – 900: Hit enemies with Halo Rings to prevent them from attacking.

Hello Halo – 1200: Can have more Halo Rings active at a time.	
Visionary Path: Improve Eye Beam attacks.	**The Ringer Path:** Improve Halo Ring attacks.
Aura Charge – 1700	**Heavy Halo – 1700**
Shoot a Heavenly Aura with Eye Beams to power it up and do more damage.	Halo Rings are larger and do more damage.
Light It Up – 2200	**Ring Shot – 2200**
Eye Beams do even more damage and have longer range.	Halo Rings shoot light beams of their own.
Bling – 3000	**Uplifting Experience – 3000**
Shoot two Halo Rings at once.	Lift enemies caught in Halo Rings up with the Heavenly Aura.

Knight Mare: "Nowhere to Hide!"

Knight Mare's Stats!

Status:	Trap Master
Element:	Dark
Maximum Health:	350
Speed:	85
Armor:	36
Critical Hit:	40
Elemental Power:	35

When the KNIGHT AWAKENS and BATTLE HORN sounds, trust that the SHADOW OF DARKNESS is on your trail!

Knight Mare is a skilled hunter and tracker who loves nothing more than chasing down evil. When a nasty gang of Bicyclopes stole The Oracle of Stones that the Dark Centaur was protecting, she galloped into action! Knight Mare knew that in the wrong hands, the magical game of Dark Skystones could doom Skylands forever. But the Bicyclopes were selfish and greedy. They wanted the enchanted game to foretell their own futures, but didn't know how to use it. They were just about to set off its cursed trap when Knight Mare tracked them down! All alone, she fought the evil creatures into submission with her huge flame-bladed sword. Now, her Battle Horn is legend, and every villain in Skylands shudders at the sound!

Attack moves:

Traptanium Flamberge: Press **Attack 1** to swing the Traptanium Flamberge sword. Press **Attack 1**, **Attack 1**, hold **Attack 1** for a combo attack.

Shadow Joust: Press **Attack 2** to charge right through enemies

Soul Gem Ability: The Shadow Realm! – 4000: Battle Horn creates a Shadow Realm, where Shadowy Clones are stronger and enemies can't see. Prerequisite: Find Knight Mare's Soul Gem in the Midnight Museum and purchase the Battle Horn.

Upgrades:

Gift Keeps on Giving – 500: Traptanium Flamberge attacks continue to damage enemies even after they've been hit.	
Charged Up Charge – 700: Hold Attack 2 to charge up the Shadow Joust attack for more damage.	
Battle Horn – 900: Hold Attack 3 to play a Battle Horn that stuns nearby enemies.	
Shadowy Clones – 1200: Hit enemies with the Battle Horn attack to make a shadowy clone who fights for you. Prerequisite: Purchase Battle Horn.	
Shadow Summoner Path: Improve Battle Horn abilities.	**Flamberge Aficionado Path:** Improve Traptanium Flamberge attacks.
More Clones – 1700	**Shadow Stab – 1700**
Increase the amount of Shadowy Clones you can have at once.	Press Attack 1, Attack 1, hold Attack 2 for a Shadow Stab combo.
It's Win-Win – 2200	**Flamberge Fragment – 2200**
Shadowy Clones now explode, hurting enemies and healing you.	Press Attack 1, Attack 1, hold Attack 3 for a Flamberge Fragment combo.
Shadowy Sacrifice – 3000	**Sword of Darkness – 3000**
Battle Horn destroys existing Shadowy Clones to power up other attacks.	Traptanium Flamberge attacks do more damage.

Blackout: "Darkness Falls!"

Blackout's Stats!

Status:	Skylander
Element:	Dark
Maximum Health:	260
Speed:	60
Armor:	24
Critical Hit:	40
Elemental Power:	35

When peril is at your door, summon the SHADOW BLADE that DARES TO DREAM.

It takes great courage to battle the demons within a mind, and this is the noble path Blackout once chose. Nightmares were created in the Realm of Dreams, a magical place that gathered all of the terrifying creatures conjured up in the imaginations of the universe. The guardian dragons then sent the nightmares into the dreams of evil creatures to scare them into behaving. But the dragon clan of Dark Stygian soon became cruel and allowed their nightmares to terrorize the sleep of all creatures in Skylands, good included. Blackout's kind nature wouldn't allow such an abuse of power. He took matters into his own hands, enlisting his own dark magic to shift into the haunted dreams himself, where he battled the evil nightmare creatures, bringing peace and hope to the sleeping Skylanders. When Master Eon witnessed Blackout's bravery, he called on the dragon to fight against the corrupt Dark Stygians. The nightmare makers were soon defeated, and Blackout joined the Skylanders to protect the dreams of his people forever more.

Attack moves:

Wing Whip: Press **Attack 1** to perform a Wing Whip. Press **Attack 1**, **Attack 1**, **Attack 1** for a combo attack.

Shadow Orbs: Press **Attack 2** to shoot Shadow Orbs, which leave behind Darkness energy and shockwaves.

Soul Gem Ability: Supernova Black Hole! – 4000: Shoot two Black Holes on top of each other to create a Supernova Black Hole. Prerequisite: Find Blackout's Soul Gem in Chapter 2: Know-It-All Island and purchase Black Hole.

Upgrades:

Black Hole – 500: Press Attack 3 to open up Black Holes that pull enemies in; hold and release Attack 3 to teleport yourself.
Darkness Overload – 700: Shoot a Shadow Orb into a Black Hole to create an explosive eruption. Prerequisite: Purchase Black Hole.
Shadow Blade – 900: Jump and press Attack 1 to turn into a spinning Shadow Blade.
Take It Black – 1200: Black Holes hold enemies longer and they do more damage. Prerequisite: Purchase Black Hole.

Wing Warrior Path: Improve Wing Whip attacks.	**Prince of Darkness Path:** Improve Shadow Orb attacks.
A Spinning Finish – 1700 Press Attack 1, Attack 1, Attack 1 for a Ground Pound combo. Press Attack 1, Attack 1, Attack 1, Attack 1 to charge ahead as a Shadow Blade.	**Dark Energy Clouds – 1700** Shadow Orbs explode into massive Dark Energy Clouds, which damage enemies.
Whip It Up – 2200 Wing Whip, Shadow Blade, and Warp Speed attacks do more damage.	**Under the Cover of Darkness – 2200** Blackout receives less damage when inside Dark Energy Clouds. Prerequisite: Purchase Dark Energy Clouds.
Warp Speed – 3000 Hold Attack 1 to repeatedly teleport through enemies and pierce them with your horn.	**Cloud Gravity – 3000** Hold Attack 2 to lift enemies inside a Dark Energy Cloud and damage all nearby enemies. Prerequisite: Purchase Dark Energy Clouds.

Vile Villains

An exciting innovation in *Trap Team* is your ability to defeat villains and capture them in the Traptanium Portal. Just like your Skylanders, each villain belongs to one of the ten elements (plus Kaos, who has his own element) and has two or three signature attack moves. All of the Doom Raiders that escaped Cloudcracker prison are roaming somewhere in the game chapters, ready for battle. Once a villain is defeated and trapped, you can play as that villain, using his or her unique fighting skills for good instead of evil. You'll find some villains have hard-hitting melee (hand-to-hand combat) attack moves, whereas others can be used strategically to strike enemies using a long-range attack.

Once you've defeated and trapped them, all villains are stored in the Villain Vault at Skylanders Academy (see Figure 4.1). Here, you can swap villains in and out of your traps. Before you begin each new chapter, decide who to bring along. This is especially important if you have limited traps. In each story chapter, there will be up to three Villain Quests you can undertake, so make sure you have traps ready with those villains inside as you play.

FIGURE 4.1 Chef Pepper Jack defeated and cooling down inside a Traptanium Dome.

If you're playing solo and have a few spare traps, it's also a great idea to choose a villain for your journey who will complement the attack moves your playing Skylander has—for example, select a villain that's good at long-range attacks, to fight with a Skylander built for close combat, or vice versa. Quickly switch between the two to take advantage of their skills in battle. This can be super helpful in Kaos Doom Challenges, where you are faced with swarms of different enemy types at once.

In certain places throughout each chapter, your villain can cause more damage than a regular Skylander, so they're always handy to have around. A villain can't die, but will run out of health faster than your Skylander (check its health bar to see how long you've got left). As soon as it runs out, you'll automatically switch back to your Skylander, but can re-engage the villain as soon as his or her health bar gets past the left-side progress line. The villain won't pick up food (you must swap back to your Skylander to eat), but any coins and experience points he or she collects will be added to the playing Skylander's bounty instead, so you never lose out.

When you complete a Villain Quest (individual locations are listed in this chapter), your villain will "Evolve." This is similar to a Skylander upgrade, but each attack move simply becomes a more powerful version of the original. Once the Villain Quest is completed, the bad-turned-good guy will also change his appearance slightly and have a longer health timer available. Villain Quests are usually mini-games or interactions with a character in a new area and are pretty easy to achieve.

In addition to the dreaded Doom Raiders, there are plenty of evil minions throughout the game ready to spring out and attack you. Let's meet some of the common ones and discuss how to defeat them:

■ **Chompies:** With big jaws and razor-sharp teeth, these dim-witted green beasties are all bite (see Figure 4.2). They come at you *en masse* and are pretty easy to wipe out before they chomp too close for comfort. If you see a silver chompy in the crowd, take it out before it sucks in some chompy-friends to create a shockwave-inducing Mega-Chompy. The Chompy Mage's favorite red "En Fuego" Chompies like to blow up in your face, so if you can, use a long-range weapon to get them before they reach you.

FIGURE 4.2 The Chompy Mage and beloved chompies are never far away. Once trapped, they make great villain allies.

■ **Grave Clobbers:** You'll find stone mummies wandering the Golden Desert, ready to smash up the place. Take them down with some swift close-combat moves.

■ **Bad Jujus:** Just like their villain leader, Bad Jujus are ghostly skeletons that strike with lightning and beckon whirlwinds of destruction to do their bidding. Keep your distance if you can!

■ **Masker Minds:** These little brain-drains can tap into the minds of nearby villains and steal their attacking skills in battle. Although it's a bit unpredictable at first, if you defeat the surrounding minions, the Masker Mind will have no one left to copycat and try to flee instead.

- **Pirate Henchmen:** You'll find these purple spiky-haired scallywags wherever the tides turn. Watch for the curled machetes on the end of their wooden clubs—they do a bit of damage.

- **Transformed Barrels:** Dodge the bombs that these stone-faced troublemakers hurl by escaping the red circle that appears, or jump into the safe green zone and stay put. How daring are you?

- **Shield Skeletons:** There are plenty of sword-wielding skeletons swarming Skylands and they're pretty tough cookies. Surprise them mid-strike to catch them off guard—even better if you can avoid their shields by attacking from behind.

- **Cyclops Spinners:** You have to be quick to kill these one-eyed wonders. Save your best aims for when they stop spinning, because you can't bring them down while they're on the move.

- **Cyclops Dragon:** Keep a high-powered villain in the portal and some Skylander backup (just in case) to take out these guys. They'll fling explosive eyeballs at you to keep themselves safe, so duck, dodge, and then deliver the longest range attack moves you've got to bring them down.

- **Evilikins:** That ingenious, lunatic Dr. Krankcase is to blame for these wooden mutant monsters. He created more than one kind of Evilikin (seven kinds, in fact) by using his glowing green goo to bring wooden objects to life. Of course, once alive, they're also evil. The best way of bringing down any Evilikin is to find its weakness. There's usually a brief moment of time needed to recharge or pause between attacks, and this is when they're at their most vulnerable. Keep a villain on hand to take the brunt of their attack and save your Skylander for the best opportunity to strike.

- **Trolls:** There are hundreds of trolls in *Trap Team*, and you'll often find them doing the malicious bidding of Kaos with a fang-faced grin. Depending on their weapon of choice (usually a heavy mace), they'll have a brief moment after an attack where they'll be slightly off balance. Keep out of their reach until the last second, then jump forward to let them have it. Trolls are great engineers, so your best bet is to go for the trolls themselves, rather than their sturdy, protective equipment.

- **Plant Warrior:** These spiky green stabbers are all over Skylands and tend to attack in groups. Keep out of reach of their pointy-pod arms and use long-range attacks to avoid damage.

Chompy: "The Classic Skylands Chompy!"

Chompies are the ultimate minion, always getting under your feet and blowing things up. High-energy, hand-to-hand combat will bring him down. Destroy the chompy pods they spawn in and watch your back!

Chompy's Stats!

Villain Quest: Workers' Chompensation	
Causing trouble at: Mirror of Mystery (Ch. 20: Adventure Pack)	
Villain Quest Location: Find Butterfly at Mirror of Mystery.	
Attack Moves:	Upgrades:
Press Attack 1 to chomp.	Travels farther and does more damage.
Press Attack 2 to summon three smaller Chompies. Press **Attack 2** again and they keep coming!	Chompies do more damage with each bite.

Chompy Mage: "The Champ of Chomp!"

Nothing is safe from the Chompy Mage and his little green spies. He can deplete your health and transform into a giant, crazy Chompy himself at will—but once trapped, his healing powers are pretty chomp-tastic. Keep your distance and jump his fire waves until he runs out of Chompies.

Chompy Mage's Stats!

Attack Moves:	Upgrades:
Villain Quest: Head of the Cheese	
Causing trouble at: Chef Zeppelin (Ch. 5)	
Press Attack 1 for a two-handed staff strike. In Giant Chompy Form, create fiery rings that ripple along the ground.	Staff swing hits harder. Rings deal more damage.
Press Attack 2 to switch forms between Giant Chompy and Chompy Mage.	No upgrade.
Press Attack 3 to summon Chompies (up to four active at a time). In Giant Chompy form, create fiery rings that ripple along the ground.	Upgrade: Chompies are more powerful. Rings deal more damage.

Shield Shredder: "The Best Defense Is a Good Offense!"

Shield yourself from the bladed Evilikin that makes splinters of his enemies! He'll release minions for a close-range attack while others shoot long-range from above. This is a good opportunity to switch between complementary Villain/Skylander attack moves.

Shield Shredder's Stats!

Attack Moves:	Upgrades:
Villain Quest: Wood-Be Band	
Villain Quest Location: Find Gilmour at Wilikin Workshop (Ch. 11).	
Press **Attack 1** to dash forward behind a spinning shield. Hitting enemies with the shield charges it up for a longer dash.	Shield does more damage and charges up faster.
Press **Attack 2** to toss up two shields. Enemies under shields take damage when they land. Shields act as defensive barriers.	Shields are larger and last longer.

Sheep Creep: "He's Baaaaad News!"

He might look innocent, but Sheep Creep will blast you into next week with his cork shooter and baaaad attitude. Dodge the corks; then attack him for an easy victory.

Sheep Creep's Stats!

Villain Quest: Mildly Irritated Sheep	
Causing trouble at: Soda Springs (Ch. 1)	
Attack Moves:	**Upgrades:**
Press **Attack 1** to fire a round of missiles.	Missiles deal more damage.
Press **Attack 2** to cover up and send out woolly projectiles.	Woolly projectiles travel farther and deal more damage.

Cuckoo Clocker: "He's Cuckoo for Clobbering!"

He's out of the cage and singing for his supper—keep off the menu if you can! Have at him while he is working up an attack, then jump out of the way before his arms come smashing down. You'll wear him out in no time!

Cuckoo Clocker's Stats!

Villain Quest: Song Bird	
Causing trouble at: Phoenix Psanctuary (Ch. 4)	
Attack Moves:	**Upgrades:**
Press **Attack 1** for a two-handed overhead smash.	Overhand smash does more damage and affects a small area.
Press **Attack 2** for a sonic shriek that damages enemies in front of Cuckoo Clocker.	Shriek does more damage.

Broccoli Guy: "Heals His Friends, Hurts His Enemies!"

This bitter green veggie-head has way too much on his plate. Take out his slobber-trap guards and he'll be vulnerable to attack.

Broccoli Guy's Stats!

Villain Quest: Broccoli Guy En Fuego	
Villain Quest Location: Find Bernie at Chef Zeppelin (Ch. 5).	
Attack Moves:	**Upgrades:**
Press **Attack 1** to fire projectiles that damage nearby enemies.	Projectiles do more damage.
Press **Attack 2** to create a healing zone on the ground for Skylanders to use (they must stand in it).	Food appears inside the healing zone.

Rage Mage: "He's All the Rage!"

Talk about anger-management problems! Only ice cream can cool this little guy's raging fury. His minions will put up a good fight, so take them down with some hand-to-hand combat, leaving him defenseless.

Rage Mage's Stats!

Villain Quest: Ice Cream in the Future?	
Villain Quest Location: Find Noobman at The Future of Skylands (Ch. 13).	
Attack Moves:	**Upgrades:**
Press **Attack 1** to swing a staff, with a small forward movement.	Staff has greater range and does more damage.
Press **Attack 2** to create an orb. Skylanders who pick up the orb enjoy a temporary boost to speed and damage.	Effects of the orb last longer and are more powerful.

Bomb Shell: "Did You Hear the One About the Tortoise and the Bomb?"

Heads up for the battle-shell with bomb power—he's no slow poke! Keep out of reach of the red bomb area and purple flames as you attack him. You'll need some agility and patience, but it won't take too long.

Bomb Shell's Stats!

Villain Quest: Demolition	
Villain Quest Location: Find Rizzo at Mystic Mill (Ch. 9).	
Attack Moves:	**Upgrades:**
Press **Attack 1** to drop some bombs.	Toss rate increases and bombs cause extra damage.
Press **Attack 2** to spin and dash. Any enemies that get hit are knocked back.	Bombs surround spinning Bomb Shell. Enemies receive more damage from explosions.

Pain-Yatta: "Filled with Candy. And Evil."

Like a kid with a blindfold, Pain-Yatta looks sweet until he strikes! Close-range attacks will bring a quick defeat if you can dodge his smashing fists.

Pain-Yatta's Stats!

Villain Quest: I'm with the Band	
Villain Quest Location: Find Bag 'O Bones at Secret Sewers of Supreme Stink (Ch. 10).	
Attack Moves:	**Upgrades:**
Press **Attack 1** to smack the ground ahead of Pain-Yatta with a lollipop.	Lollipop has more pop.
Press **Attack 2** to fill the air with candy that damages enemies.	More candy. More pain. And piñatas?

Krankenstein: "So Strong, He Fears Nothing... Except Termites!"

When you're a cobbled-together Evilikin, you're bound to get a little cranky. Although he's slow, this big lug has a long-range attack, so keep your distance or sneak up from behind to take him down.

Krankenstein's Stats!

Villain Quest: Onward Wilikin Soldiers	
Villain Quest Location: Find Wooster at Operation: Troll Rocket Steal (Ch. 14).	
Attack Moves:	Upgrades:
Press **Attack 1** to spin arm blades and damage enemies.	Hold **Attack 1** to keep blades spinning.
Press **Attack 2** to snap arm at enemies.	Attack deals more damage.

Buzzer Beak: "See What the Buzz Is All About!"

A little bird can go a long way. Especially with a hat of deadly, spinning blades. Circle him to avoid his blades; then take him down, close range.

Buzzer Beak's Stats!

Villain Quest: Family Reunion	
Villain Quest Location: Take to Buzz at Phoenix Psanctuary (Ch. 4).	
Attack Moves:	Upgrades:
Press **Attack 1** to grow and spin the blades on Buzzer Beak's hat, damaging nearby enemies.	Blades increase in size.
Press **Attack 2** to lift Buzzer Beak off the ground, creating a vortex that draws in enemies.	Buzzer Beak dive-bombs the ground to damage enemies at the end of the attack.

Dreamcatcher: "You Don't Want This Head in Your Head!"

HINT

Last seen in the final tower of Telescope Towers

OMG! The only thing she spreads faster than nightmares is gossip! This villain is all trouble, so prepare for a lot of bed-smashing and floating bows to destroy. Be as fast as you can—it's a high-energy fight. Wear her out with a full-blown attack as you near the end for a well-deserved rest.

Dreamcatcher's Stats!

Villain Quest: Sweet Dreams	
Villain Quest Location: Find Rochester at Wilikin Workshop (Ch. 11).	
Attack Moves:	**Upgrades:**
Press **Attack 1** to summon a sheep-filled dream tornado.	Tornado does more damage and can hit multiple targets.
Press **Attack 2** to summon dream devices that attack enemies they land on.	Can summon more at a time.
Press **Attack 3** to create a dreamquake.	Dreamquake lasts longer.

Bad Juju: "She'll Take You for a Spin!"

HINT

Last seen by a double-key gate in the Lair of the Golden Queen

A whirlwind of voodoo is heading your way! Take her down with a long-range attack or run in to the fray as soon as her tornado disappears to smash her before she strikes again.

Bad Juju's Stats!

Villain Quest: Remote Location	
Villain Quest Location: Find Glumshanks at Lair of the Golden Queen (Ch. 17).	
Attack Moves:	Upgrades:
Press **Attack 1** to call a lightning strike.	Lightning strike hits multiple enemies.
Press **Attack 2** to summon a whirlwind.	Summon a larger whirlwind that does more damage

Slobber Trap: "Just Your Average Plant Monster Dog!"

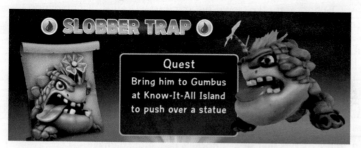

> **Quest**
>
> Bring him to Gumbus at Know-It-All Island to push over a statue

Play fetch with the slobbery dog that loves learning new tricks. After battling his evil comrades, side-step his forward attacks and catch him by surprise with your own melee moves.

Slobber Trap's Stats!

Villain Quest: Gumbus's Fortune	
Causing trouble at: Know-It-All Island (Ch. 2)	
Attack Moves:	Upgrades:
Press **Attack 1** for a belly flop that damages nearby enemies.	Belly flop deals more damage over more area.
Press **Attack 2** to leave a slobber trail on the ground that slows enemies.	Trail lasts longer and the slowing effect is greater.

Threatpack: "A Troll in a Jetpack. Now THAT'S a Threat!"

Prepare for collateral damage when bad science explodes! Keep clear of the red bomb areas and take down his minions. Then use long-range attacks to avoid the fire and bring him down, or go melee and have a bit of dodge/attack/run/repeat fun.

Threatpack's Stats!

Villain Quest: You Break it, You Fix It	
Villain Quest Location: Find Tessa at Skyhighlands (Ch. 15).	
Attack Moves:	Upgrades:
Press **Attack 1** to fire rockets that seek enemies.	Rockets deal more damage.
Press **Attack 2** to blast off and damage enemies caught in the wash.	Deals more damage and extends flight time.

Brawl and Chain: "No Chains, No Pain!"

This terrifying salty sea walrus really just wants a hug. And some hands. Start with breaking the grappling hooks on the side of the ship to limit the encroaching enemies; then use a long-range attack to bring him down.

Brawl and Chain's Stats!

Villain Quest: Fairy Night Lights	
Villain Quest Location: Find Hawk at Telescope Towers (Ch. 8).	
Attack Moves:	Upgrades:
Press **Attack 1** for a spin attack with both hook hands.	Spin lasts longer and hits harder.
Press **Attack 2** to fire a hook hand. Smaller enemies are pulled closer when hit.	Attack does more damage.

Chill Bill: "Was Evil BEFORE It Was Cool."

Quest

Bring him to Rocky at Chompy Mountain to make Troll Radio awesome again

Cool things down a little with the ice troll that rocks Skylands radio. Attack his Lob Goblin guard first, then bring him down—but be sure to avoid his freeze blast by keeping your distance.

Chill Bill's Stats!

Villain Quest: The Cold Front	
Causing trouble at: Phoenix Psanctuary (Ch. 4)	
Attack Moves:	Upgrades:
Press **Attack 1** to fire a freeze beam. Enemies caught in the beam are frozen in place.	Beam does more damage and enemies are frozen longer.
Press **Attack 2** to activate Chill Bill's jetpack. Enemies caught in its wash take damage.	Flight time is longer. Enemies take more damage.

The Gulper: "His Gulp Is Worse Than His Bite!"

Thirsty? A soda a day keeps the blob in the fray! Just swap his soda for some yucky waste sludge to bring him down to size.

The Gulper's Stats!

Villain Quest: Balloon Redemption	
Causing trouble at: Soda Springs (Ch. 1)	
Attack Moves:	Upgrades:
Press **Attack 1** to thrust trident. Trident picks up smaller targets and tosses them over The Gulper's head.	Attack does more damage.
Press **Attack 2** for a bite attack that hits multiple enemies.	Bite does more damage and swallows smaller enemies.
Press **Attack 3** to slide and leave a slime trail in The Gulper's wake. Hold **Attack 3** to charge up the attack and increase the distance traveled.	Slide goes farther and does more damage.

Cross Crow: "Don't Cross Cross Crow!"

When there's treasure to find, flock to the hunter with his eye on the prize. Attack him while he's vulnerable—when he's just about to fire his crossbow.

Cross Crow's Stats!

Villain Quest: Skylands Biggest Fans	
Villain Quest Location: Find Tessa in Time Town (Ch. 10).	
Attack Moves:	**Upgrades:**
Press **Attack 1** to fire a crossbow. Hold **Attack 1** to kneel and fire continually. Can't move while firing.	Bolts fire faster and hit harder.
Press **Attack 2** to summon a swarm of crows to attack a single target.	Swarm lasts longer and can hit multiple targets.

Brawlrus: "Brawl + Walrus = Brawlrus!"

> **HINT**
>
> Last seen hanging out with pirates just outside of Rainfish Riviera

You'll be seeing spinning starfish when the Cannonbrawl hits you! The starfish slow you down and steal your health, so dodge them! He fires in a four-shots-then-pause pattern, so take advantage of the break to attack.

Brawlrus's Stats!

Villain Quest: Submarine Bros 4 Life	
Villain Quest Location: Find Argle Bargle at Rainfish Riviera (Ch. 6).	
Attack Moves:	**Upgrades:**
Press **Attack 1** to fire a burst of tiny starfish.	Increased damage.
Press **Attack 2** to fire a giant starfish that spins and damages enemies.	Starfish does more damage and lasts longer.

Shrednaught: "2 Trolls, 1 Giant Chainsaw, Unlimited Possibilities."

SHREDNAUGHT

Quest

Bring him to Loggins at the Mystic Mill to get him back into his office

A chainsaw built for two. Shreddy, set, go! After circling you with their mega-chainsaw, they'll pause for a rest. Take the opportunity to run in and show them who's boss!

Shrednaught's Stats!

Villain Quest: Sure Beats Keys	
Causing trouble at: Phoenix Psanctuary (Ch. 4)	
Attack Moves:	**Upgrades:**
Press **Attack 1** to start up the giant chainsaw.	Hold **Attack 1** to charge up the chainsaw to run longer and do more damage.
Press **Attack 2** for a backseat driver blast.	Blast does more damage.

Dr. Krankcase: "Not the Healing Kind of Doctor."

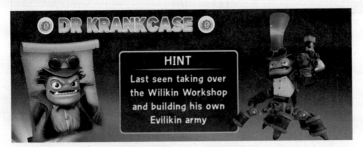

DR KRANKCASE

HINT

Last seen taking over the Wilikin Workshop and building his own Evilikin army

Unleash the maker of mayhem and glowing green goo! Smash his goo barrels before they fall to avoid more enemies appearing, and try to lure him onto the damaging grinder machines. Attack him during the vulnerable pause after he spins for greatest effect.

Dr. Krankcase's Stats!

Villain Quest: Diorama Drama	
Villain Quest Location: Find Leyland at Time Town (Ch. 12).	
Attack Moves:	Upgrades:
Press **Attack 1** to spin Dr. Krankcase's legs and slide forward.	Increased damage and distance traveled.
Press **Attack 2** to fire a goo blast.	Each blast hits more often.
Press **Attack 3** to generate lightning from Dr. Krankcase's fingertips.	Increased damage and number of hits.

Mad Lobs: "A Mabu Gone Bad? No Way!"

> **HINT**
> Last seen about to invade a peaceful Troll Village at Mirror Of Mystery

Go lob a blob at a mob for a job. Ka-boom! If you have a long-range attack move, bring him down before he throws his bomb. Easy!

Mad Lob's Stats!

Villain Quest: Fishness Protection Program	
Villain Quest Location: Find Kaos at Mirror of Mystery (Ch. 20 Adventure Pack).	
Attack Moves:	Upgrades:
Press **Attack 1** to throw three large bombs.	Bigger bombs mean bigger booms.
Press **Attack 2** to throw out many smaller bombs that explode after a delay.	More bombs covering a larger area.

Trolling Thunder: "Wears a Tank for Pants!"

Quest

Bring him to Da Pinchy
at the Nightmare
Express to reveal
beautiful art

Beware the troll in the tank, lest his tread run over your head! Take advantage of his slow rotation and attack as soon as he finishes firing.

Trolling Thunder's Stats!

Villain Quest: Statue of Limitations	
Causing trouble at: Nightmare Express (Ch. 19 Adventure Pack)	
Attack Moves:	**Upgrades:**
Press **Attack 1** to fire a shell from the turret.	Shell travels faster and does more damage.
Press **Attack 2** for a backfire that damages nearby enemies.	Backfire does more damage.

Bruiser Cruiser: "Give Him a Big Hand. Or Two!"

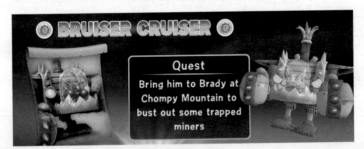

Quest

Bring him to Brady at
Chompy Mountain to
bust out some trapped
miners

When a troll boxing champion in a giant mech suit gets angry, it's gonna be a knockout! Keep him moving to deplete his health, and as soon as he tires—WHAM!

Bruiser Cruiser's Stats!

Villain Quest: Need More Than Singing	
Causing trouble at: Chompy Mountain (Ch. 3)	
Attack Moves:	**Upgrades:**
Press **Attack 1** to punch your enemy.	Punch has greater impact.
Press **Attack 2** for an explosion that blasts enemies away.	Explosions cause more damage.

Grinnade: "A Walking Time Bomb. Literally!"

GRINNADE

HINT

Last seen inside a Troll weapons lab at Operation: Troll Rocket Steal

Do you hear the pitter patter of little feet? Tick, tick, tick... run! Keep out of reach when Grinnade explodes, and then duck back in for a quick one-two punch-up. You'll take him down in no time.

Grinnade's Stats!

Villain Quest: Miner Troubles II	
Villain Quest Location: Find Diggs at Skyhighlands (Ch. 15).	
Attack Moves:	**Upgrades:**
Press **Attack 1** to start the self-destruct sequence. Don't worry, Grinnade always pulls himself back together.	Explodes for additional damage.
Press **Attack 2** to spawn Mini Grinnades that explode on contact with enemies.	Mini Grinnades explode for more damage.

Chef Pepper Jack: "For Those Who Like Their Bad Guys Extra Spicy!"

HINT

Last seen cooking up a storm in his own kitchen inside Chef Zeppelin

Stay out of the kitchen, because Chef Pepper Jack is turning up the heat! Dodge his lava peppers and tire him out by letting him hit the arena walls. Minimize your movement to focus on laser jumping and use your villain to reserve health. Jump on steaks while you attack Pepper Jack to the max; this is going to be a tough one!

Chef Pepper Jack's Stats!

Villain Quest: Head of the Cheese	
Villain Quest Location: Find Galley at Rainfish Riviera (Ch. 6).	
Attack Moves:	**Upgrades:**
Press **Attack 1** to toss out explosive peppers.	Adds more peppers to the pot to bring up the heat.
Press **Attack 2** to dash and attack with giant egg beaters.	Faster dash and more damaging egg beaters.
Press **Attack 3** for a fiery breath attack. That's spicy cooking!	Spicier breath means more pain for enemies.

Scrap Shooter: "One Creature's Trash Is Another One's Treasure."

HINT

Last seen hanging out near the end of the train tracks at the Wilikin Workshop

This Evilikin is a barrel of laughs—until you put him on the scrap heap! Jump up high to find a safer point, and dodge his inline attacks as best you can. A long-range attack back will help clear the floor.

Scrap Shooter's Stats!

Villain Quest: Pirates of the Broken Table	
Villain Quest Location: Find Yoho at Wilikin Workshop (Ch. 11).	
Attack Moves:	**Upgrades:**
Press **Attack 1** to lean forward and launch a barrel.	Fires two barrels with each attack.
Press **Attack 2** to fling four barrels along the ground.	Barrels come out faster and do more damage.

Smoke Scream: "No One Ever Told Him Not to Play with Fire."

Burn, baby, buuuuurn... and dodge the flaming barrels if you can! Take out his minions and weapons, melee style, while swapping to a long-range attack on Smoke Scream to keep away from his fiery breath. A complementary villain will make this fight easy money.

Smoke Scream's Stats!

Villain Quest: Fight Doom with Boom	
Villain Quest Location: Find Buzz at Ultimate Weapon (Ch. 18).	
Attack Moves:	**Upgrades:**
Press **Attack 1** to burn enemies with a flame thrower.	Flame thrower does more damage.
Press **Attack 2** to fire a bouncing barrel.	Barrel attack hits harder.

Golden Queen: "As Good as Gold and a Lot More Evil!"

> **HINT**
> Last seen in her own temple in the Lair of the Golden Queen

She's the ultimate greedy alchemist. Beware—when the Golden Queen wins, she gets a *very* big head! You'll need some hard-hitting attack moves and trapped villains to absorb the heat in this epic battle.

Golden Queen's Stats!

Villain Quest: Bank on *This!*	
Villain Quest Location: Find Dr. Noobry at The Ultimate Weapon (Ch. 18).	
Attack Moves:	**Upgrades:**
Press **Attack 1** for a spinning staff strike.	Staff attack does more damage.
Press **Attack 2** to fire golden rays from Golden Queen's staff.	Attack lasts longer and does more damage.
Press **Attack 3** to summon golden wings, which attack enemies.	Summon more powerful golden wings.

Tussle Sprout: "Even More Dangerous Than a Brussels Sprout!"

> **Quest**
> Bring him to Arbo at the Phoenix Psanctuary to grow some new vines

Just because he's green, it doesn't mean he's healthy. This guy's allergic to everything! (But how does he sneeze without a nose!?) Keep your distance as he releases a poisonous gas. Take out his flytrap guards first; then attack from afar if you can.

Tussle Sprout's Stats!

Villain Quest: Sproutin' Up!	
Causing trouble at: Know-It-All Island (Ch. 2)	
Attack Moves:	**Upgrades:**
Press **Attack 1** to create a gas cloud that poisons enemies. Hold **Attack** 1 to continue the attack, but Tussle Sprout can't move.	Range and damage are increased.
Press **Attack 2** to lob a spore that falls under Tussle Sprout. Spore creates a puddle on the ground. Enemies that touch it are poisoned.	Puddle is larger and damage is greater.

Chomp Chest: "Who Better to Find Treasure Than a Chest... with Teeth!"

Watch your fingers—this hungry piece of furniture will chew you up and spit you out! He's fast too, so attack him from a distance.

Chomp Chest's Stats!

Villain Quest: Hot Diggity Dash!	
Villain Quest Location: Find Flam Bam at Secret Sewers of Supreme Stink (Ch. 10).	
Attack Moves:	**Upgrades:**
Press **Attack 1** for a dashing bite attack that propels Chomp Chest forward.	Bite has more range and does greater damage.
Press **Attack 2** to search for buried treasure. **Hint**: Look for yellow crosses on the ground as you play; Chomp Chest can dig for treasure here (up to 65,000 gold coins) to fill your coffers.	Greater search area.

Grave Clobber: "A Face Only a Mummy Could Love!"

HINT

Last seen guarding the Golden Queen at the Golden Desert

After a thousand-year nap, this pharaoh still woke up on the wrong side of the bed—and he could really do with some more beauty sleep! Keep clear of the white mark that signals his next attack, but jump in to go all crazy melee on him before he raises his fist again.

Grave Clobber's Stats!

Villain Quest: Where Is Flynn?	
Villain Quest Location: Find Cali at Lair of the Golden Queen (Ch. 17).	
Attack Moves:	**Upgrades:**
Press **Attack 1** for a crouching arm sweep.	Attack deals more damage.
Press **Attack 2** to smash the ground with both hands and summon bones from the ground. Hit bones with arm sweep to scatter damaging fragments.	Attack has greater range and summons more bones.

Hood Sickle: "Blink and You'll Miss Him. But He Won't Miss You!"

HINT

Last seen in front of the first locked door at Telescope Towers

This grim reaper isn't so bad, as long as you're already undead. Keep straight ahead to miss his swinging scythe, and try to anticipate his teleport pattern. A long-range attack strategy keeps you from danger.

Hood Sickle's Stats!

Villain Quest: Hatastrophe!	
Villain Quest Location: Find Hatterson at Skylands Academy.	
Attack Moves:	**Upgrades:**
Press **Attack 1** to teleport a short distance in any direction.	Targets in the path of the teleport take additional damage.
Press **Attack 2** for a slow swing that hits a wide arc in front of Hood Sickle.	Attack causes a special state (jaded) and does more damage.

Bone Chompy: "Even Skeleton Chompies Gotta Eat!"

All teeth and no play makes Bone Chompy a very bad pet! This little beastie is super-fast, so prepare for a close-range attack. Don't keep still; dodge his forward lunges and then quickly smash him from behind instead. Swap in for a villain if you get chomped to conserve your health stats.

Bone Chompy's Stats!

Villain Quest: Paging Dr. Bone Chompy	
Villain Quest Location: Find Buzz at Operation: Troll Rocket Steal (Ch. 14).	
Attack Moves:	**Upgrades:**
Press **Attack 1** for a dashing chompy bite.	Faster dash that travels farther.
Press **Attack 2** to leave a chompy trap on the ground, which bites enemies when they walk over it.	Biting traps bite harder, or latch onto victim, inflicting damage over time.

Masker Mind: "Everyone's Entitled to HIS Opinion!"

MASKER MIND

HINT

Last seen near the docks at Rainfish Riviera

Don't be brain-drained by this tiny telekinetic terror; create an army of your own minions from enemies instead. Defeat his Bomb Shell guard twice to leave Masker Mind vulnerable to attack.

Masker Mind's Stats!

Villain Quest: Hypnosis Schnipnosis	
Villain Quest Location: Find Arthur at Telescope Towers (Ch. 8).	
Attack Moves:	**Upgrades:**
Press **Attack 1** for a moderate speed projectile that turns enemies into allies for a short time.	Affected enemies remain allies for an extended period of time.
Press **Attack 2** to push back enemies. Nice area of effect, but deals no damage.	Now deals a small amount of damage and has a larger area of effect.

Wolfgang: "His Music Is Edgy—Sharp Steel Edgy."

WOLFGANG

HINT

"Last" seen building a big, bad woofer 10,000 years in the future at the Future of Skylands

When this Werewolf strikes a chord, it'll bring you to tears. Really—his guitar skills are to die for. Keep directly in front to avoid his deadly notes, and prepare to do a lot of jumping to stay in the game. Keep your trapped villains on standby to take the hardest hits and save your health.

Wolfgang's Stats!

Villain Quest: An Inconvenience of Imps	
Villain Quest Location: Find Q.U.I.G.L.E.Y in The Future of Skylands.	
Attack Moves:	Upgrades:
Press **Attack 1** for a musical slash. Jump for an overhead smash.	Slash has greater range and hits harder.
Press **Attack 2** to slide along the ground and bask in adulation.	More distance, damage, and rocking.
Press **Attack 3** for a killer lick that produces damaging musical notes.	Notes come out faster and do more damage.

Lob Goblin: "Danger—High Voltage!"

Trap the goblin with a magnetic personality to liven up your game. All it takes is a well-timed bomb, and you'll score a super charge of grenades to shock the bad guys!

Lob Goblin's Stats!

Villain Quest: Grand Theft Plan	
Causing trouble at: Nightmare Express (Ch. 19)	
Attack Moves:	Upgrades:
Press **Attack 1** to toss electromagnetic grenades at enemies.	Grenades have a larger radius when exploding.
Press **Attack 2** to drop electric shock nodes on the ground to create electric beams that damage enemies that touch them.	Electric beams deal more damage.

Luminous: "He's Got Real Star Power. From an Actual Star!"

HINT

Last seen somewhere around Sunscraper Spire

You'll find light in the darkness of Sunscraper Spire, but beware—it can shape-shift into pure evil! Smash his light crystals to deplete his shields and then trap Luminous to ensure your path to victory is always crystal clear!

Luminous' Stats!

Villain Quest: Buzz Has a Hat?	
Villain Quest Location: Find Buzz at Sunscraper Spire (Ch. 22).	
Attack Moves:	**Upgrades:**
Press **Attack 1** for a two-fisted light blast. Hold **Attack 1** to swing the light blasts to the sides.	Light blasts do more damage.
Press **Attack 2** to summon a large crystal and drop it on a nearby enemy.	Crystal does more damage.
Press **Attack 3** to summon a floating crystal that fires a light blast and rotates.	Crystal beam attack does more damage.

Blaster-Tron: "From the Future. This Means Lasers."

HINT

"Last" seen 10,000 years in the future at The Future of Skylands

Reprogram Blaster-Tron's circuits to initiate the ultimate destructive sequence. Rocket boosters and lasers engage! Sneak up from behind and take this robot down by surprise.

Blaster-Tron's Stats!

Villain Quest: Help Diggs Dig	
Villain Quest Location: Find Diggs at the Golden Desert (Ch. 16).	
Attack Moves:	Upgrades:
Press **Attack 1** to fire lasers. Hold **Attack 1** to build up a charge. Enemies struck by blue light while charging take damage.	Lasers deal more damage.
Press **Attack 2** for a rocket-boosted charge attack.	Blaster-Tron travels farther and hits harder.

Eye Five: "Don't Recommend Playing Patty Cake with Him."

If you're pounding the pavement and getting nowhere fast, track down the mutant with the best hand-eye coordination in Skylands—even with only four fingers! You'll have to be on your toes to bring him down because he's a little unpredictable. Attack him from afar, if you can.

Eye Five's Stats!

Villain Quest: Chongo!	
Villain Quest Location: Find Doublooney at Rainfish Riviera (Ch. 6).	
Attack Moves:	Upgrades:
Press **Attack 1** to smash the ground with a fist. Continue tapping **Attack 1** to pound the ground and advance.	Ground-pound attack does more damage.
Press **Attack 2** to charge up Eye Five's fists and emit an electrical shock. Fist attacks do more damage afterward.	Electric shock does more damage.

Fisticuffs: "Speaks Softly and Carries a Big Fist!"

HINT

Last seen in the main goo control room of the Secret Sewers of Supreme Stink

Fisticuffs is an Evilikin with a stinky mission—he may be little but his rocket fist punches way above his weight! Circle his movements as he walks, avoiding his swinging fist but strike hard between punches.

Fisticuffs' Stats!

Villain Quest: Outhouse Back In House	
Villain Quest Location: Find Smeekens at Monster Marsh (Ch. 7).	
Attack Moves:	**Upgrades:**
Press **Attack 1** to shoot out a big fist attack.	Attack does more damage.
Press **Attack 2** to launch the big fist into the air. Hold **Attack 2** to aim the attack.	Fist does more damage.

Eye Scream: "We All Scream for Eye Scream!"

HINT

Last seen just outside the swamp at Monster Marsh

When you've got pretty eyes, you may as well take advantage of them—by spawning and shooting your eyeballs at enemy ranks! (It's not like she can see anyway with that crazy hairstyle.) Keep track of her eyeball spawn and smash them to smithereens before taking her out, melee style.

Eye Scream's Stats!

Villain Quest: Paranormal Captivity	
Villain Quest Location: Find Cali at Monster Marsh (Ch. 7).	
Attack Moves:	Upgrades:
Press **Attack 1** to summon five tiny eyeballs that charge nearby enemies.	Eyeballs deal more damage.
Press **Attack 2** to summon one large eyeball that charges a nearby enemy.	Eyeball does more damage.

Tae Kwon Crow: "Ninja Skills and the Fiendishness of a Bird."

It's time to ruffle some pirate feathers! Roundhouse kick this Skystones-smashing hornswoggler until he sees spinning ninja stars. Jump over his sword and keep clear of the energy bolt it creates as it hits. Use the pause after he hits to attack him and deplete his health.

Tae Kwon Crow's Stats!

Villain Quest: Gopher the Gold!	
Villain Quest Location: Find Tessa at the Golden Desert (Ch. 16).	
Attack Moves:	Upgrades:
Press **Attack 1** for a sword attack. Press **Attack 1**, **Attack 1**, **Attack 1** for a slashing combo.	Attacks do more damage.
Press **Attack 2** to throw three shuriken.	Shuriken do more damage.

Nightshade: "He'll Steal the Show. And Everything Else!"

In the ultimate game of cat and mouse, you're about to be hoodwinked by the sneakiest thief in Skylands (but at least he's polite)! Knock him off his tower to get the party started. Avoid his long-range attacks while you defeat his shadow minions on the ground, leaving him vulnerable.

Nightshade's Stats!

Villain Quest: Crown Without a King	
Villain Quest Location: Find Tessa at Midnight Museum (Ch. 21).	
Attack Moves:	Upgrades:
Press **Attack 1** to swipe at enemies and generate some cash.	Swipe does more damage.
Press **Attack 2** to toss a black bomb that explodes into streamers.	Increased damage done by explosion.
Press **Attack 3** to go into stealth mode.	Nightshade moves faster while in stealth mode.

Kaos: "Needs No Introduction...."

A little ego goes a long way as this Dark Portal Master fights with impressive skill and cunning to become the Ultimate Evil Overlord of Skylands. Prepare for a lot of dodging and jumping in the ultimate battle, and keep your backup Skylanders and villains on hand for a quick swap.

Kaos's Stats!

Villain Quest: Who Wants Kaos Kake?	
Villain Quest Location: Find Bobbers at Skylands Academy.	
Attack Moves:	**Upgrades:**
Press **Attack 1** to place a random element icon on the ground. Each icon produces a different attack. **Attack 1** becomes eye beams in Kaos's head form.	Icon attacks do more damage.
Press **Attack 2** for Doom Sharks! **Attack 2** becomes a sonic attack in Kaos head form.	More sharks are summoned.
Press **Attack 3** to assume giant Kaos head form.	Attacks do more damage.

Collectibles

Skylands isn't all just villain-chasing and brain-bending puzzles (although that's half the fun!). There are plenty of shiny rewards for you to uncover as you roam the countryside in search of a fight. From golden hordes to trophies, jewels, goblets, and scrolls, you'll find a treasure trove around every corner. Hunt them down like a hungry Chomp Chest and earn gold coins to buy upgrades or spend your loot in Hatterson's or Auric's on hats or trinkets. The harder you play, the greater your reward will be!

Treasure Chests

Four treasure chests are hidden in every chapter of *Trap Team*. When you discover and open a treasure chest, you'll be dancing in an explosion of sparkling gold, so dash around and gather it all up! Treasure chests are a super way of boosting your coffers for buying upgrades from Persephone. Each chest contains gold coins, jewelry, rings, gems, and goblets, ranging in value from 150–250 coins per chest (see Figure 5.1). If you have the Hidden Treasure magic item from the Pirate Seas Adventure Pack (released for the *Spyro's Adventure* game), you can also use this to find a bonus invisible treasure chest hidden within each chapter.

FIGURE 5.1 Boost your buying power and complete the chapter goals by finding all four of the treasure chests hidden within each chapter. Tap a treasure chest to open it and be showered in gold coins; smash any furniture you find on your travels to uncover jewels.

You'll find Persephone at her Treehouse at Skylanders Academy (you'll return here after completing each level), and she'll also be waiting for you somewhere in each of the story chapters so you can upgrade on the go.

Aside from collecting the spoils of treasure chests, you'll also find bits and pieces of individual treasure throughout the game, worth up to 1,000 coins each. These may be floating in a quiet spot waiting for you to pass by, or hidden within rooms or items as rewards for exploring all areas. Make sure you smash any furniture, barrels, and obstacles you come across as you journey through Skylands as well—chances are high that a stash of golden goodies is hidden within!

TIP

Troll Radio Alert!

In every level you'll find a Troll Radio. Spend a moment to rock out with Skylands hottest disc jockey, Chill Bill, and change the channel to hear Skylands latest news forecasts, villain theme songs, and even a chance at winning a cash prize of golden coins.

Legendary Treasure

As you progress through each level, you'll find one hidden Legendary Treasure item waiting for you to discover (see Figure 5.2). These are special statues that you'll need to take back to Skylanders Academy after you complete the level, to place in a specific room (a question mark will appear to tell you where). Once placed, the Legendary Treasure prompts a small change to the area. (For example, it may add a new decoration or pop-up feature.) In addition, each Legendary Treasure item is worth up to 1,000 gold coins, which you can use to buy upgrades, hats, and trinkets at Skylanders Academy. If there are two Skylanders present (multiplayer) when you find the Legendary Treasure, both receive the reward coins.

FIGURE 5.2 The Legendary Bubble Fish charm creates an ornamental display of floating fish in the Skylands Academy Courtyard.

Use Table 5.1 as a guide to find and place your treasures around Skylanders Academy!

TABLE 5.1 Guide to Legendary Treasures

Legendary Treasure	Location	Skylands Academy
Legendary Tribal Statue	Chapter 2: Windbag Woods	Courtyard
Legendary Chompy	Chapter 3: Nort's Rescue	Main Hall

Legendary Treasure	Location	Skylands Academy
Legendary Golden Egg	Chapter 4: Rump Feather Roost	Main Hall
Legendary Pepper	Chapter 5: Main Counter Top	Kitchen
Legendary Bubble Fish	Chapter 6: Bluster Squad Island	Courtyard
Legendary Golden Frog	Chapter 7: The Mystery Marshes	Outer Walkway
Legendary Cyclops Teddy Bear	Chapter 8: Library Lock Out	Courtyard
Legendary Saw Blade	Chapter 9: Nature Bridges West	Main Hall
Legendary Eel Plunger	Chapter 10: Digestion Deck	Outer Walkway
Legendary Masterpieces	Chapter 11: End of Line	Main Hall
Legendary Clocktower	Chapter 12: Tower Approach	Persephone's Treehouse
Legendary Rocket	Chapter 13: Containment Corner	Game Room
Legendary Parachute	Chapter 14: Troll Base Entrance	Courtyard
Legendary Geode Key	Chapter 15: Middle Defenses	Kitchen
Legendary Golden Dragon Head	Chapter 16: Dust Bowl	Main Hall
Legendary Hippo Head	Chapter 17: The Secret Vault	Upper Hallway
Legendary Weird Robot	Chapter 18: The Balloon Return	Kitchen
Legendary Gargoyle	Chapter 19: The Garden Tower	Library
Legendary Knight	Chapter 20: Crystal Chasm	Game Room
Legendary Flynn Statue	Chapter 21: Underground Ruins	Upper Hallway
Legendary Windmill	Chapter 22: Rainbow Rockside	Courtyard

Story Scrolls

There's always more to learn about Skylands, and Story Scrolls provide a wealth of information. To complete each chapter goal, you'll need to track down a scroll hidden somewhere on your journey and collect it (see Figure 5.3).

FIGURE 5.3 Piece together the heroic tales of Flynn's adventures fighting against evil in Skylands—just don't believe all you hear (he tends to exaggerate)!

In *Trap Team*, we get to delve into the lovably ego-centric philosophical musings of Flynn—our favorite flying legend. Keep an eye out for each Story Scroll to hear Flynn share his hilarious "Meditations on 'Boom!'"

You'll be rewarded with such delights as Flynn reciting the following:

> *Have you ever heard of the Seven Wonders of Skylands? Six of them are me and the other is... Ha! I was just messing with you—they're ALL me!!!*

Use Table 5.2 to help you locate all the hidden Story Scrolls and learn more about our favorite Mabu, Flynn.

TABLE 5.2 Guide to Story Scrolls

Chapter	Location	Where to Look
1	Twisting Top	Use the bounce pad to reach the platform.
2	Windbag Woods	To the right of the steam vent near Blobbers.
3	Troll Fortress	Inside a troll building opposite the arena entrance.

Chapter	Location	Where to Look
4	Hatching Hall	Use the bounce pad inside the Blocker Bird cage.
5	Bottom Shelf	Past the Super Bounce Pad near the platform.
6	Fish Bone's Card Shack	After you win a game of Skystones Smash.
7	Supply Room	Behind the windmill.
8	Watering Hole Encounter	Inside the Monster Gates on a platform.
9	Packing House	Outside the packing house on the right-hand side.
10	Outer Sewage Segue	On the left-hand side of the Chompies.
11	Spool Storage Shack	Inside the building.
12	Moon Gear Rise	At the top of the gear stack, to the right-hand side.
13	Sub-Orbital Combat Plaza	Use the Super Bounce Pad to the right.
14	Troll Weapons Lab	To the left-hand side of a bomb dispenser.
15	Landing Platforms	To the left of where you begin.
16	X's Shifting Sands	To the right at the top of the platforms.
17	The Seat of Flowing Gold	At the far right at the top of the first steps.
18	Repair Platform H	Next to the Tech Elemental Gate.
19	The Eventide Walk	Move the blocks in your way.
20	Hidden Path	Attack the Cyclops Mammoth first.
21	Hidden Cavern	To the right of the entrance.
22	Paisley Patch	Through the left-hand side fence.

Soul Gems

A collectible Soul Gem is hidden somewhere throughout each of the chapters for every Trap Team Skylander (you can often find more than one per chapter). Once you have collected the Soul Gem for a specific character, take it to Persephone to buy a new attack move or ability for your Skylander (see Figure 5.4). In addition to using the Soul Gem, you'll need to pay 4000 gold coins for the upgrade. Chapter 3, "Meet the Skylanders," has a listing of each Skylander's Soul Gem ability in their biography.

For Trap Team variants of existing characters, your new Soul Gem ability is different from any of the previous games' Soul Gem upgrades. You won't need to collect the variant character's Soul Gem to upgrade because they were hidden in the chapters of previous games. Instead, you'll have to pay 4000 gold coins. This same situation applies to Minis because their Soul Gems were previously hidden for their full-sized versions in previous games.

You found a Soul Gem!
Lob-Star

FIGURE 5.4 Search out the Soul Gem for your Skylander to be rewarded with epic new attack moves and skills!

Table 5.3 includes a quick-reference table of where Soul Gems are hidden, so you can make sure you collect them all before you complete each chapter.

TABLE 5.3 Guide to Soul Gem Locations and Abilities

Location	Skylander	Soul Gem Ability
Chapter 1: Soda Springs		
Fizzleworts Rooftop	Jawbreaker	Hypercharged Haymaker
Twisting Top	Blades	Instant Swirl Shards
Secret Ingredients	Spotlight	Light Dragons
Chapter 2: Know-It-All Island		
Patronizing Plateau	Food Fight	That's How I Roll
Shadowy Sanctum	Blackout	Supernova Black Hole
Chapter 3: Chompy Mountain		
Nort's House	Gusto	Boomerangs 4 Breakfast
Mountain Falls Lagoon	Wallop	Now That's a Hammer!
K-TROLL Troll Radio	Bushwack	Timber!

Location	Skylander	Soul Gem Ability
Chapter 4: Phoenix Psanctuary		
Hatching Hall	Funny Bone	Healing Paws
Rare Species Walk	Snap Shot	A Shard Act to Follow
Chapter 5: Chef Zeppelin		
Main Kebobs	Chopper	Ultimate Dino Destruction
Chapter 6: Rainfish Riviera		
Waste Water Cove	Lob-Star	Hard Boiled
Dire Sands	Déjà vu	Black Hole Bedlam
Chapter 7: Monster Marsh		
Haunted Approach	Krypt King	Storm Swords
Spirestone Grotto	Fist Bump	Riding the Rails
Chapter 8: Telescope Towers		
Galactic Bubble Centre	Wildfire	Lion Form
Pulseblock Pillow Pit	Bat Spin	Great Ball of Bats
Chapter 9: Mystic Mill		
First Wheelhouse	Tread Head	Rocket Boost
Waterways	Torch	The Incinerator
North Nature Bridges	Flip Wreck	Sea Slammer
Chapter 10: Secret Sewers of Supreme Stink		
Flam Bam's Retreat	Echo	Call of the Siren
Splash Station	High Five	Organic Slam Apples
Chapter 11: Wilikin Workshop		
Train Loading Platform	Fling Kong	Make it Rain!
Factory Smashing Area	Head Rush	Horns Aplenty
Chapter 12: Time Town		
Cog Family Fortune	Rocky Roll	Boulder Posse
Main Spring Fly	Thunderbolt	Lightning Rain!
Chapter 13: The Future of Skylands		
Ice Cream Planet	Gearshift	Swing Shift
Harmonic Hold	Trailblazer	Heat Wave
Chapter 14: Operation: Troll Rocket Steal		
Factory Storage	Cobra Cadabra	Big Basket Bomb
Troll Weapons Lab	Enigma	An Eye for Several Eyes
Chapter 15: Skyhighlands		
Upper Elevators	Blastermind	Lock Puzzle Psychic
Chapter 16: The Golden Desert		
The Temple of Topaz	Tuff Luck	Garden of Pain

Location	Skylander	Soul Gem Ability
Chapter 17: Lair of the Golden Queen		
The Halls of Treachery	Short Cut	Scissor Stilts
Chapter 18: The Ultimate Weapon		
Power Exhaust Ports	Ka-Boom	Missile Rain
Chapter 19: Midnight Museum (Adventure Pack)		
The Night Sky Walk	Knight Mare	The Shadow Realm
Chapter 20: Sunscraper Spire (Adventure Pack)		
Crystal Underpass	Knight Light	Brilliant Blade

Winged Sapphires

Now, here's a collectible that you'll really want to get your Skylander's hands on! Winged Sapphires are blue gems adorned with butterfly wings (see Figure 5.5). One is hiding in each game chapter—sometimes in plain sight— but you may have to crack a puzzle or get past a gate to reach it. Winged Sapphires are worth their weight in gold (literally!) so start hunting!

FIGURE 5.5 Look for fluttering purple gems while you journey through Skylands to boost your buying power with Persephone.

Every Winged Sapphire you find is worth a 2% discount on buying upgrades from Persephone. Not just once, but for all the Skylanders in your collection. The more you collect, the greater the discount—so find 20 out of the 22 hidden Winged Sapphires, and you will earn up to 40% off your upgrades (which is the maximum).

To entirely upgrade a single Skylander (with no discount), you'll need 14,200 gold coins, so the Winged Sapphires go a long way toward helping your Skylanders become the best fighters they can be.

Use Table 5.4 to collect as many Winged Sapphires as you can to earn discounts on your upgrades with Persephone.

TABLE 5.4 Guide to Winged Sapphire Locations

Chapter	Location	Where to Look
1	Hidden Flavor Grotto	In the cave (easy to see).
2	Boulder Falls Circle	To the top left of where Blobbers is waiting.
3	Mabu Landing Pier	On the right-hand side of where you begin.
4	Little Chicken Landing	Under the Traptanium Crystal.
5	Garbage Disposal	Over the edge, to the right of the waiting chefs.
6	Cheddar House	In the corner of the building.
7	Haunted Wreck	Under the Traptanium Crystal on the left-hand side.
8	Meditation Pool	In the corner at the bottom.
9	Nature Bridges North	Behind Shrednaught's fence.
10	Spoiled Sanctum	Across the metal and bamboo bridges.
11	The Old Mill	Behind the crates with Yah Har.
12	Main Spring Fly	At the top of the platforms near Florg.
13	Sub Atomic Particle Smasher	Complete the floating platform puzzle.
14	Southwest Tower	Behind the wall (smash it down).
15	Lost and Found	Inside the building, at the back of the room.
16	The Temple of Topaz	To the right of the block puzzle.
17	The Secret Vault	Past the cracked blocks, behind the gate.
18	Matter Refactoring Room	Below the pipe in front of the bounce pad.
19	The Prime Tower	Jump off the edge past the entrance.
20	Under-Island Maintenance Area	Along the tracks near the pit.
21	Cliffside Sanctuary	On the left-hand side, down behind a lock puzzle.
22	Pawn Shop	Jump onto the ledge above the garage. It's to the right.

Achievements and Trophies

Love a good challenge? Each level of *Trap Team* comes with an *extra* opportunity to earn rewards by completing certain tasks. Some are simply finishing a level, whereas others involve really tricky gameplay using all the skill, speed, and fighting prowess you've got. Only PlayStation and Xbox consoles reward trophies for completing these tasks—so if you're a Nintendo or iOS player, you'll miss out (although there are plenty of other challenges that await you).

As you play through each chapter, use Table 5.5 to help you gather trophies to show off your puzzle-solving prowess, gun-slinging skills, and villain-destroying determination!

TABLE 5.5 Guide to Achievements for Gameplay and Milestones During Story Mode Chapters

Name of Award	What to Do to Receive It	Xbox	PS3/4
Soda Saver	Complete Chapter 1: Soda Springs.	10	Copper
Now YOU Know It All	Complete Chapter 2: Know-It-All Island.	10	Copper
Chapter 3: Chompy Mountain			
Chompy Champ	Complete the chapter.	10	Copper
Statue Smasher	Destroy four stone Chompy heads.	10	Copper
Chapter 4: The Phoenix Psanctuary			
Bird Buddy	Complete the chapter.	10	Copper
Preemptive Power	Destroy one Dropship.	10	Copper
Chapter 5: Chef Zeppelin			
Master of Chefs	Complete the chapter.	10	Copper
Cannon Completest	Destroy eight Troll Transports during the flying sequence.	10	Copper
Chapter 6: Rainfish Riviera			
Squid Seeker	Complete the chapter.	10	Copper
Pipe Down	Destroy four stacks of pipes using the crane on Dredger's Yacht.	10	Copper
Chapter 7: Monster Marsh			
Swamp Survivor	Complete the chapter.	10	Copper
No Coins Left Behind	Collect 20 coins while following Marsha through the mist.	10	Copper

Name of Award	What to Do to Receive It	Xbox	PS3/4
Chapter 8: Telescope Towers			
Dreamcatcher Catcher	Complete the chapter.	10	Copper
Ball Sprawler	Knock 12 Golden Balls off the waterfall in the Meditative Pool area (tricky!).	40	Silver
Chapter 9: Mystic Mill			
Lumber Liberator	Complete the chapter.	10	Copper
Evilikin Eliminator	Shoot 20 Evilikin Runners during the flying sequence.	10	Copper
Chapter 10: Secret Sewers of Supreme Stink			
Aroma Avenger	Complete the chapter.	10	Copper
No Goo For You!	Travel to Splash Station without taking any damage from goo.	10	Copper
Chapter 11: Wilikin Workshop			
Krankcase Kapturer	Complete the chapter.	10	Copper
Ride the Rails	Ride the train to the end of the line.	10	Copper
Chapter 12: Time Town			
Clock Crusader	Complete the chapter.	10	Copper
Da Pinchy Defacer	Destroy 5 Da Pinchy statues.	10	Copper
Chapter 13: The Future of Skylands			
Back From the Future	Complete the chapter.	10	Copper
Just to be Safe	Take down every shield unit during the flying sequence.	10	Copper
Chapter 14: Operation: Troll Rocket Steal			
Rocket Recoverer	Complete the chapter.	10	Copper
Exhaust All Possibilities	Complete the arena battle without getting hit by rocket exhaust.	10	Copper
Chapter 15: Skyhighlands			
Squadron Star	Complete the chapter.	10	Copper
Look Ma, No Rockets!	Shoot down 30 Air Pirates without using rockets (tricky!).	40	Silver
Chapter 16: The Golden Desert			
Desert Dominator	Complete the chapter.	10	Copper
Garden Gladiator	Destroy ten cacti.	10	Copper

Name of Award	What to Do to Receive It	Xbox	PS3/4
Chapter 17: Lair of the Golden Queen			
Royal Flusher	Complete the chapter.	10	Copper
Highwire Act	Complete all the tile floor puzzles without falling.	10	Copper
Chapter 18: The Ultimate Weapon			
Kaos Komeuppance	Complete the chapter.	10	Copper
Do a Barrel Roll	Collect nine coins while falling down the Machine Heart.	10	Copper
Achievements for Gameplay Milestones (Easy to Super-Hard!)			
Not Out of Your Element	Unlock your first Elemental area.	10	Copper
Arena Mogul	Unlock Brock's special arena.	10	Copper
Road to Redemption	Complete a captured Villain's quest.	10	Copper
Wow, That's Tough!	Achieve Portal Master Rank 5.	20	Copper
Skystones Scavenger	Collect 20 Skystones.	20	Copper
Kaos Mode Master	Defeat 100 enemies in Kaos Mode.	20	Copper
Hero Hunter	Capture 10 villains.	30	Copper
Star Star	Earn 50 stars in Kaos Mode.	75	Silver
All the Way Up!	Level up any Skylander to Level 20.	30	Silver
Chairman of Rumble Club	Complete all Arena levels.	75	Gold
Savior of Skylands IV	Complete Story Mode on any difficulty.	150	Gold
Dream a Little Nightmare	Complete Story Mode on Nightmare.	150	Gold
IMPOSSIBLE!!!	Earn all other trophies (PS3 only).		Platinum

Learn to Play Skystones Smash

Skystones Smash is like a card game you can play throughout the story chapters. Usually one or two characters are hidden in areas of each chapter that ask you if you'd like to play with them. Sometimes, you have to beat a character in a game of Skystones Smash to unlock a gate to continue on your path, collect treasure, or evolve a villain.

Batterson, a Mabu, is waiting in the Command Kitchen in Chapter 5: Chef Zeppelin to teach you how to play, but you will find willing players in every chapter. Each time you capture a villain (it doesn't matter if you trap them or if they go to your Villain Vault), you will receive a special Skystones Smash card with their picture on it, as well as a sword and a heart (see Figure 6.1).

FIGURE 6.1 Capture villains to build your Skystones Smash collection!

How to Play

The aim of Skystones Smash is to reduce the health of your opponent to zero. Both players usually begin with ten points of health, as shown in Figure 6.2, but sometimes they start higher.

FIGURE 6.2   The number on the sword shows how much damage your Skystone can do to your opponent. The number on the heart shows how much health your Skystone is worth.

Your opponent will always go first. Once they place their Skystone, it's your turn! Place it in any spot on your side. Now the Skystones will battle against each other (see Figure 6.3).

The number on the sword of your Skystone is taken away from the number on the heart of your opponent's Skystone. You have reduced their health.

At the same time:

The number on your opponent's sword will reduce the value of your own Skystone's heart. They have reduced your health.

If a Skystone loses all of its health, it will disappear.

If your opponent doesn't have a Skystone opposite where you placed yours, their overall health will reduce by the number on your sword. This is usually more than if there is a Skystone in the way to take some of the damage.

Remember, this can happen to you, too, so try to protect your health by placing a Skystone in each spot!

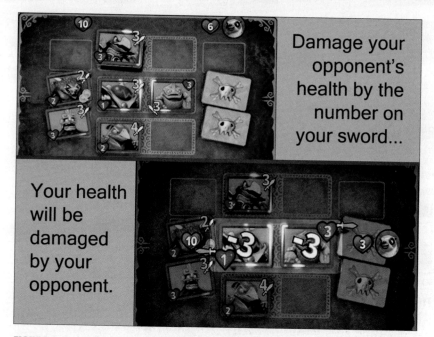

FIGURE 6.3 Place Skystones to cause the most damage to your opponent's health, but the least to your own.

Once you have a Skystone in each of the three spots, all the cards will play, from top to bottom. As soon as you or your opponent's health hits zero, the game ends.

Extra Special Skystones

You can use four types of bonus Skystone abilities in your game (see Figure 6.4). Each one has a unique strength in its special ability against the Skystone opposite it:

- **Fireball**—Need to create some big damage? This ability will damage every Skystone on your opponent's side.

- **Heart Boost**—Save this card to replenish your own health when you need it most!

- **Lightning**—Your opponent will take extra damage to their health, as well as the Skystone sword damage played.

- **Sheepify**—This Skystone turns your opponent's Skystone into a sheep! A sheep Skystone has only one health, so it's easy to defeat.

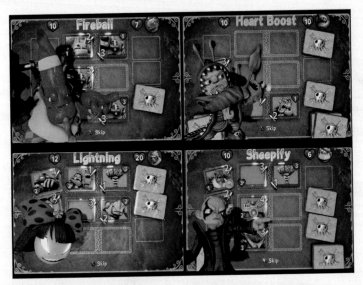

FIGURE 6.4   Not all Skystones have special abilities, so use the ones that do to your best advantage.

Skylanders Academy

You'll begin each new game at Skylanders Academy, which is a very special place. This is also the main base location that you will return to after each game level. There are characters here waiting to take you on your next adventure to new story chapters or challenges, as well as a magical gate that connects to your adventure pack locations. Within the Academy, the Main Hall leads to different rooms and paths, each one offering a new experience. Some boast games or obstacle courses while others give you the opportunity to buy accessories or learn more about the Skylanders Universe.

All Skylanders train at the Academy to learn their epic hero skills, including the Mini Skylanders who learned their craft after arriving as Sidekicks from the Skylands Miniverse. After finishing each story chapter, you'll return to the Courtyard just outside the Main Hall, where you can chase trinkets, play games, and smash coin-filled challenges! Spend some time getting to know the locals, such as Persephone, Dreadbeard, Hatterson, and Auric. If you see any wiggling cupboard doors as you search through Academy rooms, attack them to score gems and coins.

Some areas in Skylanders Academy can only be entered once between story chapters, so take care to collect as much treasure as you can each visit. If you miss out or fall too soon, don't worry—you'll be able to enter again after your next trip with Flynn or after you play a Kaos Doom Challenge (see Figure 7.1) or visit the Arena.

FIGURE 7.1   In an alcove by the Main Hall entrance is a stone statue of Kaos. Interact with this to play the Kaos Doom Challenges, which are battles that get more difficult as your experience grows.

Each time you level up a Portal Master rank, a gift box will be waiting for you back in the Courtyard with a hat, trinket, or experience orb inside. Whichever Skylander opens the box receives the bonus, so you may like to swap before you interact with it.

There are so many fantastic places to explore on the island of Skylanders Academy; let's discover some secrets together in this chapter.

The Courtyard

In the center of the courtyard is the Villain Vault (see Figure 7.2), the prison where all your defeated enemies are sent, whether you trap them during the game or not.

You can interact with villains here to transfer them into your traps, ready for an upcoming Villain Quest or a play-through of a story chapter. The villain health bar doesn't decrease while you're in Skylanders Academy, so take your time and have fun getting to know their abilities. You can track your uncaptured villains down by interacting with the Tree Stump across the cobblestone bridge (see Figure 7.3).

FIGURE 7.2 Before you begin a new story chapter, visit the Villain Vault to transfer any villains that would be useful during your game. Once you've begun a new level, you can't transfer them without starting again.

FIGURE 7.3 If you want the inside scoop on which villains are still on the loose in Skylands, or where to track down their Villain Quests, take a look at the Wanted Posters on the tree stump to the left of the Courtyard entrance.

Buzz will introduce you to the swirling purple Mystery Gate to the left of the Villain Vault (see Figure 7.4). As you add each of the four Adventure Packs to your collection, a statue for each will appear in this area. You can enter the story chapter for the Adventure Pack that you place on the Traptanium Portal, through this gate. The four Trap Team Adventure Pack locations are the Nightmare Express, Mirror of Mystery, Sunscraper Spire, and Midnight Museum.

Spotlight
510
2851

FIGURE 7.4 Use the purple swirling Mystery Gate to enter your Adventure Pack destinations. Continue past this area along the red carpet to reach the Courtyard Tower.

Persephone's Treehouse

On the right side of the Courtyard, the fairy Persephone floats around her Treehouse (see Figure 7.5). Chat with her to buy upgrades for your Skylanders with the coins you earn while playing. Collect Winged Sapphires throughout the story chapters for a discount on upgrades, and find each Skylander's Soul Gem to unlock a special attack. Practice attack moves with your new Skylanders and villains using the dummies-on-a-spring outside Persephone's Treehouse. This is a good place to test a new characters' damage capabilities and learn their attacks without decreasing your health.

Inside Persephone's Treehouse, bounce up a line of coins to land on the upper-level balcony. If you see any wiggling cupboard doors, attack them to score gems and coins. You'll also find the Elemental Diamond trinket here.

FIGURE 7.5   Persephone is always close by if you want to buy upgrades. There is no limit to the number of upgrades you can make per visit, as long as you have enough coins to purchase them.

The Courtyard Tower

Out in the courtyard, to the far left of the Main Hall entrance, is a little door at the end of a red carpet (see Figure 7.6). This door won't appear until you have completed Chapter 2: Know-It-All-Island. You'll have to go past the Mystery Gate, then jump a gap to reach it. The Courtyard Tower is a super-fun mini-game full of coins, with elevators that take you higher and higher. There are multiple exits (and remember once you leave, you can't return until later). Hidden somewhere in this area will also be a new trinket—Iris's Iris.

FIGURE 7.6 You can visit the Courtyard Tower once per story chapter, and it will be stocked with coins each time.

The Main Hall

The Main Hall is a central area leading to the Upper Hallway (and Defense Tower), the Kitchen, Game Room (through to the Observatory), the Outer Walkway (through to the Library), as well as mini-games such as Skaletones Showdown, Brock's Rumble Club (the Arena Challenges), and Hatterson's and Auric's stores.

Auric's Shop is the first area to open in the Main Hall after you complete Chapter 2: Know-It-All Island (see Figure 7.7). As you return to Skylanders Academy after each story chapter, Auric's inventory expands, so be sure to pop back each time to buy some trinkets, hats, and lock puzzle keys.

There's a fireplace at the back of the Main Hall (near Auric's Shop). Floating close by is a hot-air balloon, which you can interact with to create a handy quick-trip portal back out to the Courtyard.

To the right of the Main Hall entrance, Mags is waiting with her new slot machine after you return from Chapter 3: Chompy Mountain. Try your luck to collect 25 gold coins. Continue past her to visit the Academy Defense Tower.

After you return from Chapter 4: The Phoenix Psanctuary with the Legendary Egg, place it above the fireplace. Jump up from the left to reach the egg. If you attack it, it will open up to reveal two smaller eggs, which you can push around. You'll also be able to visit the Rumble Club with Brock and play Skaletone Showdown now.

Ready to hit that Rumble Club again?

FIGURE 7.7 The Main Hall provides a fun space to brush up on your gymnastics skills while filling your purse, without the pressure of enemy attacks.

The Great Chimney

You can visit the Great Chimney once per story chapter. Head into the Main Hall to find a small switch near the fireplace on the back wall (near the portrait of Kaos). Interact with it to discover a new area (jump down the fireplace) where you can score a heap of coins in a bouncing mini-game, shown in Figure 7.8, and earn another trinket—the Big Bow of Doom (that sounds like Dreamcatcher's fashion style!).

FIGURE 7.8 Take a dive into the Great Chimney for a bouncing coin extravaganza! Just don't bounce out of the area until you're finished—you can only enter once per visit.

Academy Defense Tower

Inside the Main Hall, immediately right (up the stairs past Mags' slot machine) is a little open elevator that will carry you up to the Courtyard Tower. Walk along to find the Academy Defense Tower (see Figure 7.9), which opens after you complete Chapter 7: Monster Marsh.

Skaletone Showdown

Crossbones is waiting in the Main Hall, hoping for an epic musical battle of Skaletone Showdown with you (see Figure 7.10). Chat with him as either a Skylander or a villain, and then head to the right-side platform where you can interact with one of six statues to descend into the basement underneath. Each statue character has its own unique style of music. Choose your level of difficulty and show those rattling renegades your rhythm!

The aim of this game is to copy your competitor's musical talent by pressing your controller buttons in time with the music. The notes will move along the bottom of the screen as they are played, from left to right (see Figure 7.11). Hit the button indicated as it passes through the empty box on the right. You'll earn applause from your audience of enthusiastic Mabu as you play! You can win increasing amounts of coins, as well as rock out to your own tune with Rattlin' Rhoda for extra badges.

FIGURE 7.9 The Academy Defense Tower is an airy room overlooking beautiful Skylands, which boasts a Troll Radio, a new trinket, and a stash of loot floating above bounce pads.

FIGURE 7.10 You have six statues to choose from as your guides to Skaletone Showdown.

FIGURE 7.11 Your badge will appear on the statue you interacted with after playing Skaletone Showdown.

Outer Walkway

Inside the Main Hall, walk through the big wooden doors on the left near the Skaletones statues to enter the Outer Walkway. This will take you to the Grand Library and Archives, and little Quigley who can show you the Reading Room.

The Grand Library

You'll find a book inside the Grand Library (top of stairs to the right) that contains all of the Skylanders and magic items you have played with so far, so you can keep track of your collection. The entrance to the library is shown in Figure 7.12. Inside, there are plenty of wiggling cupboards to attack, a hot-air balloon teleporter, and a secret entrance to the Archives. In the center of the room, Quigley is looking for a Mini Skylander to explore the Reading Room with him.

The Reading Room

After you complete Chapter 9: Mystic Mill, the Grand Library opens. Swap to a Mini Skylander and chat with Quigley. You'll be teleported to a series of ramps and ladders in a secret part of the library (full of coins, of course)! When you reach the end of the ramp/ladder trail, interact with the wall on the left to open the secret Reading Room, shown in Figure 7.13, where you can gather coins and score a new trinket called Stealth Elf's Gift. The wall on the right will return you to Quigley.

FIGURE 7.12 Ready to read? The Grand Library is revealed upon your return from Chapter 9: Mystic Mill.

FIGURE 7.13 Don't lose your balance on the way to the Reading Room! This little treasure trove is tricky!

The Archives

Inside the Grand Library, sneak down a set of stairs on the right, then turn left to find a hidden area where a new trinket awaits—Billy Bison (the cuddliest Cyclops teddy in town)! Just like the Reading Room, the Archives are a coin-fest of fun with lots of bounce pads and platforms to discover (see Figure 7.14).

FIGURE 7.14 Bounce your way through the Archives, but don't fall— you can only enter this area once per visit to Skylands Academy.

The Kitchen

Down the right-side set of stairs below Auric's shop is the Kitchen (see Figure 7.15). This area opens up after you return from Chapter 5: Chef Zeppelin, with plenty of special features to explore. You'll find an enormous cauldron bubbling away over a stone pit with some floating orbs above it. Attack the cauldron with a Skylander to match each of the orbs (you'll need to swap Skylanders to access all the orbs). After each one has fallen into the cauldron, you'll be rewarded with a shower of gems.

Blobbers is busy cooking in the Kitchen, but he needs Kaos to help. After you capture Kaos in Chapter 18: The Ultimate Weapon, take him back to visit Blobbers to complete his Villain Quest (Who Wants Kaos Kake?). Yummy!? I'm not too sure about eating a cake that has a face with sharp, pointy teeth, though. Eek!

Quest Discovered: Who Wants Kaos Kake?

FIGURE 7.15 The Kitchen has a few fun mini-games and a locked gate to the Crystal Caverns. If you find the Legendary Pepper Chest during Chapter 5: Chef Zeppelin, this will appear as a decoration.

The Crystal Caverns

Inside the kitchen to the right (up high) is a fancy, locked, circular gate with glittering purple crystals inside. You'll need to complete Chapter 15: Skyhighlands and find the Legendary Geode Key to open this gate. A Mini Skylander can enter to bounce around a purple wonderland of shining coins (see Figure 7.16). It's easy to fall, but you can always return on your next visit to Skylander Academy.

FIGURE 7.16   Gathering the coins in the Crystal Caverns is a bit tricky. Return on each visit to Skylands Academy to search different platforms for the Wilikin Windmill trinket.

Upper Hallway

Just beside the stairs leading down to the Kitchen is another set of stairs heading up. These lead you to the Upper Hallway, where you'll find Hatterson's Hat Store, the Game Room, and the Observatory.

Hatterson's Hat Store

You can reach Hatterson's Hat Store through the Upper Hallway after you return from Chapter 6: Rainfish Riviera. Here, you can buy all sorts of crazy hats from Hatterson to boost your power stats. (A full inventory of hats can be found earlier in this book in Chapter 2, "Ready, Set, Go!")

After you capture Hood Sickle in Chapter 8: Telescope Towers, visit Hatterson to complete his Villain Quest. In this quest (called Hatastrophe!), Hood Sickle must run through a series of areas destroying counterfeit hat machines (see Figure 7.17). There are eight machines to destroy in ten minutes, which sounds easy enough. But beware: The Trolls are determined to protect their illegal hat-smuggling activities!

FIGURE 7.17 Poor Hatterson is going out of business—those nasty Trolls are making counterfeit hats and selling them! Set Hood Sickle loose on the Trolls to destroy their giant hat machines with his scythe.

The Game Room

After you have completed Chapter 6: Rainfish Riviera, you can access the Game Room through the Upper Hallway (see Figure 7.18). Brush up on your Skystones Smash skills with Dreadbeard (for a coin bounty!) or do some exploring. A self-playing piano will entertain you on the top-right ledge, featuring all of Skylands' sensational music.

Inside the Game Room, you'll find another teleporter (floating hot-air balloon) on the lower-left balcony, which takes you to the Courtyard (you can also teleport from the Courtyard to the Game Room using the Skystones Smash hologram).

Care for another game of Skystones Smash, matey?

Dreadbeard

FIGURE 7.18 Beat Dreadbeard at Skystones Smash in the Game Room or try the Elemental Steps mini-game.

You'll discover a series of platforms on the right-side balcony called the Elemental Steps. Groups of platforms lead to rewards of gold, so start climbing! The trick is, you can only progress from one platform to the next by swapping Skylanders (or villains) to match the elements of the steps. There are ten sections to this stepping game, and at the end you'll earn a big pile of gold—but it will take quite a while to get there.

Next to the piano is a Legendary Rocket statue, which teleports you over to the Observatory.

The Observatory

There's a new trinket (Spyro's Shield) waiting for you in the Observatory, but you won't be granted access to this area (through the Game Room) until you have recovered the Legendary Rocket in Chapter 13: The Future of Skylands. Inside, there's a telescope to look through with an impressive view of the awesome Toys for Bob rocket circling the moon, as well as a room with plenty of coins and gems to collect.

Battle for Skylands!

It's time to begin the ultimate adventure into Skylands! There are 39 villains to capture in your travels throughout the 18 Story Chapters, as well as an additional six to track down in the Adventure Packs, which we'll cover in Chapter 9, "Expand Your Adventure!" Chapters 8 and 9 include a complete walkthrough of each game level in detail. There are many ways to explore Story Chapters; however, in this guide, I'll outline the most direct route to take to the conclusion of each level, ensuring you have access to all areas on the way.

One of the ways to increase your Portal Master Rank is by earning a "Collectibles" star within each level. To accomplish this, you'll need to find all of the hidden collectibles in each Story Chapter. To help you out, each chapter summary that follows begins with an image of the collectibles to keep your eye out for, including specific Soul Gems, Hats, and Legendary Treasure. You'll also need to uncover three Treasure Chests and one Villain Stash per level, as well as a Story Scroll and Winged Sapphire. Also shown in your collectibles image are the villains you must defeat to complete the level.

From there, we'll cover tips and tricks for getting through obstacles, discovering hidden areas, and fighting strategies to bring down enemies. Each time a Lock Puzzle appears in your way, always try to solve it yourself first. If you need a helping hand, you can flip to the Appendix at the end of this book called "Lock Puzzle Cheats" to find directions.

Are you ready to explore? Let's get going!

Chapter 1: Soda Springs

Disaster has struck at the Grand Opening of Skylander Academy! Oh no! One of the villains, The Gulper, who escaped from Cloud Cracker prison, is on a rampage in Soda Springs. He is tearing apart the village in an attempt to steal all of their prize-winning soda! Now this is a very cranky monster with a serious sugar craving—yikes! Before you can capture him, though, you'll have to make your way through some new areas and challenges. Sheep Creep has his rocket launchers aimed at you (he's not as innocent as he looks!) and there are some collectibles along the way (see Figure 8.1). In this Story Chapter, you'll need to find the Turtle Hat, Weather-Vane Hat, Melon Hat, and the Bucket Hat. There are hidden Soul Gems for Blades, Jawbreaker, and Spotlight, as well as a Villain Stash, three Treasure Chests, a Winged Sapphire, and Story Scroll.

FIGURE 8.1
Gather these collectibles as you explore Soda Springs to capture Sheep Creep and the Gulper.

TIP

Grab Some Loot!

As you play, explore every area you enter. Smash up barrels, furniture, wheelbarrows, and vegetables for easy treasure. Use your coins to buy upgrades, trinkets, and hats.

Sugar Plateau   It's time to begin your adventure with Buzz. Straight ahead, you'll find a barrel with a cork in it. Blow up the gate. (Treasure Chest alert!) Beyond the gate, push the turtle forward to form a bridge. Arrows will appear to show you the direction in which the turtle can be moved.

Cola Stream & Backwash Spillway   Jump off the right side of the turtle and float downstream for a treasure stash. A bounce pad will fly you back to the start. Retrace your steps to the turtle bridge and cross to find a Troll Radio. Change the channel a few times for a shower of golden coins. Push the stack of turtles to create a bridge. Cross over to find Buzz.

Soda Flats & Hidden Flavor Grotto   It's time to defeat your very first villain, Sheep Creep! Trap him in a Life Trap so that you can choose to play as Sheep Creep by tagging in with your controller. Once he's defeated, the battle gate near Buzz will drop, revealing a bounce pad. Jump up to find a nervous-looking turtle. Just beyond him is a doorway to Hidden Flavor Grotto, where you'll find your first Winged Sapphire! Give the sheep a shove into the gap ahead, then bounce up and follow the path onward.

Natural Ingredients Tree & Seltzer Pit

Down below is a huge Traptanium Crystal protected by a swarm of Chompies. Whenever you come across one of these crystals, smash it with a Trap Master's attack to reveal a surprise underneath. Now gather your wits—it's fighting time! Once the enemies are defeated, a gate will open, revealing a bounce pad. First, smash up the Traptanium Crystal, which will collapse the ground beneath you, revealing the **Seltzer Pit** and hidden **Treasure Chest** (see Figure 8.2). Grab the gold and double-bounce up! Buzz is waiting for you at a **Water Gate**. You'll find a few Elemental Gates in each chapter—you'll need a Trap Master of the same Element to open each one.

FIGURE 8.2

Smash the Traptanium Crystal to fall into a horde of treasure at the Seltzer Pit.

Carbonated Plant

Inside the gate, follow the water path to find three turtles. Push them so you can knock the turtle closest to the edge right off—don't worry, he floats! Jump onboard to reach the Hat Box; then mash your controller to earn a Turtle Hat (+7 Armor)! You can choose to wear this now, or just store it in your inventory. Take the bounce pad back to your turtles; then use the second bounce pad to gather some extra coins before you leave.

Twisting Top & Melon Flavor Farm

Next to Buzz is a purple Super Bounce Pad. Jump over to Twisting Top to claim the **Soul Gem** for Blades (see Figure 8.3). Prepare for a quick Chompy fight when you jump down. Buzz is waiting next to a **Life Gate** called **Melon Flavor Farm**. Simply push pumpkins onto the scale to raise the lift. Kill the Plant Warrior and jump up to claim a Melon Hat (+5 Elemental Power). Head back out the gate and drop off the edge of **Twisting Top**, where you see a trail of coins. This ledge holds a **Story Scroll** and a **Light Gate** (Secret Ingredients Cavern). If you don't own a Light Trap Master, this gate will appear as a "Mystery Gate" instead.

FIGURE 8.3

Super-bounce to the highest point on Twisting Top to claim the Soul Gem for Blades before exploring.

Secret Ingredients Cavern

Smash the Traptanium Crystal to reveal a bounce pad. Use the cork cannon to smash a wall ahead, revealing a Soul Gem for Spotlight (see Figure 8.4). Push the golden block on your left to the right once and then forward twice to create a step. Use the bounce pad to grab a stash of gold and jump across to the gold block to claim a very cool Weather Vane Hat (+25 Armor). Head back out the elemental gates to Twisting Top and bounce back up to Buzz.

FIGURE 8.4

The Light Gate (Secret Ingredients Cavern) offers a Story Scroll, Weather Vane Hat, and a Soul Gem for Spotlight. Light and Dark Gates will appear as Mystery Gates unless you have a Light or Dark Trap Master in your collection.

Sugar Free Landing & Really Secret Spot

Can you hear The Gulper in the distance? It's nearly time to sort him out! First, use the super bounce pad near Buzz. Head down to your right and defeat the Plant Warrior to drop a Battle Gate ahead. Ignore it for now and dash down the left-side ramp toward a Tech Gate. Halfway down the ramp, though, jump over the left edge to reach a tiny island of coins, bounce across to a second island for more, and then bounce back up to the ramp.

Zero Calorie Cavern

You'll hear The Gulper getting cranky at the Soda Festival, but hold off on exploring that area until you've investigated the Tech Gate. Inside is a room of platforms. You need to hop from one to the next across the front (left to right) and then the back row (right to left) to reach a Bucket Hat (+5 Armor). Great work! Back outside, follow the ramp through the Battle Gate up to Buzz.

Grape Flavored Vista & Bottleneck Balcony

You're about to meet your second villain, The Gulper, a giant blob-monster that really loves soda (see Figure 8.5)! Buzz explains that you have to destroy the soda vat before The Gulper drinks it. First, smash the Traptanium Crystals for a reward. (Treasure Chest alert!) Nearby, Pibbs wants to play a game of Skystones Smash next to a super bounce pad. (Batterson will teach you how to play in Level 5: Chef Zeppelin, or you can read Chapter 6, "Learn to Play Skystones Smash," in this book). Super-bounce over to Bottleneck Balcony. (Troll Radio alert!) Across the rooftops, just past the windmill, is your first Villain Stash. You'll need to tag in your trapped Sheep Creep to open it. Continue along and time your jumps across the floating corks so you don't fall off as they rise and fall.

FIGURE 8.5

The Gulper is furious—he wants soda! Switch the orange soda barrel for eel-flavored green goop to save Soda Springs from disaster.

Fizzlewort's Rooftop

It's time to face The Gulper! Aim the cannon at The Gulper's fingers to knock them out of your way; then smash the barrel behind his hand that is blocking the steps. Bounce up a step. There's a ledge to your right (leap down) next to the step bounce pad with a Soul Gem for Jaw Breaker. Claim it and then bounce back up to Buzz. You need to push the orange vat of soda off the rooftop and then replace it with the green vat. Yum, yum! Grab your Water Trap to take The Gulper as your prisoner. For completing your first chapter, you've earned a Soda Saver Trophy. Tremendous effort, Skylander!

Chapter 2: Know-It-All Island

There's trouble afoot! Kaos has created an evil Frequency Modulator of Doom to break the Doom Raiders out of Cloud Cracker Prison... but things don't go to plan when the Golden Queen takes over! In this Story Chapter, your mission is to rid Know-It-All Island of the nasty Trolls that have taken over. Three new villains will try to stop you from succeeding, but you'll find a series of stone carvings called Knuckleheads on your path, willing to offer you advice about the Doom Raiders. Keep your eye out for the first piece of Legendary Treasure in this chapter, the Legendary Tribal Statue, as well as three new hats (Sleuth, Hedgehog, and Skipper hats). You'll uncover hidden Soul Gems for Food Fight and Blackout, as well as the general collectibles you find in each chapter (see Figure 8.6).

> ### TIP
>
> **Standard Collectibles**
>
> In every new Story Chapter, there are certain collectibles that are always hidden somewhere along your path. These collectibles include three Treasure Chests, one Villain Stash, one Winged Sapphire, and a Story Scroll. Unique collectibles such as Legendary Treasure and Magic Hats may also be hidden, but each of these looks different and has a special purpose.

FIGURE 8.6

Gather these collectibles as you explore Know-It-All Island to capture Tussle Sprout, Slobber Trap, and Buzzer Beak.

TIP

Be Prepared!

Have Slobber Trap and The Gulper in traps ready for their Villain Quests. (You'll battle Slobber Trap in this level if you don't have him from a previous game. As you defeat villains during play, they'll be stored in your Villain Vault for use in new chapters and to revisit previous ones.)

Pompous Point
Buzz has some great news—you can learn secret info about the Doom Raiders from Stone Heads, so keep an eye out for them as you explore!

First up, head right to find Mags to complete The Gulpers **Villain Quest** (called **Balloon Redemption**). Swap in to the trapped Gulper to begin. For this quest, The Gulper must deliver ten balloons to sad Mabu children—they'll float away with happiness! Tussle Sprouts and Slobber Traps will try to stop you. Throw small enemies over your shoulder with the trident and stab the big guys.

Easy! Once this is completed, you can play the **Troll Radio** for coins and head back across the bridge. On the left-side ledge, you'll see a **Golden Key**—use it to open the gate.

Told You So Terrace
Swap to The Gulper again to score the Villain Stash to your left. Ahead is a Traptanium Crystal pit full of Buzzer Beaks. Attack them and smash the crystals to come face-to-face with the stinky earth villain Tussle Sprout. Take out his minions but try to hit Tussle Sprout long-range while he's moving. Avoid the poisonous gas cloud he creates! Once clear (Treasure Chest alert!), bounce back out of the pit.

The Weighting Room & Stuck Up Steppes
Explore the right path first to visit Arbo at the Earth Gate (The Weighting Room). Each block (from the landing platform and top-left ledge) can be pushed onto the circular rock in the middle to make it rise, creating steps to reach the Treasure Chest. A third block (above the treasure chest) must be dropped down onto the rock circle to raise the main rock platform again. You'll be rewarded with the Sleuth Hat (+7 Critical Hit). Use the teleport pad to get back to Stuck Up Steppes.

Travel left this time. The bounce pad will take you to your first Stone Head for a fun poem about the Chompy Mage (see Figure 8.7). Bounce up another level to find a gate. There is a golden key on each island to your left. Push the block heads to build bridges to reach them. The left island has another talking Knucklehead **Stone Head** (grab the key!) and **Persephone** is waiting on the other island. Use both keys to open the gate.

FIGURE 8.7

Interact with the talking Stone Heads to find out all about the Doom Raiders and earn coins.

Windbag Woods

This area is guarded by Buzzer Beaks. Pick up the bomb and run—you've got ten seconds to throw it at the gate. As soon as the barrier breaks, a Troll megatank appears. Blow it up with a second bomb to bring down the battle gate to your left. Explore behind the tank to discover a Story Scroll.

Enchanted Forest

Arbo is guarding a Life Gate to your right. Bomb the bulldozer to make a bridge, but be prepared to battle a few waves of Trolls to reach a Treasure Chest. Jump over the spinning blades to reach another platform holding a Shrednaught and dash to the bounce pad. Jump again over the second spinning blade to earn a jewel. There's another bounce pad leading to a bomb on a hanging terrace—grab it and launch it at the Shrednaught. It will break and form a bridge to a third platform, where you can score a Hedgehog Hat (+2 Speed, +2 Elemental Power). Jump on the teleport pad to return to Windbag Woods.

Blobbers is waiting with bad news—Trolls have taken over the Hall of Records! Smash the Traptanium Crystals to reveal a pathway where the villain **Buzzer Beak** and his minions will attack you. Take them out with a long-distance attack, keeping clear of his blades. You'll be rewarded with a **Legendary Tribal Statue**.

Steam Vent Junction & Boulder Falls Circle

Jump up the steam vent and turn right. There's a trail of coins dropping off the edge, so follow them down to find another Stone Head with some background on Wolfgang. Now back to Blobbers! Push the boulder onto the steam vent to increase pressure underground and—wham!—away flies the boulder (see Figure 8.8)! Ride the steam vent up to reach Boulder Falls Circle to earn a Winged Sapphire. Before you continue up again, explore along the right side to find a Dark Gate.

FIGURE 8.8

Push the giant stone balls off the edge of the platform and roll them onto a vent to create a high-pressure steam ride up to the next level.

Shadowy Sanctum

If you have a Dark Trap Master, you can enter this gate. First up, jump on the left-side button to raise a bounce pad block; then push the block into the gap next to it. There's a block in front to the right—push it to the left to form a pathway to the back platform. Bounce up to reach Black Out's Soul Gem (see Figure 8.9). While you're there, push the block forward onto the floor in front, then drop back down. Dash to the back and then jump on the left-side button three times to release the purple orb. Push the floor blocks to make a row leading to the alcove at the back of the room. Switch the lever at the entrance to launch the orb up and into the alcove. Use the bounce pad to jump up and push the orb further into the hole to drop the gate. You've earned a Skipper Hat (+5 Armor).

FIGURE 8.9

Use the big button on the floor to raise a bounce pad block, then later to release the glowing orb in Shadowy Sanctum. Your rewards are a Soul Gem for Black Out and a Skipper Hat.

Patronizing Plateau

It's time to take another ride on a steam vent! There's a Stone Head waiting to tell you about the Golden Queen, and to your right, Gumbus is ready to take Slobber Trap on his Villain Quest. Simply push over a statue to reach an island of coins. Super easy! If you haven't captured Slobber Trap yet, you'll find him very soon, so you can backtrack for this.

To the left is a **Soul Gem** for Food Fight, so grab it and run to Buzz. He'll explain how to use the cannon turret to shoot down Troll Ships (see Figure 8.10).

FIGURE 8.10

Aim the turret with your controller to shoot down enemy Troll Ships. Line your blue target mark up to the yellow targets on the ships to bring them down.

Embellisher's Retreat

A battle gate will drop to reveal Slobber Trap and his minions. He'll join in last, so be prepared to dodge his lunging attack, and then move in as he regroups. If you have a long-range attack move, it will come in handy now. Trap him in a Water Trap. If you haven't completed his Villain Quest back at Patronizing Plateau, do it now before returning to Buzz at the final gate. Buzz will lead you in one final turret attack before he declares victory. Spectacular work, Skylander! Know-It-All Island is safe again, and you just earned a Now YOU Know It All award!

TIP

Legendary Treasure

In every story chapter, a Legendary Treasure is hidden somewhere for you to find. Each time you return to Skylander Academy, you'll be prompted to place your new treasure somewhere special. Check Table 5.1 in Chapter 5, "Collectibles," if you're not sure where to place yours.

Chapter 3: Chompy Mountain

The Chompy Mage is up to no good again! He and his bitey green hordes are taking hostages at Chompy Mountain. You must save the day! Bruiser Cruiser and the Broccoli Guy will try to keep you from reaching the Chompy Hatchery, but never fear—with your three brave Mabu helpers, you'll recover the Legendary Chompy Statue and tame that puppet wielding wizard in no time! Keep an eye out for your collectibles along the way (see Figure 8.11), including a Paperboy Hat, Horns Be With You Hat, and a Hunting Hat as well as Soul Gems for Bushwhack, Gusto, and Wallop.

FIGURE 8.11

Gather these collectibles as you explore Chompy Mountain to capture Bruiser Cruiser, The Chompy Mage, and Broccoli Guy.

TIP

Be Prepared!

Have Sheep Creep (Life), Bruiser Cruiser (Tech), and Chill Bill (Water) in traps ready for their Villain Quests. (You'll battle Bruiser Cruiser in this level and capture Chill Bill in Chapter 4: Phoenix Psanctuary.)

Mabu Landing Pier & Old Mabu Town
Before you move forward, turn right to find a Winged Sapphire close by. Great start! Now you can chat with Gumbus, who wants to take Sheep Creep on a Villain Quest. This one is super-fun, but remember—the clock is ticking! You have nine minutes to destroy 15 buffalo by shooting Sheep Creep from a cannon into the stone buildings. Awesome work!

Back at the start, smash down a wooden gate to find Buzz in **Old Mabu Town**. Snuckles is looking scared outside his house. Follow him inside to play a **Troll Radio** and then walk back outside. Up the stairs, poor Rizzo is locked in a jail cell in his own house. Use a bomb to release him. Smash the barrier to your left to find a **Magic Gate** inside his house.

Crystal Caves
Now for a tricky task (see Figure 8.12). On the first circular platform, you'll find lots of coins and a Treasure Chest. The second platform, however, involves some dodging to collect the coins. Avoid the rolling orbs—they'll damage your health if you get hit. It's the same again on the third platform, with faster orbs. Blow them up or smash them to survive.

Your reward is a Horns Be With You Hat (+7 Elemental Power). Teleport back to Rizzo's house and grab another bomb. You'll want to move fast with this cargo!

FIGURE 8.12

Attack or avoid the magic orbs as you collect treasure in the Magic Gate to earn a new hat.

Wishing Well & Nort's House
Take the bomb outside and throw it at the Wishing Well to smash the roof. Dive inside (bombs away!) to score a Treasure Chest hidden beneath a Traptanium Crystal. Back on the surface, it's time to visit Nort's house. Nort is another timid Mabu, and he's stuck on a ledge and needs help getting down. Jump on the green button to raise an elevator. Ride it up a second time to retrieve a Soul Gem for Gusto. Before you leave, unlock the Villain Stash by the door.

Spinner's Landing & Overgrown Ramparts
Outside, Snuckles, Nort, and Rizzo will open the gates to Spinners Landing. A few nasty Trolls will be waiting to fight you. As soon as you defeat them, a battle gate will open revealing a coil that spins, unlocking one part (of three) of a distant gate. The Mabu build a bridge for you to cross to Overgrown Ramparts. Oh no! The Chompy Mage is back! Fire the cannons at him until he flees. (Don't step on the yellow crosshairs!)

A new bridge appears with a wooden gate at the end. To its left is Bruiser Cruiser's **Villain Quest**, but first you need to capture him! **Bruiser Cruiser**, shown in Figure 8.13, will attack you once you reach the wooden gate, so be prepared! He is strongest while he is driving forward in attack mode, so take him out as he turns and spins. Defeated! Now return to Brady for his Villain Quest and clear the avalanche of rocks to earn a Paperboy Hat (+4 Speed).

FIGURE 8.13

Bruiser Cruiser is a dangerous enemy, but if you catch him out while he's turning, he'll topple over.

Mountain Falls Lagoon
There's a new spire near the waiting Mabu to interact with, unlocking the second part of the distant gate. Head over the new bridge to Mountain Falls Lagoon. It's time to get your feet wet! First up, get smashing—hit the Traptanium Crystal to recover a Soul Gem for Wallop. Well done! Up the left-side steps is a Lock Puzzle. The aim here is to hit the blocks in your way until they shatter, and then zap the little player around the board until you land on the exit.

Okay, deep breath, it's time to battle again! Chompies, Trolls, and Lob Goblins will swarm you. There's plenty of room to move, so get creative with your attacks and have fun. As soon as you see the Broccoli Guy join in, get rid of him before he has the chance to heal enemies. Phew, that was close! Well done. If you're ready for an upgrade, **Persephone** is waiting up the stone steps for you. After you've had a chat with her, look for the green buttons to the left side of the bridge. On their left is a grass path leading to a small house. Keep your eye out for a **Story Scroll** here.

K-Troll Radio
Duck inside the house to find Chill Bill's Villain Quest (called The Cold Front). Rocky is on the lookout for a new DJ, so bring him back here later to earn bucket-loads of coins from the Troll Radios. Back outside, near the stone path, is another bonus—Bushwack's Soul Gem.

Chompy Mountain
It's almost time to face the dreaded Chompy Mage himself, but first you'll need to rescue the Mabu prisoners in Chompy Mountain. Head into the fortress to find Buzz for the latest update. There's a wooden gate nearby—smash through to reach a second wooden gate, this time guarded by Chompy statues. Use the cannon to blow up the statues, then the gate itself. Uh oh, there's trouble brewing in Rizzo's Rescue! Chompies and a Slobber Trap will greet you with a swarm of biting teeth. As soon as you defeat them, Rizzo will lead you to the elevator. Before you join him, though, let's do a little more exploring. Smash the Traptanium Crystals to reveal a new room called Artillery Storage. Inside you can challenge Bungo

to a game of Skystones Smash. Gather the coins and have a smash-fest with barrels to uncover a Treasure Chest. Back in the main room, there's an Undead Gate to your left.

Undead Vista   A pack of Chompies is holding guard here, but the real hold up is a Lock Puzzle. A gate will drop with a Hunting Hat (+2 Critical Hit, +2 Armor).

Rizzo is waiting patiently at the elevator shaft. Join him to enter **Nort's Rescue**. Where you start, smash a wooden fence on your right to score the **Legendary Chompy Statue**. There's a cannon to your left. Blow up the Chompy-head statue and a few Trolls guarding Nort. When he wanders off, don't follow him just yet—grab the treasure and run around the far side of the cannon wall to jump on a button that will drop the wall. Push the cannon across and destroy the gate on the far-left holding cell so you can enter.

The Chompy Hatchery   Inside this cell, you'll be faced with Broccoli Guy. Take out his two Slobber Trap guards first—he can't actually defend himself, so once they're history, he's an easy target. As soon as he's defeated, trap him in a Life Trap and dash back out to Nort. It's time to rescue poor Snuckles!

Drop down onto a ledge to your left to score some treasure; then bounce back up. Shift the three boxes nearby so that the middle block falls over the edge, smashing the Chompy Statue below. If you've already smashed the three you passed outside, you just earned a **Statue Smasher** achievement—awesome work! Two waves of enemies will spring forward, so fight back to free Snuckles from his cage.

TIP

Complementary Attacks!

Remember, you can swap Skylanders mid-fight, or choose a villain to swap in that boasts a skill your Skylander doesn't have. In heavy battles, make good use of your villains—your Skylander will regain precious heath while your villain fights instead. A villain will automatically return to his trap to recharge when he sustains too much damage, so let him take the worst of it if you can't avoid being hit.

Chompy Head Spire

Follow Snuckles to the elevator to take your final ride up to Chompy Head Spire. The Chompy Mage, shown in Figure 8.14, is waiting to attack you! Waves of Chompies bombard you here, so make sure to choose a Skylander with a strong long-ranged attack (if your Skylander can fly, even better). Keep clear of the red crosses. In the second wave, Chompy Mage joins the fight as his alternate form, Mega-Chompy. Jump (or fly, if you can) over the flaming rings to keep safe, but attack him as often as it's safe to wear down his health. The third wave is even harder—Chompy Mage transforms into a Magma Chompy and brings lava-covered minions into the fight! Battle hard and keep out of fire's reach. As soon as you bring him down, you'll learn that the Doom Raiders are acquiring Traptanium to make "The Ultimate Weapon." Glumshanks and Kaos are, of course, plotting a mutiny. There's trouble ahead!

FIGURE 8.14

The Chompy Mage transforms into Magma Mega-Chompy to throw rings of lava across the floor.

Chapter 4: The Phoenix Psanctuary

The Evil Chef Pepper Jack is hunting down the Phoenix Chicken, so it's up to you to save her! All kinds of feathered fiends will try to stop you from rescuing her, including the big, bad Cuckoo Clocker. Shrednaught and Chill Bill have a score to settle, and Buzzer Beak needs to fly in for a family reunion. Collect the Legendary Egg for your collection (see Figure 8.15) as well as Soul Gems for Snap Shot and Funny Bone, and the Parrot Hat, Daisy Crown, and Ceiling Fan Hat. You'll begin at Outer Plumage with Flynn and Tessa.

FIGURE 8.15

Gather these collectibles as you explore the Phoenix Psanctuary to capture Chill Bill, Shrednaught, and Cuckoo Clocker.

TIP

Be Prepared!

Have Buzzer Beak (Air), Tussle Sprout (Earth), and Cuckoo Clocker (Life) in traps ready for their Villain Quests. You'll capture Cuckoo Clocker during this chapter, but might need to play through again to evolve him.

Outer Plumage, Fledgling Rise, & Paradise Highway

Let's get off to a smashing start (Traptanium Crystals!) to uncover a hidden area full of golden coins and a **Treasure Chest**. Destroy fruit for extra loot. Pick up the glowing nut and plant it in the marked ground. A flower bridge will grow, leading to some nasty Eggsecutioners ready for battle. On the second platform, you can open the cage to retrieve another nut. Plant it and cross over to **Fledgling Rise**, collecting coins on the way. You'll find a caged bounce pad and a third floating nut, which you can plant to create a new bridge. The left fork of the bridge takes to you **Paradise Highway**, where Buzz has a simple **Villain Quest** for Buzzer Beak called Family Reunion. He just needs to show up! You'll earn a Parrot Hat (+7 Speed) as a reward. Smash the empty cage to collect golden eggs before you leave.

Rump Feather Roost

Follow the right-side path now, where you can switch a lever to release the bounce pad back on the middle platform. Be prepared for a fight before you bounce—Shrednaught is up there waiting for you!

He's easy to bring down in close combat because he moves s-l-o-w-l-y. As soon as Shrednaught is trapped, Trolls and Eggsecutioners take his place. A single Lob Goblin will throw bombs at you, so use a long-ranged attack to take him out. (Ignore the **Treasure Chest** for now, you can come back later.) Ride the blue platform down (near the bounce pad) to drop over the side and score a **Legendary Egg**. Well done! Gather coins and then bounce up to the next level, **Hooked Bill Ascent**. Plant a nut to draw the guarding Blocker Birds away from the gate. The coast is clear, so it's time to move!

Down Feather Wash & Rain Flower Grotto

Drop over the right side of the bridge where Arbo has a Villain Quest for Tussle Sprout called Sprouting Up! It's time to repent for his evil ways. He came, he saw, he tussled (see Figure 8.16)! Plant Tussle Sprout to reveal a new bridge with a Villain Stash. (Beware the Eggsecutioner ready to hit you with his mace!) Defeat the enemy and head back across the bridge. There is a Water Gate next to a bounce pad. Enter the gate (Rain Flower Grotto) to discover a lovely Daisy Crown (+5 Critical Hit, +2 Speed) to adorn your head (very stylish on Lob-Star!).

FIGURE 8.16

Uncover a Villain Stash by completing Tussle Sprout's quest—but watch your back!

Hooked Bill Ascent

Bounce back up to Hooked Bill Ascent, where the Blocker Birds will still be distracted eating. Some Trolls and a Chill Bill are waiting to get their battle on, so go for it! When they're out of your way, plant the nut to create a new bridge. Long-range attacks can defeat the new wave of Trolls and a Lob Goblin to uncover a bounce pad on the final platform. Bounce up to the Aviary Gate, drop off the left edge near Flynn, and enter a tunnel.

Rare Species Walk & Aviary Gate

Eek! You'll be greeted by some nasty Trolls and a Shrednaught. (Keep clear of his rotating blade!) As soon as you defeat them, a battle gate will drop, revealing Snap Shot's Soul Gem. Continue along the path to return to Aviary Gate, where you can now reach the Treasure Chest you passed earlier. Bounce back up to Tessa and Flynn.

Clockwork Nest

Drop to the right-side circular battle arena. Use a long-ranged attack to destroy the grappling hooks as they clamp onto the perimeter so that the Trolls fall before they reach you (see Figure 8.17). If you can trick the Chill Bill into harming his own Trolls (quick dodge!), you'll double your effectiveness. Shrednaughts fall from the sky—use long-range attacks to keep clear of their rotating blades. If you attack a drop ship before it delivers its Shrednaught, you'll earn a Preemptive Power trophy.

FIGURE 8.17

Destroy grappling hooks as quickly as possible to keep enemy numbers down in battle.

Hatchling Hall

Once the nest is safe, follow the tunnel to Hatchling Hall, a room full of bird cages. Persephone is here with upgrades. Shift the cages around to create a path leading to a golden key; then take it outside to Clockwork Nest. Chill Bill will attack you with a couple of Lob Goblins. Attack him from behind to avoid his icy blast. If you get hit, mash your controller to break the ice. The Lob Goblins are easier to take down. Attack as they prepare to throw a bomb; then jump out of way before it lands. Plant a nearby nut to uncover a bounce pad to Aviary Gate. Plant a second nut to feed (and distract!) the Blocker Birds. Use your key to unlock the gate. Before you enter the cave, use the bounce pad in the cage to your right to score a Story Scroll. When you jump down again, you'll notice another nut near the left of the cavern. Plant it and follow the flower bridge to earn a Soul Gem for Funny Bone.

Feather Bed Hatchery & Fan Wing Thermals

Enter the Aviary Gate. To your left is an Air Gate, where you'll be sucked through tubes into Fan Wing Thermals. Ride the fan's breeze to collect floating coins. (Have a high-flying adventure with Chill Bill's icy blast jet-pac!) On the highest ledge to your left is a switch to uncover a bounce pad. Run along the platform (note the coins at the far right) and then take the bounce pad up to earn a Ceiling Fan Hat (+5 Critical Hit, +5 Armor). Jump to the ledge and follow a trail of coins back to the suction tube to return to Feather Bed Hatchery. Straight ahead, Da Pinchy has a musical Villain Quest for Cuckoo Clocker. This super-strong songbird needs to sing!

Onward with your quest! Chef Pepper Jack has stolen the Phoenix Chicken, and it must be rescued. There is a ramp with tumbling eggs nearby. Dodge or destroy them so you can reach the glowing suction tube safely; then jump in. You'll be whisked away to **Little Chicken Landing** (**Troll Radio** alert!), where a **Winged Sapphire** waits to be discovered underneath a Traptanium Crystal. Suction-tube rollercoaster time again!

Free Range Rollers

Trolls and Lob Goblins will be waiting for you to land this time. Avoid the rolling eggs, or destroy them for a golden reward. Dive off the far end of the platform to fall to Wishbone Landing. Destroy the Traptanium Crystal to claim a Treasure Chest; then bounce back up to Aviary Heights. Follow the steps to find a suction tube that will whisk you away to battle!

FIGURE 8.18

Baby birds pop up from under circular mats in the nest to peck at enemies and Skylanders alike. If you can lure your enemies in, then jump away, they'll get a nasty surprise!

When you arrive, Chef Pepper Jack is standing in a nest, ready to make a super spicy omelette from the Phoenix Chicken eggs! There are three waves of enemies to face here. First, you'll have a round with some Lob Goblins and Trolls. (Dodge the bombs!) Then Shrednaughts will join the fight. There are three circular areas where baby birds lift the nest floor up to poke their heads through (see Figure 8.18). As they peck around the edges, you and your enemies are both in danger of losing health if you get bitten. The third wave brings the villain **Cuckoo Clocker** into the fray. Keep your distance because his fist-smash leaves an aftershock of damage. If you've got a quick-moving Skylander, jump in behind and attack him as he regroups after his attack. Success? Of course! Well done, Skylander. It's time to head back to the Academy.

Chapter 5: Chef Zeppelin

Hot-tempered Chef Pepper Jack is up to no good again! Track him down to the blazing kitchens of the Chef Zeppelin airship to make him toast. But first, there are Trolls defending the ship that need to cool off and some Chompies in hot water. Find the Legendary Pepper Chest to display in the kitchen at Skylanders Academy, and collect the Scooter, Colander, and Juicer Hats, as well as a Soul Gem for Chopper (see Figure 8.19).

FIGURE 8.19

Gather these collectibles as you explore the Chef Zeppelin ship to capture Bomb Shell and Chef Pepper Jack.

TIP

Be Prepared!

Have the Chompy Mage (Life) and Broccoli Guy (Life) in traps ready for their Villain Quests.

The Landing Pan   As Flynn flies you toward the Chef Zeppelin airship, you are given command of the cannon turret. Aim to destroy the Zeppelin's air defenses by shooting back at the Troll transport ships firing at you. (If you hit eight, you'll earn a Cannon Completist achievement.) This turret works the same as the ones you have used with Buzz. There are four winged gems floating around the sky. They're a little tricky to see, but if you shoot them all down, it will double your total coin score.

Main Counter Top   As Flynn flies you in the Landing Pan, a handful of Trolls will attack you straight up, so bring them down. There's a deck gun on the Main Counter Top platform; use it blow up the three barricades in the distance (change direction using the lever on the ground). Take a jump over the right side of the deck gun (the bread roll with filling railing). You'll fall to a ledge with a Legendary Pepper Chest. Teleport back using the blue pad. To the right of the sandwich railing is a second platform and deck gun. Aim the cannon at the distant barricade and destroy it. There are two extra areas to discover from this platform. To your right is the Side Spinner. Jump over the flaming kabobs and grab gold coins as you bounce back up. Drop off the opposite ledge (follow the coin trail).

Bottom Shelf, Peculiarity of Light, & Tail Winds

You land on Bottom Shelf, where there are two Elemental Gates to explore, but each is guarded by a Troll. To the right is a Light Gate (Peculiarity of Light, see Figure 8.20) with a Story Scroll floating outside (enchiladas, anyone?). Inside the gate is a Troll Radio and Hat Box. Shift the blocks to clear a path to the bounce pad; then bounce up to score a Juicer Hat (+12 Armor, +5 Speed). Well done!

Now follow the Bottom Shelf walkway to the left end, where you'll find an **Air Gate**. This place is called **Tail Winds**. Jump onto the bounce pad to land on a floating balloon; then hop off at the first platform to recover a **Villain Stash**. Again, ride another floating balloon to reach a third balloon and be rewarded with a Scooter Hat (+10 Elemental Power). Use the super bounce pad to return to **Main Counter Top**.

FIGURE 8.20

A simple block challenge will score you a new hat in the Elemental Light Gate.

Main Kabobs

Run left to leap into Main Kabobs. Jump, jump, jump! There's a Soul Gem for Chopper over the edge, so drop down and claim it before bouncing back up. Past the spinner is a ramp with coins over the side. Drop down to find Chopping Block. Complete the Lock Puzzle to enter a secret door.

Kitchen of Shame & Topside Burners

The first person you meet is Bernie (see Figure 8.21), who's in search of Broccoli Guy for his Villain Quest (called Broccoli Guy En Fuego). Swap in Broccoli Guy to upgrade (no challenges here). Return to Chopping Block and Main Kabobs. Persephone is waiting up the ramp at Topside Burners. Grab the bomb near her, take a deep breath, and then leap over the edge to face the Trolls.

FIGURE 8.21

Little chef Bernie has a Villain Quest for Broccoli Guy in the fiery Kitchen of Shame.

Smorgasbord, Top Shelf, & Bottom Shelf
Waves of enemies will descend. There is plenty of room to battle, so dance around and have a bit of fun with your attack. When you've destroyed them all (of course you can!), chat with Cookie. He has a Villain Quest (called Free the Chompies) for the Chompy Mage. Ready, set, go! Dash in and drop down to Top Shelf, attacking all the bags holding Chompies to free them. There's a Lock Puzzle to complete first.

Tricky! You've earned a **Treasure Chest** for that effort! Jump down to reach the coins on **Bottom Shelf** and then super-bounce back up. There is a ramp to the left of Bernie called **Cheese Graters**. Meet Tessa there for an update.

The Cooling Rack
Run onto the battle field where Chill Bills, Trolls, and a Bruiser Cruiser will be waiting to fight back. Use a long-ranged attack for the best effect. Bomb Shell soon joins in, so keep clear of the red rings on the ground and the purple fire that bombs leave behind. Dash in to attack him after each bomb lands. Once he's defeated, a battle gate drops. Pick up the golden key and dash down the steps beside the Cooling Rack to Port Gangway. Grab a bomb and bounce up to the barricade outside Auxiliary Kitchen. It's battle time again! Trolls and Chill Bills will attack you—your reward for defeating them is a Treasure Chest. Head back to Port Gangway (where you found the bomb). Trolls and Grinnades are guarding a door at the end of the walkway. Use your golden key to enter.

Command Kitchen & Garbage Disposal
Batterson is here, lamenting his mean boss Chef Pepper Jack. (Troll Radio alert!) He's a nice guy, though; he'll teach you to play Skystones Smash. In the kitchen behind Batterson is a Fire Gate leading to The Oven. Inside, begin at your far right (dodge the flames, they're unpredictable) to find the final Treasure Chest. Shift each of the baking pans over the flames to cook dough into bread; then hop across them to reach the Colander Hat (+10 Armor). Back in the kitchen, opposite Pot Roast (the Skystones Smash Mabu) is a kitchen

sink tube called the Garbage Disposal. Dive in to find a Winged Sapphire, and then bounce back up. It's time to take on Chef Pepper Jack, but first you need to beat Pot Roast in a game of Skystones Smash to drop the battle gate. Good luck!

Chef Pepper Jack

The final battle against Chef Pepper Jack is the most difficult so far (see Figure 8.22), but you can definitely win! There are a few waves of attacks, each a bit trickier than the last. First, he'll throw exploding lava peppers at you. Next, you need to jump over moving lines of heat that crisscross over the grill. If you have a flying Skylander such as Chopper or Full Blast Jet-Vac, they'll come in really handy here! Chef Pepper Jack then kicks it up a notch with more lava pepper bombs and lines of fire.

FIGURE 8.22

Chef Pepper Jack uses fiery and explosive attacks in stages. If your Skylander has flying skills to keep up off the ground, you can avoid the worst of the lava rings and exploding chops.

In the next stage, Chef throws some chops on the grill. Jump onto them to escape the heat—but watch your head! (They fall from above.) Chef Pepper Jack will throw peppers onto the chops so they explode while you're standing on top of them (sneaky), so hop from one to the next to escape damage as they blow up. As soon as you land on a safe steak, take the opportunity to attack Chef Pepper Jack while you can. You need to keep your attacks constant to wear his health down over time. After a good effort of smashing him up between jumps, you'll win and send him howling into your trap!

Look out! There's trouble in the ranks of the Doom Raiders when Kaos challenges the Golden Queen in an "Evil Off." Instead, she turns him into a golden statue in need of rescuing by the Skylanders. It looks like the tides have turned!

Chapter 6: Rainfish Riviera

Mags desperately needs your help! Her Information Squid has been stolen and is about to meet a terrible fate! Travel to Rainfish Riviera to rescue the beast before it's too late. Things get fishy when Brawlrus and Brawl and

Chain both drop in to keep you from saving the day. Keep your wits about you to take on Masker Mind and uncover the Soul Gems for Lob-Star and Déjà vu. Collect some crazy new hats on the way (the Imperial, Steampunk, and Metal Fin Hats) and search out the Legendary Bubble Fish (see Figure 8.23) to adorn Skylanders Academy Courtyard upon your victorious return!

FIGURE 8.23

Gather these collectibles as you explore Rainfish Riviera to capture Masker Mind, Brawlrus, and Brawl and Chain.

TIP

Be Prepared!

Have Chef Pepper Jack (Fire), Brawlrus (Tech), and Eye Five (Light) in traps ready for their Villain Quests. You'll capture Brawlrus during this chapter.

Monsoon Point & Waste Water Cove

Dive over the rocks to the left of Mags (smash a few barrels in your way). You'll land on a small beach below that's hiding a Soul Gem for Lob-Star. Easy start! Explore this area to find treasure stashed in a secret cave. Bounce back up to Mags and then smash the wooden gate near her to enter Blowhole Beach.

Blowhole Beach & Steel Fin Balcony

It's Chompy time! Chompy Pirates will attack, and then the starfish-spinning villain Brawlrus and some Pirate Henchman will attack as well. This is a great melee-style fight, so jump in and have at them! Mags needs to you to build a bridge to continue on, so pick up the floating wood and deposit it on the left side of the pier where you see the purple sign. Cross over and remember to gather your bridge to use it again—there's a tiny shack across the water to your right with a golden key hidden inside. Smash the fence and put your first key in the double-locked gate near the old shack.

Steel Fin Balcony & Fishbone's Card Shack

Head down to the left to Steel Fin Balcony and then chat with Bucko inside the shack. He has a second key to give you, but not until you beat him at Skystones Smash. Give it a go! Not only will you earn another golden key, but a Story Scroll too. As soon as you leave, the villain Masker Mind will attack you (see Figure 8.24). Take out his henchmen first—so he has no one left to control—and then smash him. That's mind-bending work, Skylander!

FIGURE 8.24

Masker Mind controls minions by increasing their power to attack you. He has no offensive moves himself, though, so when you get him alone, attack before he disappears.

Brackwater Falls

Dive over the edge of the pier where you see trailing coins to find a Villain Quest for Eye Five. Doublooney wants him to play a game of Chongo. You won't have Eye Five in a trap yet if this is your first time through, but if you've played before and have him handy (ha, ha!), give it a go. You must defeat all enemies and collect the treasure while being taunted by the awful chatterbox Dreamcatcher. Smash them with Eye Five's huge fists. Dreamcatcher is generous enough to give you a flamethrower, though, followed by a lifetime supply of bombs and a zapping flying saucer, so use everything you've got. This is a big task. You have ten minutes to gather up to 5,000 presents during progressively harder rounds. Stick to the doorways whenever you can; that way, you'll be able to smash the majority of enemies as they first come into the arena.

Undead Gate—Fish Bone's Retreat

Across the bridge you'll find an Undead Gate with an eerie bone-filled cavern inside. This challenge takes a bit of practice. Dodge or jump over the magma balls that come flying toward you as you run diagonally across to the floor square with a skull on it. This square is your safe spot, so rest here while you plan your attack. You'll have to be fast to reach the Treasure Chest in the back corner. Go for it! Return to the skull square when you've collected the treasure. Your next stop is the open block space along the back wall of cannons. This is tricky because you need to run straight toward the back wall from the skull square and then jump across to your left, landing in the square in front of the gap as the square beside you shoots up from the sand. A second square in front of the gap will block your way if you aren't fast enough. Behind the squares is a Metal Fin Hat (+12 Critical Hit).

Fish Eyed Walk & Fish Eyed Control
Bounce back up to Steel Fin Balcony and open the gate with your second golden key. Mags is here to explain the path ahead is blocked. Head inside to Fish Eyed Control, where Bomb Shells and Pirate Henchmen are itching to fight you. Defeat them all to drop the battle gate, revealing a green button that will unlock the outside gates. (Troll Radio alert!) Follow Mags to a crane to play drop-the-henchmen-into-the-sea. Super fun! Once the deck is empty, pick up Mags with the crane and pop her over onto the deck instead. She'll unlock the bridge so you can cross over. Create a bridge leading to the bomb gate with Mags. You can't get any further, though—yet.

Clam Tower, Submarine Pen, & Starfish's Sub
Drop off the side of the deck platform where you see coins. A bounce pad will take you to the top of the tower. Pick up the ticking bomb. Jump back down and run inside the door to the Submarine Pen. Quick! Launch it straight down the stairs to explode the wooden barricade and score a Treasure Chest. Bucko is waiting patiently nearby for a game of Skystones Smash. Follow the wooden path to find Persephone. Further on, Argle Bargle has a Villain Quest for Brawlrus (called Submarine Bros 4 Life). Once Brawlrus has evolved, dive inside the submarine to reach Starfish's Sub. There is a heap of treasure here as well as a Steampunk Hat (+17 Armor). Don't forget the Troll Radio on your way out.

Dredger's Yacht
Remember the bomb gate across your newest bridge? Let's get rid of that. Bounce back up to the tower, grab another bomb, and then run back to the main platform and launch it at the gate. Mags is here with another crane challenge. For this one, pick up the pipes and drop them on the pirates or drop the pirates overboard instead. If you destroy all the pipe bundles, you'll earn a Pipe Down achievement. Jump down to the Traptanium Crystal, but be ready to battle. A ship of trouble-makers pulls up beside yours, ready to board! Blast off their grappling hooks before the pirates climb over. Uh, oh! You have a very villainous visitor now—it's Brawl and Chain! Launch your attack as soon as he stops spinning his chains. If you can swap in a trapped villain to take some of the heat, go for it. Victory! Now you can smash up those Traptanium Crystals. Shift the blocks aside for access into the tunnel underneath. There's more fighting afoot Below Deck! Unlock the Villain Stash before you go back up.

Dire Sands & Barnacle Shoal
Back up on deck, break the wooden fence down and talk to Mags. There are timid snail friends to your left. Push them to create a path where you'll find a Soul Gem for Déjà vu. Down the sand path to your right is an Earth Gate. Let's explore it now. This is another snail-shifting game. The aim is to make a square-shaped bridge through the water to reach an Imperial Hat (+7 Armor, +2 Speed).

Bluster Squall Island & Cheddar House

To your left is another path with a bridge. Cross to battle some Chompy Pirates; then pick up the bridge and put it down on the right side to cross over to Bluster Squall Island. Battle some Bomb Shells to get past. Inside Cheddar House, Galley has a Villain Quest for Chef Pepper Jack (called Head of the Cheese). Chef Pepper Jack dashes around, picking up cheese and dropping it in a basket, avoiding the minions of an angry talking Stone Head. There are six pieces of cheese to collect while the Stone Head chases Pepper Jack, so run fast! Burn enemies in your path with Fire Breath and use the final bounce pad to return home. Once Chef Pepper Jack has completed his Villain Quest, you'll have access to the Treasure Chest and Winged Sapphire in Cheddar House.

Big Hook & Fish Mouth

Pick up your bridge once more and drop it near the path to reach the last house. There's a Traptanium Crystal outside with a Legendary Bubble Fish hidden underneath. Follow the path around the house of Big Hook until you find a crane. Pick up the bait and drop it onto the Rainfish to get him to stay still (see Figure 8.25). Then use the crane to pick up the giant beast before he swims away. Drop him and duck inside his mouth to retrieve the Information Squid (see Figure 8.26). Awesome work, Skylander! You saved the day!

FIGURE 8.25

You have three chances to use the crane to pick up a bundle of fish and drop it on the Rainfish to get it to stay still. Pick it up as quickly as you can before it swims away again.

FIGURE 8.26

Enter the mouth of the Rainfish to retrieve the Information Squid for Mags. All is not what it seems....

Chapter 7: Monster Marsh

That Information Squid you rescued had a nasty surprise hiding inside him. Kaos! Even worse, you're headed for the unluckiest place in Skylands, where everyone makes bad decisions. Uh, oh! There's a terrible sleeping magic that has fallen over all the villagers of Monster Marsh. In your quest to wake the villagers, you'll have to take on Eye Scream, Chomp Chest, and Eye Five. As you explore some truly creepy places in this Story Chapter, gather your wits, as well as Soul Gems for Fist Bump and Krypt King. Lurking in dark places are the Dragon Skull Hat, Classic Clown, Shadow Ghost Hat, and the Legendary Golden Frog (see Figure 8.27).

FIGURE 8.27

Gather these collectibles as you explore Monster Marsh to capture Chomp Chest, Eye Five, and Eye Scream.

TIP

Be Prepared!

Have Eye Scream (Dark) and Fisticuffs (Dark) in traps ready for their Villain Quests if you've played before. If this is your first play through, you'll capture Eye Scream in this chapter and Fisticuffs in Chapter 10: Secret Sewers of Supreme Stink.

Haunted Wreck & Haunted Approach

You'll start right next to a Traptanium Crystal, so smash it for an easy Winged Sapphire and play the Troll Radio. Gomper is waiting with some scary news: This place is cursed! There are wooden blocks to the left of the Troll Radio. Shift them to reveal a wooden gate leading to Haunted Approach.

Down the wooden ramp closest to you, Cali has a **Villain Quest** for Eye Scream called **Paranormal Captivity**. Unless you've been through the game already, you won't have Eye Scream trapped—but in case you have, let's look at her quest. Eye Scream is given ten minutes to run around a haunted graveyard to free ghosts that are trapped in pottery. Watch out for the Plant Warriors and nasty minions waiting to attack. If they do, your captured ghosts will be scared off and you'll have to search for more. Try to jump over your enemies and avoid them to save time. You can collect more than one ghost at a time, but you'll have to be fast not to lose them. Two slow grave clobbers will guard the spaceship you deliver them to, so dash around them and keep out of their way.

Spirestone Crypt & Haunted Wreck

The path to your right ends at scattered boxes. Shift them to create steps to jump up to the deck of a ship called the Haunted Wreck. Up here you'll find a Troll Radio and a Soul Gem for Krypt King.

Jump down off the Haunted Wreck. At the end of the path past the boxes (to the right) is an **Undead Gate** leading to **Spirestone Crypt**. Inside this gate, shift the low-lying boxes first and then jump on them to reach the top levels. (Attack the tiny eyeballs for coins.) Along the back ledge on the far right is a Dragon Skull Hat (+5 Critical Hit, +10 Armor).

Spirestone Cliffs, Spirestone Grotto, & Spirestone Graveyard

As you leave the Undead Gate, there's a break in the fence to your right. Dive down to find a cave with a wooden gate inside. Collect the gold and smash a second gate to reveal a Treasure Chest. Head outside and bounce back up. There's an iron gate leading to Spirestone Graveyard. You have to complete a lock puzzle to get through. The battle gate will drop, and you'll be free to grab the Soul Gem for Fist Bump inside.

Hungry Isle & Spirestone Mausoleum   Ride the super

bounce pad to Hungry Isle where Chomp Chest is waiting to chomp you (see Figure 8.28)! Each time you attack him, he drops treasure (so no hurry!). If you have a Skylander that summons minions, you can let them cause damage while you step back from his bite. He's quick! Once he's defeated, super-bounce back to Spirestone Graveyard. Break down the gate to Haunted Approach and wander over to Spirestone Mausoleum. There are bucket loads of little bouncing eyeballs here to attack you (but they're kind of cute). Defeat them to drop the battle gate and free poor Headwick. When you succeed, the iron gates will open. As you cross the bridge, some Eye Screams will throw explosive barrels at you. Jump over (or smash them) to reach the other side.

FIGURE 8.28

Chomp Chest attacks in the Hungry Isle, but take your time defeating him—each chomp drops coins!

Windmill Hill, Supply Room, & Secret

Basement   There's a blocked gate with an open door next to it lead-

ing to the **Supply Room**. Inside, Millington wants to play **Skystones Smash**. Go for it! Once you defeat him, the gate outside will open. Explore through the gate to reach a spinning windmill. If you get hit, you lose health. At the top right is a **Story Scroll**. There's a lower ledge between the windmill blades and the platform that you can drop to. Its door opens to a **Secret Basement**. Inside you'll find a **Troll Radio** and **Persephone**. Climb back up the top of the windmill and pull the lever to lower the swinging platform.

The Little House on the Misty Marshes & the Misty

Marshes   Jump onto the platform to fall down to The Little House

on the Misty Marshes, where an epic fight begins against a group of weird-looking creatures (see Figure 8.29). Defeat them to lower a battle gate. Cross over the bridge.

Headwick is waiting for you, worried because Marsha is locked in a lantern. The only way to free her is to complete a lock puzzle. Marsha will guide you through the poisonous swamps under her magic shield to keep you safe.

Gather 20 coins as you follow to score a **No Coins Left Behind** trophy. She'll stop twice so you can leave the protective bubble and complete a challenge. The first time, there are stone blocks behind her to shift. Create a path to an island to claim a **Legendary Golden Frog**. Continue with Marsha to reach her second stop, a **Dark Gate**.

FIGURE 8.29

There's an abundance of ferocious eyeballs waiting to attack you at the Little House.

Dark Hollow   Inside the Dark Gate, you'll find two levers and a single glowing orb down below (see Figure 8.30). This is super-fun; it's just like an enormous game of Pinball! As the orb rolls, time your levers to hit the back-left and right-side panels. It can help to have two players, one on each lever. The panels will eventually crack open, revealing a hollow for the orb to fall into. A second orb will appear to knock into the second hollow. Finally, a third orb must be rolled up the central ramp. Your reward is a Shadow Ghost Hat (+20 Critical Hit, +7 Armor). Awesome work! Now let's head back out to Marsha. Follow her through the swamp to a Traptanium Crystal with a super bounce pad underneath.

FIGURE 8.30

Use the levers on either side of the stage to maneuver the glowing orbs into the left, right, and central gates to score a new hat.

Empty Isle, Village Approach, & Smuggler's Hideout

Battle time! **Eye Scream** and her evil bouncing eyes are ready. A long-range attack is best to avoid her exploding eyeballs. Trap her in a Dark Trap and bounce back to **Village Approach**. Shift the blocks next to the bounce pad to create a path. Some mini-eyeballs and odd-looking enemies will chase you around. There are a few waves of attack here, each getting a little bit harder. If you have a Skylander who can fly or jump high, it will really help. This is a melee-style battle, and you'll need your wits about you! **Eye Five** will join the fray. Keep out of his swinging arm reach, and tackle him as he recovers with his hands together. Once he's down, the other enemies will disappear, too. There's a Traptanium Crystal at the back right of this playing field. As soon as Eye Five is defeated, smash the crystal. You'll uncover **Smuggler's Hideout**, where a **Treasure Chest** is hidden. There's a lock puzzle guarding the loot.

When you smashed the Traptanium Crystal, the battle gate at the back left dropped also, leading to a ramp. As you run up, Eye Scream throws exploding barrels down the ramp that you need to jump or smash. At the top of the ramp is a sleeping Mabu called Winkle. Wake him up to open the gate.

Sleepy Village, Grocer Jack's, & Boots the Cobbler

Inside the gate is Sleepy Village. Smeekens is another sleepy Mabu who has a quest for Fisticuffs. He has to pull in the outhouse that's floating away to earn a Clown Classic Hat (+20 Elemental Power). Rip is sleeping on the ground nearby. Wake him up and head into Grocer Jack's for a game of Skystones Smash with Bing. Back outside is a Traptanium Crystal to smash, earning you the Villain Stash behind it. Along the path, there's another little house to the left. Wander in to find a Troll Radio and Krueger, who is having a snooze. Back outside, York is terrified! Dreamcatcher is putting all the Mabu to sleep and stealing their dreams. Follow the coins outside to find all the Mabu and wake them up. As soon as you do, Dreamcatcher is hanging (or floating?) around for a fight.

Dreamcatcher's Arena Challenge
This is huge! Enemies swarm endlessly while Dreamcatcher splits the ground underneath you (see Figure 8.31). If you can jump or fly, you'll manage the crumbling earth better, as well as the lines of electricity enemies throw at you. There isn't much time for recovery here, so keep at it. All types of enemies are after you. Swap between long-range and melee Skylander/villain combos to keep your fighting skills complementary. As soon as you defeat all the other enemies, Dreamcatcher will disappear so you can't trap her. Still, you've saved the Mabu from the nightmarish clutches of evil. Brilliant work, Skylander. Keep fighting!

FIGURE 8.31

Fly or jump over the crumbling ground to battle the nightmarish minions of Dreamcatcher.

Chapter 8: Telescope Towers

The terrifying villain Dreamcatcher has put all the Mabu scientists to sleep. She wants to steal crazy inventions from their dreams and use them for evil. What a nightmare! Collect the Legendary Cyclops Teddy Bear along with three new hats (the Rugby Hat, Old-Time Movie Hat, and Synchronized Swimming Cap) as you hunt down Dreamcatcher (see Figure 8.32). Beware of Pain-Yatta and Hood Sickle, who will haunt your attempts to claim the hidden Soul Gems for Wildfire and Bat Spin as you climb to the highest towers.

FIGURE 8.32

Gather these collectibles as you explore Telescope Towers to capture Hood Sickle, Pain-Yatta, and Dreamcatcher.

TIP

Be Prepared!

Have Brawl and Chain (Water) and Masker Mind (Undead) in traps ready for their Villain Quests.

Galactic Bubble Center & Pulseblock Plains   Shhh...

there are sleeping Mabu everywhere! Head for the red floating pillows first to pick up a Soul Gem for Wildfire. Easy! Okay, down to business. Follow the island edge behind you to the right to find a sleeping Mabu called Hawk (he is snoring just past Cali). He has a Villain Quest for Brawl and Chain called Fairy Night Lights. In this quest, you need to deliver seven night lights to the Mabu houses before darkness falls. Each time you reach a house, enemies erupt from the trees (so leafy trees mean new houses!). Use the super bounce pads to reach the night lights after each delivery because he's a very slow-mover. Smash stone walls between buildings to find new places. You have a ten minutes to complete the quest.

Wake up and chat with the sleeping Mabu. Headwick is near a broken bridge waiting to show you the way to Dreamcatcher. Jump on the glowing button to raise the pulse blocks; then push them to activate a second button. Hit the second button to raise up to a new series of red floating platforms where you can activate the bridge for Headwick and follow him across.

Embroidered Bridge & Back-to-Back Stack-N-Jack   Move fast! Three jack-in-the boxes on the bridge will try to knock

you off. On the other side, Headwick has another pulse generator. Head up the path to your left. To the right is a group of floating red platforms with Persephone right at the top. Continue along the path. (Watch your step—more jack-in-the-boxes!)

Watering Hole Encounter & Hypnosis Pocus   At the

end of the path, Dreamcatcher's minions are bouncing to fight you again. This villain is big trouble. Destroy her mini-eyeballs to drop two sets of battle gates. To their right is a button on a floating platform that raises you to a Story Scroll. There's a doorway in the middle with swirling magic. It leads to a Villain Quest for Masker Mind. Arthur wants Masker Mind to hypnotize Stanley into thinking he's a chicken—it's pretty funny! Grab your winnings and try the left side of the battle gate instead. Jump on the pulse button to reach some new red platforms. There's treasure up here, as well as a new button to jump on. It raises some blocks down at the Chamber Entrance. Hop down and push them into an L shape to reveal a new button that raises you to a golden key in a floating bubble. Take it to the door in the tower below.

Cosmic Chamber, Pulseblock Pillow Pit, & Observation Terrace   Wow! A shimmering rainbow-colored door

appears in its place. Enter to wake the sleeping scientists. The platforms will appear and disappear as you move forward. Jump on the button to reach a higher platform and follow the arrow (see Figure 8.33).

Across the red bridge, Dreamcatcher is up to her old tricks. Enemies will float inside bubbles to attack you, so fight back! Once they are defeated, a pulse button will be revealed. Jump on it to bring up pulse blocks; then shift them to create a current that reveals a new button leading to a platform with a

Soul Gem for Bat Spin. The button on the next platform will extend a bridge with a super bounce pad at the end. Time to leap!

FIGURE 8.33

Interact with the buttons to raise and lower movable pulse blocks.

What a ride to **Observation Terrace**! A Pain-Yatta and his eyeball friends are waiting to fight, so dash right into it. A battle gate drops, revealing a Traptanium Crystal to your right, which forms a new bridge. Before you cross, talk to Galli, who's locked in a cage. Beat him at Skystones Smash to earn a golden key for a locked door to the left of his cage. Don't go in yet. You'll want to cross the bridge first.

Observation Loggia & Meditation Pool   Awesome! Two
Elemental Gates in one place! (Troll Radio alert!) Let's start with the Tech Gate (Grinding Gears). There are two pump buttons up high: one on the left and one on the right. You have to reach them in turn, by jumping from one spinning gear to the next while avoiding the smashing machines. Once you have activated both buttons, the center gear will start shifting back and forth in front of the original platform. Hop on and ride across to the back, where you can earn an Old-Time Movie Hat (+15 Elemental Power). Ride the gears back to the entrance.

Now let's visit the **Magic Gate** (**The Magic Frame Game**). Smash all the paintings until a new platform appears. Your reward is a Rugby Hat (+3 Speed, +7 Critical Hit).

Let's explore! Jump on the button on **Observation Loggia** to ride down to the **Meditation Pool** underneath. You'll discover a **Winged Sapphire** and a new game. There are golden balls floating in the pool here—don't smash them! If you can nudge 12 of them across the water and over the waterfall edge, you'll earn a **Ball Sprawler** trophy. Okay, now to that unlocked door back across the bridge on **Observation Terrace**.

Impossible Gravity Collider   Wake up the sleeping Mabu. More
phantom platforms that appear and disappear as you draw close—don't fall off! Duck across to ride the steam vent at the end of the platform to reach

some coins, and then the platform expands again. Dreamcatcher returns to bombard you with bad guys, but this time, Hood Sickle is leading the charge (see Figure 8.34)! You'll have to attack him as soon as he finishes swinging his weapon to avoid the hit. Be fast—or he'll vanish. He'll always teleport behind you, so as soon as he disappears, spin around. The platform crumbles beneath your feet, so stay on the safe green blocks. Follow the expanding path to reach a Villain Stash past the sleeping scientists. Another pump button is nearby—it's time to take a jump! Ride up high to wake up more snoozing scientists. Step closer to the right to make a path appear; then loot the area before returning the newest pump button. Ride up again. A magic door awaits—but beware—so does a new battle!

FIGURE 8.34

The Impossible Gravity Collider has vanishing platforms and disappearing villains.

Roof Observation Deck & Framing an Art

Attack   There are two exits, but both are blocked by battle gates until you defeat the enemies. The whirling rainbow portal on the end will lead to you to a secret room called Framing an Art Attack. Attack more paintings to earn a Treasure Chest above a steam vent. Now high-tail it back to the Impossible Gravity Collider using the super bounce pad, and take the super bounce pad next to the giant telescope.

The Great Spiral Observatory & Feng Shui

Shove   Pain-Yatta is on the loose, and he's anything but sweet. Beware the candy he offers you—it'll damage more than your teeth! Keep your distance, but he's slow enough to melee attack from behind as he smashes the ground. Head down the ramp to the tower entrance where you'll find a lock puzzle on a gate.

Inside the gate, a room called Dream a Little Dream has more snoring scientists. Wake them up to reveal a push button to ride up to a **Treasure Chest**. Jump on the pump button again to drop down into **Feng Shui Shove**. Ride a steam vent to discover another hidden **Treasure Chest**. Smash (and rearrange) the furniture on the platform to earn your reward.

Stairway to the Stars, Spiral Balcony, & Library

Lock Out   Back in Pain-Yatta's lair is a series of platforms to ride up using steam vent and push buttons. Right at the top, you'll land on Spiral Balcony. Before you talk to Headwick, activate the Water Gate. This is a really fun game called Waterfall Fall. Jump off the super bounce pad to start. You'll fall through a series of rings. If you can hit every one, your reward is a Synchronized Swimming Cap (+10 Critical Hit, +10 Armor). Before you leave Spiral Balcony, jump off the side of the platform to recover a Legendary Cyclops Teddy Bear. You'll have to pass a lock puzzle first. Okay, let's track down Headwick for our final epic battle against Dreamcatcher!

Battle Against Dreamcatcher   This nasty girl will shoot torna-

dos made of nightmares at you while she breaks the platform out from under your feet (see Figure 8.35). You need to break Dreamcatcher's shield by waking up (in other words, attacking) the sleeping Mabu. As soon as her shield is down, go for it! A ranged attack is really helpful, especially if you can use multiple homing ranged missiles like Chopper or Déjà vu for a heavy attack.

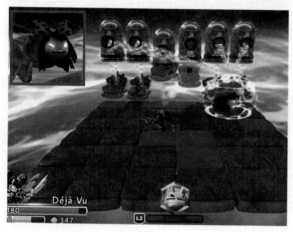

FIGURE 8.35

Watch your step! Dreamcatcher attacks while tearing the ground away from underneath your feet.

Chapter 9: Mystic Mill

The Great Captain Flynn is back—it's Hero Time! The Doom Raiders have overtaken Mystic Mill, and Rizzo and the Mabu Defense Force are trapped. Search the Lumber Mill to dig up Soul Gems for Flip Wreck, Tread Head, and Torch; then build bridges to reach the Legendary Saw Blade (see Figure 8.36). There are three new magical hats to collect: the Garrison, Volcano, and Mountie Hats—if you can get past the wooden fists of Krankenstein and Shield Shredder! Let's get to work!

FIGURE 8.36

Gather these collect-
ibles as you explore
Mystic Mill to capture
Krankenstein and
Shield Shredder.

TIP

Be Prepared!

Have Shrednaught (Tech) and Bomb Shell (Magic) in traps ready for
their Villain Quests.

Mabu Flagship
Crates are falling from the sky, and the storm is ris-
ing. Shift the crates into the gaps on deck as they fall. Your aim is to make
your way to the spinning wheel so you can regain control of the ship. Once
you have control, use the turret on Flynn's ship to shoot the cannons and
Evilikins guiding them. If you shoot 20 of them, you'll earn the Evilikin
Eliminator trophy. Keep your eye out for four winged gems as well. The Mabu
Defense Force is here to help you take back Mystic Mill.

Loading Docks
Before you run off, Rizzo has a Villain Quest for
Bomb Shell. You have ten minutes to pick up eight bundles of dynamite and
deposit them into special spots around the Troll fortress. It sounds simple,
but the clock's ticking! Luckily, the dropping spots are well marked. There's
a secret storage spot with bombs to use and plenty of dynamite. Trolls will
attack as you run past, so be quick! You'll earn a Garrison Hat (+20 Armor).

Lumber Mill Office
And there's a second Villain Quest ready for
you here—this time for Shrednaught. Loggins needs a giant load of wood
chopped, and you've got just the Trolls to do it! These repented villains will
come in handy later in this chapter, so keep them close.

Okay, let's let the Mabu Defense Force get to work. They'll build a set of
steps to reach the golden key on the **Loading Docks**. Unlock the gate but
walk up the ramp to your right before you enter.

Packing House and Wheelhouse A

There is a Story Scroll here, as well as two small houses. In the left-side house (Wheel House A) is a Soul Gem for Tread Head and a Troll Radio. In the right-side house (Packing House) is another Troll Radio and Packard, who wants to play Skystones Smash. Okay, let's continue exploring the path through the gate.

Mudder's Corner, Western Storage Unit, & Sawdust Processing

You'll see a few buildings here. There's a Troll Radio on your left between two houses. The first house on the left is Wheelhouse B. Inside you'll find a Villain Stash.

The second house (**Western Storage Unit**) is full of enemies. Evilikin Cannons will drops bombs on you from above, but the real fun begins when **Shield Shredder** joins in. Keep clear of their spinning shields and move in when they pause.

The third entrance (**Sawdust Processing**) can only be opened by an upgraded (evolved) Shrednaught (you visited Loggins at the Lumber Mill Office a bit earlier for this). Smash up the barrels inside.

Waterways

Back in Mudder's Corner, dash underneath the red metal bridge to your right into Waterways. At the end of the path, the gate is double-locked. First, wander to your right. Interact with the pile of wood on the ground to create steps up into the Power House. Inside, you'll see switches on the floor. Flick them to create steps at the back of the room to retrieve the first key. Take it to the lock.

Back to the left is a big aqueduct (tunnels of water flowing down the hill). Run up the first two ramps (jump bombs and falling logs), and then hop over the end onto a platform with coins. Leap down to a **Fire Gate**.

Fire Falls

This is a fun jumping game (see Figure 8.37). Hop your way to the top floating platform to earn your Volcano Island Hat (+15 Critical Hit).

FIGURE 8.37

A lava-filled cavern awaits you at Fire Falls—but don't fall in!

There are two little houses, and a **Life Gate** just before the **Power House** (right side). The first door doesn't open. The second door (**Eastern Storage Unit**) can only be opened by evolved Shrednaught and hides a **Treasure Chest**. Go and explore the Life Gate.

Flying Flora & Plant Processing... Plant

Cross a bridge to the grassy island and bounce up; then pick up the magic nut (see Figure 8.38). Bounce again to a smaller platform to plant it and grow a flower bridge. Cross over and hop onto a balloon (right side) to float to a Treasure Chest and a second nut. Take the nut back to the central platform, and then ride the left-side balloon up to plant it. A new flower bridge will take you to a chimney inside a room with the Mountie Hat (+15 Armor). You'll exit through the first little (previously closed) house!

FIGURE 8.38

Grow magical flower bridges to access Treasure Chests, Soul Gems, and Hats in Flying Flora.

Run back to the red metal overpass and climb the wooden ramp to the right side. There's a super bounce pad on the top—let's go! You'll land on the top of a tree truck with a **Soul Gem** for Torch. Alright! Now run right to the very top of the aqueduct to find that second golden key. (Beware the rolling logs and falling bombs!) Once you've got it, drop back down to unlock the gate.

Saw Mill Main Gate & Nature Bridges – North

It's battle time! Chompies and Shield Shredders are waiting for you. As soon as you defeat them, a battle gate will drop. While the Mabu Defense Force keeps the bad guys busy, smash up the Traptanium Crystals. It builds a bridge across to Nature Bridges - North. Destroy the second crystal to create a new bridge and cross over. Pick up the wooden bridge and carry it across the platforms until you reach a Treasure Chest. Pick up the bamboo bridge behind you and relocate it to build a bridge to the original platform. Run back and grab the wooden bridge that you used to reach the Treasure Chest. Carry it around, over the Traptanium bridges to reach the Soul Gem for Flip Wreck.

It's time to go help the Mabu Defense Force at the **Main Gate**. Evilikins will attack you while the Mabu open the door. Once the door is opened, jump the boxes to reach a **Winged Sapphire** behind a door that only evolved Shrednaught can open. Keep running down the ramp, past the battle gate (which will drop when you defeat the Evilikins). Don't go up the red ramp yet; instead, head to the left instead to find **Persephone**. Smash the Traptanium Crystals to build a new flower bridge.

Nature Bridges – West
Cross the flower bridge and gather all the coins to reach each new platform. Pick up the bamboo and metal bridges until you reach the Legendary Saw Blade on the furthest platform. It's time for our final fight. Head back to the red ramp past Persephone.

Pulp Shredder
I hope you've got your wits about you, Skylander— these guys are tough! Shield Shredders and Evilikins are your main enemies here—a long-ranged attack to shoot the cannons would be a great start (see Figure 8.39). Go for Krankenstein as soon as he jumps down onto your platform to end the battle completely. Congratulations, you saved Mystic Mill from the Doom Raiders! Time for a well-deserved rest at Skylanders Academy.

FIGURE 8.39

Evilikin cannons damage from a distance. Take them out before Krankenstein weighs into the fight.

Chapter 10: Secret Sewers of Supreme Stink

There's a big mess at the stinkiest place in Skylands! Dr. Krankcase flooded the sewers with toxic goo, and the workers don't believe you really want to help them. Prove your mettle and shut down the goo to save the day. Before you get to take that bumpy ride through the sewers though, Echo and High Five's Soul Gems are buried somewhere in the stink for you to find, along with a Rubber Glove Hat, Trash Can Lid, Shower Cap, and the Legendary Eel Plunger (see Figure 8.40). While you've got your hands dirty, take out Fisticuffs and Rage Mage with the trash before they can put up a fight. Good luck, Skylander!

FIGURE 8.40

Gather these collect-
ibles as you explore
the Secret Sewers
of Supreme Stink to
capture Rage Mage
and Fisticuffs.

TIP

Be Prepared!

Have Chomp Chest (Earth) and Pain-Yatta (Magic) in traps ready for
their Villain Quests.

Goober's Trail & Outer Sewage Segue

Flynn drops
you near wooden fence (those purple pumpkins have coins in them). Once
the fence is broken, you'll be faced with Goo Chompies and trails of toxic
goo across your path. Jump or fly—just don't touch it! Grab the bomb and
blow up the gate at the end of the path to enter Outer Sewage Segue. A few
Chompies will come out; smash them and head around the left side (jump
the goo!) to discover a Story Scroll. Super easy. Okay, back around to the
right side of the tower, you'll see a tunnel. There's a second tunnel hidden
straight underneath (you'll need to jump down to the lower entrance), but
first you'll need to bring a bomb from back out at Goober's Trail. Run back
and grab the bomb; then jump off the ledge in front of the top tunnel.

Effluent Deck & Flam Bam's Retreat

Enter the second
tunnel and throw the bomb at the barrier inside to score a Treasure Chest.
Bounce back up to the top tunnel.

A dragon called Flam Bam has a **Villain Quest** for Chomp Chest called **Hot
Diggity Dash** (see Figure 8.41). The goal is to eat 75 hot dogs (and any ham-
burgers that get in your way). Your timer extends with each hot dog you eat.
Smash rock walls and trolls if you have to, but dodge enemies whenever you
can to save time. Awesome work, Skylander!

FIGURE 8.41

Chomp Chest is super hungry! The more food you eat, the longer you have to search.

Back to **Flam Bam's Retreat** to smash up those Traptanium Crystals. Bounce up a level and exit through the tunnel to find a **Soul Gem** for Echo. Drop off the outside ledge (Chompy alert!) and head right. There's a circular platform nearby. To raise the platform, walk in the direction of the arrows. The goo falling from the roof will shut off, making it safe to jump across to the house. Great work! One more thing—a lock puzzle with three stages guards the door.

Grit Chamber & The Storm Drain

Your newest host Verl will meet you with an aversion to germs. Hop onto the green platform and float across the goo. Some Goo Chompies will be there to meet you. Jump onto the floating barges and jump off again down in Backflow Alley. Wander up the ramp to find a Troll Radio and a skeleton called Bag O' Bones who has a Villain Quest for Pain-Yatta. Pain-Yatta needs to escort scuttling geckos out of harm's way by smashing up enemies that cross your path. You'll earn a Rubber Glove Hat (+12 Armor, +12 Critical Hit) for your trouble.

Run along the floating barges back to the **Grit Chamber**. Take out the enemies to release more floating barges in the second channel. Jump across to the other side and flick the switches on the floor. A giant circular door will open, but don't go in yet. To your far right is a wooden fence. Smash it and dash up the ramp to find a Villain Stash in **The Storm Drain**. (Be wary of the spouting goo and Goo Chompies!) Let's return to the big tunnel you opened in the Grit Chamber.

Flow Drain Dropoff & Spoiled Sanctum

Enter the tunnel for a big fall down into Spoiled Sanctum! As you fall, dodge the goo and reach out for treasure. Beware—you'll fall into a nasty surprise! Chompies, Goo Chompies, Evilikins, and a Scrap Shooter are here to make things difficult. If you have a long-ranged attack to shoot them as they fall onto the platform, you'll get it done quickly. When all the enemies are defeated, a battle gate will drop. Hop across rows of floating barges to reach the other side where Persephone is floating on a platform to your left. Follow the path to the right. Pick up the bamboo bridge to create your own path to a metal bridge, which you can shift to reach a Winged Sapphire and some gold. Drop the metal bridge back where you found it and bounce up into Drainage Vista.

Drainage Vista & Catwalk Cubby   First, explore to your left, down the path called Catwalk Cubby to score a Treasure Chest. Back on the main platform, flick the switches closest to where you bounced in first to create a laser square. Then flick the switch near the stone block to complete the circuit and blow it up, revealing a super bounce pad.

Drainage Central   You are dropped into an arena called Drainage Central. All manner of evildoers will attack you, but the hardest to take out are the Shield Shredders with their spinning blades. Keep your distance—if you have a Skylander that can shoot missiles or bombs, make good use of them. Evilikin Cannons drop bombs at you from pedestals—unless you can fly, you'll need to destroy their wooden stands to make them fall so you can attack. Rage Mage is waiting behind a battle gate for most of the fight, boosting their efforts with angry magic (see Figure 8.42). When he joins you with the Scrap Shooter, he's super-fast, zipping around the arena. Focus on destroying the Scrap Shooter first. Even after Rage Mage has been captured, there's one more wave of bad guys to take out. When all the enemies have been defeated, a battle gate drops, revealing an enormous gear. Hop on and start walking to raise it. Well done, Skylander! You shut down Dr. Krankcase's goo supply!

FIGURE 8.42

Rage Mage increases the speed and damage of other enemies around him. Destroy all enemies to drop the battle gate and shut down Dr. Krankcase's goo supply.

Inner Headworks   Jump off the giant gear toward the metal ramp leading to a Fire Gate (Inner Headworks). Inside, you'll see a lock puzzle straight ahead. To your left is a bomb and to your right is a bounce pad on a block. If you shift the bounce pad block across into the floor gap, you can bounce up to a higher level where a stone wall is blocking a treasure stash. Grab a bomb, bounce up, and blow the wall to collect your loot! To the right of the treasure trove is another bounce pad, so jump up and head left

to retrieve a golden key. There's a second key to collect before you can unlock the gate. Drop down and go left to grab the bomb, and then continue on to a bounce pad and jump up to a higher ledge. Blow up the stone wall and push a bounce pad block off the ledge to ground level. Drop off, grab another bomb, and bounce up high to reach the second key behind another stone wall. There are a few other stone walls to blow up while you're on the job. Drop back down and use your two keys to open the gate and score a Trash Lid Hat (+10 Armor, +10 Elemental Power).

Digestion Deck & Going Down

When you leave the ramp for Inner Headworks, drop to your right to grab some coins. There are two pipes on the ground level you can explore. Start in the right-side tunnel, Digestion Deck. Rows of exploding goo shoot up from the platform as you walk across, so time your moves. Flam Bam the dragon wants to play a game of Skystones Smash. Continue down the path to find a Legendary Eel Plunger and some gold. Left of Flam Bam, the platform continues around and exits through the second tunnel coming from Drainage Central.

Between the two tunnels is an enormous hole in the ground with coins leading inside. Take a flying leap! This is **Going Down**. Grab the coins as you fall. It's a long ride down to **Splash Station**. If you've managed to dodge the goo up until now, well done! You've earned a **No Goo For You!** Trophy.

Splash Station, Aqua Deck, & Barge Basin

There are pipe blocks scattered on the deck that need rearranging. Shift them around to form a new path for the water to flow through (see Figure 8.43). The water will knock a Soul Gem for High Five. Head right. There are more blocks to push here; this time, shift them to fill the nearby basin with water. Run up the path of blocks you created and down to your right to enter the basin. Hop over the barges to reach a Water Gate on the other side (Aqua Deck). There are lots of yummy treasures in here, as well as a few Chompies. Shift a single block to reach the back platform and earn a Shower Cap (+6 Speed).

Prove You Are a Skylander Arena Battle

Epic battle time! This is an arena to prove your mettle, so be prepared for a big fight. Waves of Chompies come in first, with some Shield Shredders. Another Rage Mage jumps in during Stage 2; try to smash him before he disappears. He will leave you a diamond, though, so that's a bonus! Knock your opponents off the platform into the goo to get rid of them, and try to take out the Shield Shredders as they jump in, before they have time to spin their blades. A giant slug pops up his eyeball in warning. Watch out! It leaves slime trails across the arena ground, which will slow you down (see Figure 8.43). If you have a flying Skylander, he or she will definitely come in handy here. Stage 3 is where Fisticuffs jumps into the fight. Try to attack him while his arm is outstretched. Alternatively, use a long-range attack, which is even better. Choose a Skylander that's quick on his or her feet, and you'll have this battle done and dusted in no time.

FIGURE 8.43

In your final battle against Fisticuffs, the arena floor is divided as a giant Cyclops worm leaves a trail of slime to slow you down.

Chapter 11: Wilikin Workshop

Poor Glumshanks is now a slave for the Doom Raiders! They aren't happy that you stopped their supply of stinky goo, but Dr. Krankcase has a solution—10,000-year-old stinky cheese! Now they're hunting down Kaos to open a portal into the future! It's time to teach them a lesson they won't forget.... You'll begin in a creepy little village where young Kaos made some friends— literally, made them out of wood! How odd.... Search out the Legendary Masterpieces to hang at Skylanders Academy, collect a Clown Bowler Hat and Lil' Elf Hat, and find Soul Gems for Head Rush and Fling Kong (see Figure 8.44).

FIGURE 8.44

Gather these collectibles as you explore Wilikin Workshop to capture Scrap Shooter and Dr. Krankcase.

> **TIP**
>
> **Be Prepared!**
>
> Have Dreamcatcher (Air), Scrap Shooter (Fire), and Shield Shredder (Life) in traps ready for their Villain Quests. You'll capture Scrap Shooter during this chapter.

Wilikin Worker's Town & Wilikin Band Café

First up, you'll start with a little treasure hunting! There's a ledge behind you (dive over and then bounce back up). The house on your right is called Wilikin Band Café. There are some wooden puppet-style friends of Kaos inside with a Villain Quest for Shield Shredder called Wood-Be Band. All he has to do is turn up and play some special music (which sounds suspiciously like a circular saw) to evolve. Great start!

Spool Storage Shack & Wilikin Break Room

Head down the hill toward Kaos and take a right into the first house (Spool Storage Shack) to find a Story Scroll. There's a hidden red button under some barrels that will drop a battle gate revealing a Treasure Chest. It's not here, though—you have to explore the next house on the left (Wilikin Break Room). Kaos is going through a secret tunnel to open the main door for you from the inside, but don't worry about him for now—you'll catch up soon.

Railcar Repair Station & Railcar Repair Shop

Outside are a couple of pipe blocks to shift into line and then one on top to drop down, creating a bridge across to Railcar Repair Station. On your left is the Railcar Repair Shop. (Troll Radio alert!) Straight ahead you'll see an Undead Gate leading to Toy Returns. Go inside.

Toy Returns

Walk through the gate and then into a tunnel full of bones. Gates will rise in front and behind you, trapping you with presents that fall from the sky. It's not all nice surprises, though—some of them have enemies inside! After you defeat the enemies, the front gate will drop and you'll move to a second, then third battle area, collecting coins as you go. Smash the bad guys, melee style—you haven't got much room, but there's plenty of opportunity to level up here. Your reward is a Clown Bowler Hat (+20 Critical Hit). Teleport back to the gate to exit.

Railcar Gauntlet & Railcar Arena

Back outside the Railcar Repair Shop was a big switch on the ground. Let's flick it! The rail gates open up so you can pass through. Watch out! Railcars come speeding toward you as you dash toward the main gate at Railcar Arena. A battle gate stops you from going further as you're bombarded with enemies. Keep clear of the spinning Evilikins until they pause—another super-fun melee attack. As soon as you defeat them all, Scrap Shooter joins in the fun. He will do three barrel-roll attacks in succession; that's when you charge in for your attack. Every so often, he braces on the ground with his hands and flips back his head to shoot high barrels. As soon as he has finished this move, dash around the back to take him out.

Big Train Loading Area

Kaos is standing on a barrel just inside the battle gate, but first drop off the ledge near the wooden fence (to your right) to score a Soul Gem for Fling Kong. Bounce up! There are coins near Kaos, so do a bit of exploring and jump on the train for a quick getaway when the Evilikins start running to attack you. The train will stop very soon at the End of the Line.

End of the Line & Safe Toy Disposal

At the End of the Line, jump off to claim your Legendary Masterpieces statue. (How easy was that!?) Smash the Traptanium Crystals to reveal a Traptanium Bridge (see Figure 8.45); then dash over to the floating ship and grab some gold.

FIGURE 8.45

A floating ship of golden treasure next to a magical gate full of gifts—what more could you ask for?

There's a **Magic Gate** off to your left (**Safe Toy Disposal**). Inside, you get more presents—this time full of gold. There's a Lil' Elf Hat (+8 Speed) as a bonus. Use the Super Bounce Pad outside the gate to bounce back up to **Big Train Loading Area**.

Sneaky Pete's Saloon

It's time to deal with these Spinning Evilikins now, so attack them as you make your way up the platform beside the railway, heading toward the main building. On your right, there's a little house called Sneaky Pete's Saloon, where Yoho has a Villain Quest for Scrap Shooter (called Pirates of the Broken Table). He has to repair a broken Skystones Smash table, and then he automatically evolves. Too easy. Stay for a game if you like, or keep exploring.

Rochester's House, Sweet Dreams, & The Old Mill

Next up, keep running along the rail line, and then swap to the left side of the tracks to gather piles of coins. At the end of the line are two little houses opposite the main entrance. Scrap Shooters and Evilikins will take the opportunity for a mass attack—keep on your toes and watch out for the passing railcars! The left-side house is The Old Mill. Smash up all the boxes to reach a Winged Sapphire and a Skystones Smash player named Yar Har. In the right-side shack (Rochester's House) is a Villain Quest for Dreamcatcher called Sweet Dreams (see Figure 8.46). Poor Rochester needs her help to fall asleep and have a nice dream. Follow Rochester into the Dream Portal to collect treasure and evolve.

FIGURE 8.46

It's time for Dreamcatcher to make amends for her evil ways. Visit Rochester's House to settle him in for a nice, long nap.

The Factory

Kaos has been waiting ever so impatiently—so take him inside the Wilikin Factory to deal with these Doom Raiders now. Ride the conveyer belt to the end of the room (stash that cash on the way!). Some Spinning Evilikins will join the party; as soon as they're down, a bounce pad will appear. Whip out your villain to open a Villain Stash; then smash the Traptanium Crystals to reach a Treasure Chest. Bounce up to the next conveyer belt. Persephone is waiting to offer you an upgrade. Let the conveyer belt bump you over to a lower level with more coins. Watch out for the smashers as you ride the belt and hop off when you reach a new bounce pad in the Smashing Area; then bounce up again.

Smashing Area & Crane Loading and Dropping

Straight ahead is a battle gate with a Treasure Chest inside. But first you need to continue along the conveyer belt and take the mini-platform to the right (before you reach the end). A red button will drop the battle gate so you can claim the treasure. Now, ride the belt to its end and bounce up another level. There's a Traptanium Crystal to the left; smash it up to score a Soul Gem for Head Rush.

Cross the conveyer belt to reach a second battle gate with enemies in front. Destroy them all to drop the gate; you'll see a raised ramp ahead and the lever you need to switch to lower it. But beware—it's a mine field ahead (under the boxes)! Knock the switch to lower the ramp and run up it. Okay, here Kaos wants you to do the "old pick 'n drop" trick. Use the crane to drop bombs on the barriers, to create a path (see Figure 8.47). Run through it to reach Dr. Krankcase, exploring every room for gold.

FIGURE 8.47

Pick up the bombs and drop them onto barriers (and enemies!) to make a path to Dr. Krankcase.

Path to Dr. Krankcase

Beware! Hordes of Evilikins will make this difficult. As you defeat enemies in each section, a rock wall will drop, allowing you to move a bit further toward Dr. Krankcase's house. More Evilikins and a Krankenstein will attack you, and there's not much room to move. If you have a heavy-handed Skylander who moves fast, now's the time to whip him or her into action. When your last rock wall drops, run for the house.

Dr. Krankcase is full of energy and is a hard villain to beat. His legs spin in a circle around his body, causing damage, so try to keep clear of them. Team up with a long-range attacker or villain if you can.

In Stage 2 of the fight, Dr. Krankcase drops barrels into goo to create green barrels that spin in the same way he does and explode (see Figure 8.48). Try to blow up the barrels before they get slimed. Stage 3 shows Kaos trapped in a barrel as Dr. Krankcase drops goo onto the platform from above. Keep off the goo because it will slow you down while you attack the barrels falling from the conveyer belt. An Evilikin drops in to play. Wolfgang steals Kaos; then your platform gets smaller as a giant spikey roller takes over (see Figure 8.49). Stay on the platform you have left and keep attacking Dr. Krankcase whenever he drops in—you have to wear down his health from here. As soon as he's defeated, it's back to Skylander Academy.

Brilliant work, Skylander!

FIGURE 8.48

Poor Kaos! Dr. Krankcase has him trapped in a barrel—until Wolfgang kidnaps him from the kidnapper!

FIGURE 8.49

Dr. Krankcase lets his exploding goo-barrels do most of the hard work, but keep clear of his spinning legs when he joins in the fight.

Chapter 12: Time Town

Dr. Krankcase won't cause any more trouble, but it seems Kaos is back *in* trouble. Wolfgang has him trapped in Time Town and he's up to no good. Hunt down the Legendary Clocktower as you prepare for your ultimate battle with Cross Crow. You'll discover Soul Gems for Rocky Roll and Thunderbolt, as well as a very helpful Alarm Clock Hat and a Skylanders Bobby Hat (see Figure 8.50). You may come face to face with the outlaw Wolfgang, but be warned—he won't stick around for long. A Skylander's work is never done!

FIGURE 8.50

Gather these collectibles as you explore Time Town to capture Cross Crow and rescue Kaos.

TIP

Be Prepared!

Have Dr. Krankcase (Tech) and Cross Crow (Water) in traps ready for their Villain Quests. You'll capture Cross Crow during this chapter, but might need to replay to evolve him.

Grand Approach   Whoa! That was a crash landing. There's a Traptanium Crystal to your left, so smash that up first. You'll uncover a platform that you can hop onto and ride over to a small island with a Soul Gem for Rocky Roll. There are numerous statues of Da Pinchy around Time Town—and the first three are here! Smash five statues during this chapter to receive the Da Pinchy Defacer trophy. Ride back to Grand Approach (another Da Pinchy statue straight ahead!). Dive off the edge behind your landing spot to visit Father Cog's Patio.

Father Cog's Patio & Cog's Family Fortune   You'll drop down to find a bounce pad (that's your ride home) and a door leading to Cog Family Fortune. There are jewels hanging off the biggest gears. You need to jump on the big gold button on the floor to rotate the gears, bringing the jewels into reach. Once you've got the loot, head outside and bounce back up to Grand Approach to chat with Da Pinchy, who's waiting at the gate.

Pendulum Bob's House, Moon Gear Rise, & Musical Terrace   Through the gate, there's a little house on the left. Inside, you'll find Hans hoping for a game of Skystones Smash. (Da Pinchy statue alert!) There are two gear blocks outside on the platform. Push them both forward to raise gears up to use as stepping platforms (Moon Gear Rise). A Story Scroll is on the right-side gear. There are two bounce pads on the smallest gear; bounce left (jump higher then fall down to Musical Terrace) to find a Treasure Chest. Bounce back up and head right (bounce again) to score some coins.

Chime Hammer Square, Diorama Drama, & Wayward Cog Storage

Run past the flipping scenery wall to reach Chime Hammer Square. Da Pinchy is in dreadful strife—he's being held hostage by a Cross Crow and some Buzzer Beaks. There is lots of room to move here, so it's an easy win. Before you follow Da Pinchy, leap backwards off the platform behind you to fall into Diorama Drama, a Villain Quest for Dr. Krankcase. (Da Pinchy statue alert!) He just has to show up to see Leyland's diorama to evolve him, but each time you come across a diorama in Time Town, tag him in and spray the stage with goo (see Figure 8.51). Secret areas will appear that you can enter. This time, you can actually walk inside the diorama (Wayward Cog Storage) with evolved Dr. Krankcase to claim a Skylanders Bobby Hat (+20 Armor, +7 Elemental Power). Okay, let's bounce back up to Da Pinchy.

FIGURE 8.51

Each time you see a diorama in Time Town, swap in to Dr. Krankcase and spray the stage with his evil green goo. A secret location will appear that you can enter.

Backstage, Main Spring Fly, & Skylands' Biggest Fans

There is a new type of lock on this gate—a steam lock. Use the hammer to punch the turning gold pots, right on the white steam tube. (If you miss, you have to start again!) The gate will open—be prepared for a Buzzer Beak battle! A Cross Crow joins in (destroy the grappling hooks as soon as they land). When all enemies are defeated, the Battle Gate button will turn gold and stairs will appear. Climb up and drop off the right side to visit another diorama. Tag in as Dr. Krankcase and spray the skeleton. A door will appear, leading to Backstage. Start at the left to ride the spinning platform to reach a Villain Stash. There are two more Da Pinchy statues in here to smash. Okay, back outside you can bounce up a level. Before you super-bounce, explore left to claim the Soul Gem for Thunderbolt. Okay, super-bounce time!

Florg is here to greet you with some worrisome news. To his right along a wooden ledge is Tessa with a **Villain Quest** for Cross Crow (called **Skylands' Biggest Fans**). If this is your first play-through, you won't have captured him yet, but if you've been through before, give it a go. Cross Crow needs to take out the Trolls and fix ten fans (by mashing) in ten minutes, so that the birds can fly again. Super-bounce between areas and use a good melee fighter to battle Eggsecutioners and Bomb Shells as you move. It's a bit tricky, but you can do it, Skylander. Ready, set, go!

There's a conveyer belt to the left of Florg. Jump off halfway along (quick!) to land on a gold button that activates stairs leading to a **Winged Sapphire**. Bounce back to the conveyer belt and dash through the moving wall.

Sunny Side Narrows

Run up the conveyer belt, but don't let it carry you down yet! You'll find a Jeweled Apple, Troll Radio, and a second platform you ride to visit Persephone underneath. A teleport pad will take you back to the top platform, where you can return to the conveyer belt and ride it down. Enemies are waiting for you. Run to the end of the platform and drop down to the gold button. This will rotate the gear on the platform above and bring the swinging platform closer to the edge (see Figure 8.52). Bounce back up (grab the swinging gold) and run on the giant gear to raise it up. Before it closes again, jump inside the hole in the ground underneath.

FIGURE 8.52

Walk the giant gear up off the ground in Sunny Side Narrows, and then quickly drop underneath into the room below to battle enemies for a reward.

Clockwork Innards

A big fight is brewing down here. Bird enemies attack from all sides. A couple of crows shoot bombs from a high ledge. It's a good idea to get rid of them quickly, so run on the giant gear to reach them. The battle gate hiding a Treasure Chest won't fall until all enemies are destroyed. To exit, run the giant gear right as high as it will go and head right to get back to Sunny Side Narrows.

Remember that big gear you jumped underneath? Run it up to its highest point now and jump into a new area. Through the flower wall, Da Pinchy has another **Steam Lock** for you to hit with the hammer. A new section will open, but before you enter, explore the **Earth Gate** to your right.

Broken Toe Plateau & Waterfall Cave

Run across the bridge into Broken Toe Plateau and fight some enemies on your way into a watery cave. Collect the pick and shift the block to reach the gold pile at the back. Outside, use the pick to break up the rocks on the left side of the entrance to reveal a step. Run up and around the front right of the monolith, breaking rocks in your way as you go. Reach the top for your reward, an Alarm Clock Hat (+10 Armor, +4 Speed). Teleport back to the bridge to exit the gate. Ride the super bounce pad over to Clockwork Courtyard.

Clockwork Courtyard & Retired Clock Storage

Da Pinchy has another Steam Lock for you here. Inside, Buzzer Beaks are on the attack, so watch out! Battle gates won't drop until your enemies are destroyed. Run to your right to find one more diorama for Dr. Krankcase to enter (Retired Clock Storage). Smash away, and then return to the fight. As soon as the battle gate drops, some Cross Crows shoot arrows at you.

Cogsworth's Bed & Brunch

A little house on the left (Cogsworth's Bed and Brunch) has furniture to smash. When the Cross Crows are defeated, a second battle gate will drop. Shift the gear blocks onto the spinning floor gears to lower a new rotating platform like a Ferris wheel. Jump on to reach a Troll Radio, and then take the right-side platform for a new Steam Lock (or three!). Beware! Cross Crow is waiting to take you out (see Figure 8.53)! Smash him, melee style, and you'll destroy him fairly quickly—but the fight isn't over until all the other bird fighters are defeated. (Watch out for swooping attacks!) There's a Treasure Chest behind a dropped battle gate as your reward.

FIGURE 8.53

Cross Crow and his evil minions will keep you from rescuing Kaos for as long as they can.

Tower Approach

Hop on the rotating platform again for your last trip—this time, jump off at the very top. A new fight starts. When the enemies are gone, a battle gate drops to reveal a Traptanium Crystal. Smash it to claim your Legendary Clocktower. Da Pinchy has one last Steam Lock for you to reach your final destination.

Owl Clock Gallery   Hang in there, Kaos (see Figure 8.54)! Your rescue team is on the way! Jump on the gold button to spin the stairs to the left. Climb up to reach a second gold button; then jump away. The stairs will spin to the right this time; run up there and jump on a third gold button. Run up the center stairs to rescue poor Kaos (still hanging upside down)!

Well done, Skylander. Time for a well-deserved rest. Head back to **Skylander Academy** for some fun exploring.

FIGURE 8.54

Oh dear! Wolfgang certainly has Kaos hanging by his toes! He's not happy at all.

Chapter 13: The Future of Skylands

Wolfgang has zapped into the future and invented the "Big Bad Woofer," an epic music speaker that blows everything up. It's going to destroy Skylands! Travel 10,000 years into the future with Da Pinchy to thwart his evil plans! (But whatever you do, don't let Kaos see a clock!) There are hidden Soul Gems for Gearshift and Trailblazer, a Legendary Rocket, and three new hats (a Kokoshnik, a Tin Foil hat, and an Extreme Viking Hat, shown in Figure 8.55). This isn't going to be an easy ride, but there will be lots of giant lasers to make up for it!

FIGURE 8.55

Gather these collectibles as you explore The Future of Skylands to capture Wolfgang and Blaster-Tron.

> ## TIP
>
> **Be Prepared!**
>
> Have Rage Mage (Magic) and Wolfgang (Undead) in traps ready for their **Villain Quests**. You'll capture Wolfgang during this chapter, but might need to replay to evolve him.

Arrival Platform
There's an electric field buzzing across the entrance to **Ice Cream Planet**. You have to pull the switch on the deck to shut it off and get past—but first, leap over the edge of the railing where you landed to drop down to a **Light Gate**.

Museum of Important Rockers
Run inside to interact with the switch on the wall next to the Troll Radio to bring a floating platform close to you. Hop on and ride it across to a second switch at the back of the room. Each time you flick a switch, it changes the arrangement of the floating platforms, bringing them closer or further away from each other. Use them to make your way to the back platform, where you can grab some gold and use the bounce pad to jump up high, scoring a Kokoshnik Hat (+30 Elemental Power). Drop back down and ride a platform to your left to find a Treasure Chest.

Ice Cream Planet & Ice Cream in the Future
Leave the Light Gate and bounce back up to where you began. Okay, time to explore the ramp now that the electric field is clear. Watch out! A Blaster-Tron is on guard! He's pretty slow to move and turn, so you've got the upper hand if you keep out of his line of fire. He has a shield on the front of him, so shoot him from behind. When the coast is clear, jump on the left-side robot taxi for a flying visit to score a Soul Gem for Gearshift. Jump overboard to land back on the Arrival Platform. There's another robot taxi on your right— but first, look at the sphere in the middle. Noobman has a Villain Quest for Rage Mage (called Ice Cream in the Future). The angry little guy just waves his sign around for a bit and then—Bam!—he's upgraded! Great work. Now take a ride on the right-side robot taxi.

Electro Bridge Controls & Astro Bug Zapper
You'll end up on a platform with nowhere to go. Flick the switch under the enormous light bulb to build a path to the next platform, but be careful—bombs shoot across as you run. Another electric field stops you from going any further. Jump down from the right-side ledge to land in Astro Bug Zapper (see Figure 8.56). There's a switch to the right to shut down the electric field. Dash through the barrier to find a Troll Radio.

FIGURE 8.56

Dodge the bombs through the Astro Bug Zapper to shut down the electric barrier into Sub-Orbital Combat Plaza—but be ready for battle!

Sub-Orbital Combat Plaza

Battle time! A flying Skylander here will keep you safe above the electric lines that cross the battle floor. Future Brawlruses and zapping enemies will keep you on your toes here. When they are all defeated, you can enter the Fire Gate.

Mini Sun

This is fantastic! Inside this Fire Gate, a burning sun will emit harmful rays as you walk around the outside collecting coins (see Figure 8.57). Stay just ahead or behind the rays to reach an Extreme Viking Hat (+15 Critical Hit, +10 Elemental Power). Exit the same way you came in.

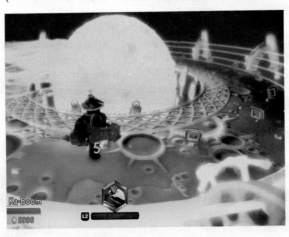

FIGURE 8.57

Fancy a walk around the sun? Just be careful not to get sunburned!

Back in **Sub-Orbital Combat Plaza**, hop the fence to the right of the Mabu to ride a super bounce pad up to reach a **Story Scroll**. Back on the main deck below, there's one more robot taxi to ride. Let's go!

Containment Corner & An Inconvenience of Imps

On the platform, you'll find a Villain Quest for Wolfgang called An Inconvenience of Imps. If this is your first time through, you may not have him yet (you'll capture him in this chapter). If you do have him already, then let's take a look. Q.U.I.G.L.E.Y. is worried about the overpopulation of Imps. Destroy the blue grain bags they feed from to capture their attention and lead them to the vacuum suction tube. Play Wolfgang's music—they'll be sucked right up. Your reward is a Tin Foil Hat (+10 Armor, +15 Elemental Power).

Back on the **Containment Corner** platform is a Traptanium Crystal to smash, which reveals a bridge. Cross over to find another two crystals to smash (and bridges) both leading to a larger platform with a hologram of Wolfgang. Grab the metal bridge at the end and lay it down at the mark off the middle platform to score a **Treasure Chest**. Cross back (pick up your metal bridge) and return to the first platform, where there's a place to lay the bridge opposite Q.U.I.G.L.E.Y. From here, you can super-bounce to reach a **Legendary Rocket** for your collection. Brilliant effort! Another super bounce pad will take you back to Q.U.I.G.L.E.Y.

Your last stop here is the robot taxi to the left of Q.U.I.G.L.E.Y., who will return you to Sub-Orbital Combat Plaza.

Anti-Grav Truck & Space Dog Field

Catch a lift in the yellow Anti-Grav truck parked on the other side of the plaza, with a Mabu called Snuckles X9. He'll take you to meet the undercover operative in the great resistance fight against Wolfgang. When the platform is caught up in a grabber beam, you need to knock the blocks off the side of the platform, so shift and shoot the cannon at the two yellow arrows to knock the grabbers off. Keep moving to reach Space Dog Field, where Persephone is trapped behind an electric field (the switch is on the opposite wall under the ramp). Cyclops Spinners and Future Brawlruses, then a mutated Chompy, attack you. If you can double-up with a second player, you'll defeat them quickly. Switch off the barrier so Persephone is free to upgrade you if you're ready.

It's time to track down that musical mischief-maker, Wolfgang. Follow Zeta Blobbers up the ramp to your left. When you pass the Future **Troll Radio** and reach another electric fence, jump over the right-side railing to score a **Villain Stash** and switch the barrier off. Run past the barrier, but wait—oh, no! You've been caught in the Atom Smasher!

Subatomic Particle Smasher & Planet Ham

Avoid or destroy the floating atoms as they drop into the smasher while Zeta Blobbers runs for help. Switch to your villain to avoid some damage when the going gets tough. After a while, an electric field drops, and you can bounce out to safety.

Before you follow Zeta Blobbers, push the double-stacked blocks to his right, over to the left where he stands, to fill the gap in the stairs leading to a platform above him (see Figure 8.58). There's a **Winged Sapphire** up there!

More block shifting—knock the blocks to your right now over the edge to create a little bridge between platforms. Push a third block straight across the bridge to the back of the second platform to make a step. Climb up to reach a **Treasure Chest** and some food on **Planet Ham**.

FIGURE 8.58

Make sure you shift the double block to the left first to collect the Winged Sapphire. Then right off the edge of the platform to create a path to Planet Ham.

Harmonic Hold

Zeta Blobbers directs you to a new atom smasher called Harmonic Hold. There's another hologram of Wolfgang and some enemies to fight—Cyclops Spinners and a Blaster-Tron. The aim here is to find the blueprints of the Big Bad Woofer to identify its weak points for destruction. Smash the Traptanium Crystal to the right of the battle gate. Dash over to meet your ultimate robotic opponent, Blaster-Tron! Take out his Future Brawlruses and attack him from the back to capture him in a Light Trap.

Cross the central metal bridge for a game of **Skystones Smash** with Gumbus the 10,000th. Cross back (carry and reuse the metal bridge) to reach a **Troll Radio** on the left-side platform, which leads to another hologram of Wolfgang next to a **Soul Gem** for Trailblazer. It's battle time again back on the main platform at Harmonic Hold. Defeat the enemies to drop the battle gate, and follows Zeta Blobbers to reach the blueprints. Carry the metal bridge over to the blueprints. The loudest music concert in Skylands history is about to go down—quick! Escape into the spaceship with Zeta Blobbers and use the turrets to blow up every hexagonal force field surrounding the Subwoofer Ship. (You earn a **Just to Be Safe** trophy for your effort!) Bombs will come at you, so just keep shooting to clear them, too.

The doors will open to reveal more conduits to shoot. This is tough work! A robot is creating a new force field from the inside, so as soon as you've cleared the space in front of the main conduit, reverse your direction and blow it up.

Battle with Wolfgang!
Uh, oh! Wolfgang is furious! This is the big villain fight to end them all (see Figure 8.59). His dangerous music notes will attack first—if you can fly you'll be spared these nasty little health-stealers. Each time Wolfgang attacks, he needs a moment of recovery, so get in quick with your attack. Keep it up—he has a lot of health to wear down. You'll switch to a narrow platform fairly soon, where there's less room to move. While he's near you, attack as much as possible. Soon he'll attack you from a platform above where you can't reach.

FIGURE 8.59

Wolfgang has a huge amount of health to use. Keep your attacks constant to wear him down.

Next up, lasers shoot down onto the platform, which are pretty hard to dodge. While they are thin lasers, you're safe, but as they transform into thick lasers, they cause big health loss. Make sure you swap in to your indestructible villain to share the damage. Wolfgang is nearly at his damage limit now, so put in that last ditch effort toward victory! Trap him in an Undead Trap. Awesome work, Skylander. That was tricky! You definitely deserve a break.

Chapter 14: Operation: Troll Rocket Steal

Miserable Glumshanks is still a slave for the Golden Queen. He accepts a special delivery from the future—terrible-smelling cheese that will doom Skylands. The Golden Queen is dishing out rules for all Skylanders, and if they don't comply, she'll shrink the towns and trap them in a glass ball! Worst of all, the Trolls have a rocket and are making evil plans. This Story Chapter requires military precision to seek out and claim the Kepi, Nurse, Sunday, and Cubano Hats (see Figure 8.60), a Legendary Parachuting Mabu Statue, and Soul Gems for Cobra-Cadabra and Enigma. Skylanders at Attention!

FIGURE 8.60

Gather these collectibles as you steal the rocket back from the Trolls and capture Grinnade and Threatpack.

TIP

Be Prepared!

Have Bone Chompy (Undead) and Krankenstein (Air) in traps ready for their Villain Quests. Bone Chompy won't be captured until The Golden Desert, so unless you've played through before, you'll need to replay this chapter later to evolve him.

Mabu Main Base & Paging Dr. Bone Chompy

Before you even get started, Buzz is at the soldier tent, ready to take Bone Chompy on a Villain Quest (called Paging Dr. Bone Chompy). If this is your first run-through, you won't have captured him yet (he's in Story Chapter 16), but if you already have him trapped, go right ahead. You are rewarded for your help with a Nurse Hat (+30 Armor). A few steps down the path is a Troll Radio (guarded by Trolls!), and at the end of this path is Snuckles in a cage. When the nearby Trolls have been defeated, his cage will open.

Crawler Canyon
Back up a bit and take the right path to find an Earth Gate called Crawler Canyon (see Figure 8.61). Glowing Traptanium plates are being carried around a dirt mound by little spider—type insects, but with only four legs! You have to time this challenge well to succeed—if you get knocked off, you have to start again! The platforms come from alternating sides—right, then left, the right again, and so on—so stay focused. Wait right in the middle of the plate and jump onto progressively higher plates until you reach the top of the mound to claim a Monday Hat (+10 Critical Hit, +10 Elemental Power).

FIGURE 8.61

The creepy crawlies in Crawler Canyon scuttle in opposite directions. Choose a Skylander with fast speed to conquer this quest.

Back outside at **Mabu Main Base**, dash up the right-side path to find a **Villain Quest** for Krankenstein called **Onward Wilikin Soldiers**. Wooster just wants to chat with Kranky in a secret language, and then—Bam!—he's evolved. Super easy! You earn a **Kepi Hat** (+25 Critical Hit) for your troubles.

Head back down the hill to **Mabu Base Entrance** and past Snuckles (who is now free). Tortellinas explains how a Health Regenifier works (stand on top and mash it) to increase your health when you're low. There are a handful of these around the battlements in this chapter, so whenever you see one, jump on to fill up your health bar.

Smash a few Trolls to free Nort from his cage; then grab the bomb from the platform just near Tortellinas. Throw it at the gate to bring it down. Some more Trolls will escape, so deal with them too. You'll find stone entrances on either side of the gate. You'll explore these now.

Southwest Tower & Southeast Tower   Take a bomb with

you into the left entrance (Southwest Tower) to blow up the internal gate, earning a Winged Sapphire. The right-side entrance (Southeast Tower) has a lock puzzle with a Treasure Chest behind it.

Battlements & Troll Firing Range   Through the bombed

gate is the Battlements area, which has another Lock Puzzle to crack to get through a second battle gate.

As soon as the battle gate drops, Trolls swarm in. Defeating them frees Rizzo, who explains that you need to reach the recharger to get the bomb machine working. The Mabu soldiers build some steps on either side of the road for you (see Figure 8.62). Climb up to the right to reach a Health Regenifier (mash!) and Traptanium Crystal up on **Troll Firing Range**. Smash it up for a **Treasure Chest** reward.

FIGURE 8.62

Free the captive Mabu soldiers so they can build steps to reach rewards and help you fight.

Tank Factory, Factory Power Plant, & Factory Storage

Take the left steps to meet Rizzo for a jumping game to wind down the fan so that you can reach the Tank Factory. There's a Tech Gate here to explore called Factory Power Plant. This challenge is a lot trickier than it looks! You have to be really quick and focused with your jumps to make it across to the Cubano Hat (+7 Speed, +7 Elemental Power). There are two spinning platforms—jump from the lower one to the higher one and then straight back over the other side before boxes slide in and squash you.

Back outside the gate, run to the left of the new stairs (up the ramp) to discover a **Treasure Chest** and a **Soul Gem** for Cobra Cadabra in **Factory Storage**.

Okay, so you still have a battle gate to destroy out in the Battlements area, so grab a bomb and blow it up. Watch out! A group of Trolls have been waiting for this opportunity! Rizzo shows you a catapult you can use to parachute Mabu soldiers into the fight. Destroy the enemies blocking your path, only to find another Lock Puzzle on the gate!

Troll Base Entrance, Northeast Tower, & Northwest Tower

As soon as the battle gate drops, another fight begins. There's a little stone platform to the right of the Health Regenifier. Dash up to claim the Legendary Parachuting Mabu Statue. Fight your way into Troll Main Base, where there are heaps of challenges. There are entrances on either side of the battle gates. There is another Lock Puzzle required to reach the Northeast Tower. Inside, you'll find a treasure stash. Northwest Tower has some more loot.

Troll Main Base & Troll Weapons Lab

Battle time! You can see these guys coming through the gate, but don't be intimidated—you have a platoon of Mabu soldiers at your side (see Figure 8.63). Trolls, Trolls, and more Trolls! Smash through two sets of wooden gates on the left to reach the Troll Weapons Lab cave with a nasty surprise inside—the villain Grinnade! A heavy melee attack will take him down quickly—just keep clear of his bombs if you're standing up front.

FIGURE 8.63

Hordes of enemy Trolls attack, but you're not alone—the Mabu soldiers are on your side.

Head to the right when you leave Grinnade's hideout to a small platform with a **Story Scroll** floating next to a Mabu; then hop on the teleport pad for a quick trip across the battle field to a **Soul Gem** for Enigma.

Mech Factory & Mission Con-Troll
Back down the main path, the house on the right fork is called the Mech Factory. There is a Troll here waiting to shoot at you with his robotic walking tank (see Figure 8.64). You'll get a bit of treasure when you destroy him. Through the main battle gate you go, to an arena battle! The crazy Professor Nilbog (aka Threatpack!) is pretty cranky that you want to steal his (stolen) rocket. He employs all of his evil minions to stop you reaching it.

Grinnades and Trolls attack you in groups—this is an epic melee battle with lots of room to move, so make the most of it! (You also want to impress your audience of Mabu soldiers watching from the sidelines, don't you?) Keep an eye on the yellow skull hatches on the back wall. When they lift up, a stream of fire bursts out. Dodge the bombs when some Lob Goblins appear, but your main opponent is Threatpack. He shoots scores of bombs at once, with small red circles on the ground where they will land. Go hard with your attacks, and you'll wear his health down quickly. Your success means you've saved the rocket from the evil Trolls! Next up, you battle the Air Pirates in Skyhighlands!

FIGURE 8.64

Beware the shooting flames in this arena battle as Threatpack and his minions attack you!

Chapter 15: Skyhighlands

Those miserable Air Pirates are causing havoc in Skyhighlands. Teach them a lesson they won't forget while you race to claim the Prism before Hawkmongous (soon to become the terrible Tae Kwon Crow!) reaches it first. Find the right gear to claim a Soul Gem for Blastermind and uncover the Legendary Geode Key to open the Crystal Caverns back in the kitchens of Skylanders Academy (see Figure 8.65). Fight pirate henchmen and scallywags to earn two new hats (the Radar and William Tell Hats).

FIGURE 8.65

Gather these collectibles as you explore Skyhighlands and capture Tae Kwon Crow.

TIP

Be Prepared!

Have Threatpack (Water) and Grinnade (Fire) in traps ready for their Villain Quests.

Defend the Dread-Yacht

What a start! You're piloting the fighter ship! Shoot at incoming pirate ships that will try to destroy you and Flynn's ship (see Figure 8.66). If you need a boost of health, fly close to Flynn's ship and through the yellow heart shape above it. When Mags joins in, zoom over her ship to collect a rocket and—Boom!—shoot it at the enemy ship. Your aim is to destroy 30 airships. If you can do it with cannons only, you'll be rewarded with a Look Ma, No Rockets! trophy.

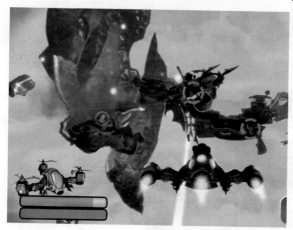

FIGURE 8.66

Line up your pointer with the red target on enemy ships. This is a bit easier in single-player mode.

Landing Platforms & You Break It, You Fix It

As soon as you hit the Landing Platforms, you'll see a Story Scroll on the left platform. Tessa lands nearby on her giant bird. She has a Villain Quest called You Break It, You Fix It for Threatpack. A cannon needs fixing, but you don't have to do anything. From now on, each time you use a turret, you'll be given homing rockets instead of standard rockets, as long as Threatpack's trap is in your portal. Awesome! As you explore this chapter, you'll see some large, purple crystal blobs around. Smash or blow them up for hidden treasure.

Stolen Property Room

Dash up the ramp to dive into a quick melee fight with some Buzzer Beaks. On the left of a locked gate is a little round house; duck inside for a look. This is the Stolen Property Room. (Troll Radio alert!) Some feathered fiends will attack you straight up. Shift the boxes at the back of the room to reach a golden key and carry it outside to the locked gate. A few more feathered pirates attack, along with a Bad Juju. Destroy them—but beware, the great Hawkmongous is itching for a fight. Luckily, he settles for a game of Skystones Smash. Beat him to get past.

Lower Defenses, Lower Elevator, & Digger's Dungeon

Tessa flies past the top platform with enemy pirate ships on her tail. Settle yourself in the turret to shoot them down (see Figure 8.67). Remember—if you did Threatpack's Villain Quest, you have homing rockets now! Shoot as many pirate ships as you can (and a couple of gems) to make Tessa safe. Once you're done, hop out and go through the now opened gate to the Lower Elevator.

Just use that cannon over there to blast them into next week. Or next month even.

Quest Discovered: Miner Troubles II

FIGURE 8.67

Help Tessa escape the enemy pirate ships to access the elevator gears.

Digger's Dungeon & Miner Troubles II

There's a big gear on the ground that you can run on (follow the arrows' direction). Nearly at the top (not quite), to the left, you'll be able to access Digger's Dungeon. This is a small room with treasure and a Villain Stash. Diggs has a Villain Quest for Grinnade (called Miner Troubles II). All he has to do is bomb some ore and—Zap!—he's evolved. That was an easy one.

Middle Defenses

Up high, at the very top of the gear (to the right of Digger's Dungeon) is another ramp. Hop off the gear and run down to Middle Defenses. A Cuckoo Clocker meets you at the top platform with an iron fist. Flynn needs some more help with a turret. Shoot down Air Pirates (and three gems) to move on. If you don't reach your target, you'll play the turret again. As soon as you reach your target, a gate will open on the platform. Dash up the steps to meet Hawkmongous for another angry game of Skystones Smash. Beat him to score a Legendary Geode Key on the top platform (see Figure 8.68). Great effort, Skylander!

Upper Elevator

At the top of the stairs is another giant gear. Jump on and run to raise it to reach a platform midway that has a Soul Gem for Blastermind. Explore the little door to the left. It's a little room called the Greenhouse. There's a Life Gate in here (see Figure 8.69). Just shift the two blocks so one can move across the ground to drop into a hole near the green metal ramp; then use it as a step. Your reward is a William Tell Hat (+25 Critical Hit), which looks good enough to eat.

FIGURE 8.68

Grab a glittering geode in Middle Defenses.

FIGURE 8.69

Opening the Life Gate is the only way to reach boxes that you must shift to jump to the Hat Box.

The Waterworks

At the very top of the giant gear, jump onto the platform with The Water Gate. Inside The Waterworks, shown in Figure 8.70, is a little old shack with a Treasure Chest and a Hat Box. There's a trick to reaching the Hat Box, though. Run up the steps around the inside wall, standing on the button to release more water into the room. A box will float up, creating a new step on your path—continue along the stairs, using an elevator block to get up higher. There's another button to stand on that will add more water to fill the room. Keep climbing higher and pressing buttons. By the time you reach the top, the room will be flooded and a ramp will extend to the middle so you can claim a Radar Hat (+5 Critical Hit, +15 Armor). Run across the opposite ramp and press the button to drain the room, and then jump down to exit.

FIGURE 8.70

Climb ramps to flood the tunnel with water and claim a floating Hat Box at The Waterworks.

Upper Defenses & Lost and Found

To reach this area, jump on the small gear near the Water Gate and ride it up high to the Wooden Stairs. Villains are waiting for a quick melee. Next, visit the small door in the circular house. In this room (Lost and Found) is a Winged Sapphire, a Traptanium Crystal, and some gold. Smash the crystal and drop into a pit to claim a Treasure Chest. Bounce back out for some more fun with a turret.

Cutting Platform

Climb up to the highest platform you can see because... it's BIG battle time! Hawkmongous is really angry now! He hates to be disturbed when he's using his special prisms for evil, especially by Skylanders. Hang on, he's not Hawkmongous anymore. He's TAE KWON CROW! Prepare for a fight (see Figure 8.71)!

FIGURE 8.71

Defeat enemies to claim the magic prism—it will point the way to the evil Golden Queen!

Buzzer Beaks attack you first, closely followed by a Bad Juju. Pirate Henchman drop from the sky, so fight back as hard as you can. There aren't too many at once, but the white prisms on the side of the arena shoot beams of light at you to cause damage. Keep an eye on them and dodge the incoming light when they begin to glow. Tae Kwon Crow is a worthy enemy; he springs around the room with ninja moves, reappearing in another spot. Keep smashing him as often as you can catch him to wear down his health. It won't be long until you win! Congratulations, Skylander. With this prism, you'll soon find out where the Golden Queen's evil lair is and track her down. Now it's back to Skylanders Academy for some more exploring.

Chapter 16: The Golden Desert

In this chapter, you're on the hunt for the Golden Queen. Cali has found a way into her temple, but the Golden Queen is guarded by huge, leaping, slithering Chompy Worms! This might get dangerous Skylander—hope you're ready for some serious sand fighting! Sift through the ruins to find a Legendary Dragon Head, the Desert Crown and Batter Up Hats, and a Soul Gem for Tuff Luck (see Figure 8.72). Be warned, though, Cali may not come out of this fight looking quite the same!

FIGURE 8.72

Gather these collectibles as you explore The Golden Desert and capture Grave Clobber and the Bone Chompy.

TIP

Be Prepared!

Have Blaster-Tron (Light) and Tae Kwon Crow (Dark) in traps ready for their Villain Quests.

X's Shifting Sands
Old Diggs is waiting on a giant rock near your starting place with a Villain Quest for Blaster-Tron called Help Diggs Dig. Switch in your Light Trap to let Blaster-Tron pull treasure up out of the ground (and keep it)! On the top of the opposite rock is a Story Scroll. (Gee, that Flynn is a handsome fella!) Okay, ready for a super bounce? Let's go!

A couple of Bone Chompies come snapping as soon as you land. There's plenty of room here, so take them out and head to the right-side rocks where Tessa has a **Villain Quest** for Tae Kwon Crow (called **Gopher the Gold**). You captured him in the last chapter in a dark trap. For this quest, Tae Kwon Crow needs to attack the Hazard Birds that are trying to steal and eat gophers (see Figure 8.73). Meanwhile, Tessa is busy trying to find one golden gopher in each of four colonies and tag them. You'll bounce between colonies as the timer counts down from ten minutes. Your health will decrease as the Hazard Birds steal gophers, so keep an eye on the health bar and attack birds that eat gophers as quickly as you can. This one is tricky!

FIGURE 8.73

Attack the Hazard Birds before they run off with gophers in Tae Kwon Crow's Villain Quest.

Back in **X's Shifting Sands**, a huge grave block opens up on the main battle area and some Grave Clobbers emerge to fight you (see Figure 8.74). Bone Chompies join in, but there aren't many enemies here. Smash up the grave stone to prevent any more from climbing out. They are pretty easy to defeat, so you'll have the battle gate button uncovered quickly. Super-bounce over to Cali on the next platform.

FIGURE 8.74

Grave Clobbers and Bone Chompies rise from the Undead to attack you.

Dust Bowl   The Dust Bowl is infested with a giant Chompy Worm! Cali will clear a path so you can cross safely, but you need to make good use of the catapult on the side of the platform while she does. Jump on that turret and spin it around to shoot the Chompy Worm every time it surfaces (see Figure 8.75). Each time it dives back under the sand, aim at the cactus trees to leave behind a trail of jewels. If you shoot ten cacti, you can earn a Garden Gladiator Achievement. Soon enough, the Chompy Worm has enough fighting and flies away, leaving you to dash around, collecting your new treasures.

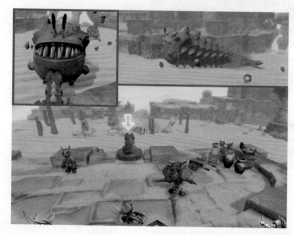

FIGURE 8.75

Argh! Watch out for the Chompy Worm. He's getting closer and closer!

On the far left of the field, drop off onto a ledge to recover a **Legendary Dragon Head**. Super-bounce back to the main area to find a switch against the back-left rocks. This activates some dynamite to blow up the rocks that are blocking a super bounce pad near Cali.

Take a flying leap to the entrance area of a temple. A Grave Clobber is your main adversary here. These guys are slow but really powerful, so keep out of their reach. One good clobber with their arm will take your Skylander out of the game. A long-ranged attack will help, unless you have a super-quick Skylander who can attack him from behind. A troop of Shield Skeletons with bombs join in. Melee combat will take them down easily (see Figure 8.76).

Next, the doors of the temple open to release the **Bone Chompy**! This little biter is fast and very persistent! Get rid of any other enemies first; then wear him down and trap him in an Undead Trap. A super bounce pad appears under the battle gate button.

FIGURE 8.76

Look for hidden treasures around the Temple of Topaz before you shift blocks to extend the ramp.

The Temple of Topaz

Cali needs your help again. Shoot cactus balls out of the cannon at the charging Chompy Worm. There are Masker Mind Bomb Shells throwing explosives at you, so whenever the Chompy Worm goes underground, aim at these bad guys instead. Like before, the Chompy Worm will fly away when you've caused enough damage to it. Brilliant work. You've successfully cleared out all the Chompy Worms!

There are plenty of jewels to collect on the playing field, as well as two Traptanium Crystals to smash. The left crystals just hide jewels, and the right will create a series of Traptanium bridges leading to a **Soul Gem** for Tuff Luck. Super-bounce back to Cali.

Now flick the switch to blow up the rocks blocking your entrance into the temple. (**Troll Radio** alert!) Claim the **Winged Sapphire** on the right side of the wall and then shift the directional blocks around the floor to drop them into the three holes to create steps. On each of the three platforms is a gold button. Climb up and jump, jump, jump! A ramp will extend so you can enter the temple.

The Howling Caverns & Hole in the Wall

This big battle room is full of treasure and enemies. Shielded Skeletons and a Grave Clobber attack you first. Attack the Grave Clobber from behind if you can—use speed to your advantage. Chef Pepper Jack and Short Cut both do really well in this area. Two bounce pads are uncovered when all of the enemies are defeated.

The left-side bounce pad leads to an alcove on a higher platform called **Hole in the Wall**. Floor spikes prevent you from reaching a **Treasure Chest**. Just time your run across the floor as they drop and rise to claim it. **Persephone** is waiting on a ledge to your left. Use the right-side bounce pad to reach a higher ledge with a Lock Puzzle blocking a door.

The Earthen Alcove

Enter the Golden Springs and head straight for the Earth Gate (The Earthen Alcove). First claim the Desert Crown Hat (+27 Elemental Power) on the floor. Now shift the blocks left and then back to create stairs to reach some extra treasure.

The Golden Springs

Move the block in the center of the room and flick the switch next to it. Flick the second switch twice (wait for the electric pulse) to create a laser that breaks down the blocked wall. Run up the uncovered steps to find a new Lock Puzzle gate on your left.

The Howling Caverns

Enter this new area to smash a Traptanium Crystal with a Treasure Chest underneath. The path on the right leads to a stone entrance called The Howling Caverns. Take it slow, though—wherever you see holes in the floor, spiked spears shoot up from the ground as you pass through. There's a Villain Stash to your right on the lowest level. Watch your back—Shielded Skeletons are headed your way.

There are two other exits in this room, so be careful which one you choose.

The Windy Watch

At the left of the lowest level down the ramp is an open doorway leading to a single platform that is part of The Golden Springs. Let's explore this first. Ribz the Skeleton wants to play Skystones Smash out here. Next, enter the Air Gate (The Windy Watch). Ride the balloons across to the furthest floating platform to reach a Batter Up Hat (+15 Critical Hit, +12 Armor). Jump your way back to the Golden Springs and take the stairs again to reach the Villain Stash.

The Windy Heights

The exit closest to the Villain Stash will take you back to the Temple of Topaz. If you leave through this door, you're heading for the end of the game, so make sure you've already covered all other areas. As soon as you get through the door, explore left to find another Treasure Chest. Off the ledge here (straight across from the door) are a series of islands called The Windy Heights. Make your way across by placing bridges between them. There are three types of bridges: metal, bamboo, and wood; you can tell which kind is required by the attachment points. Plan ahead to make sure you carry the correct bridge for your next crossing (see Figure 8.77). Begin by heading to the far left and then work your way toward the Coliseum, then right toward The Windy Watch again. From there, head in a straight line back to reach the Coliseum.

FIGURE 8.77

Carry and place the wooden, bamboo, and metal bridges to create a path to the Jeweled Coliseum.

The Jeweled Coliseum   The epic, final battle is here! Evil Golden Queen has turned our beloved Cali into a golden statue, and you must fight to get her back (see Figure 8.78). Cheering skeletons watch from the arena walls. Waves of Shielded Skeletons attack first (only a few at a time) and then a Bad Juju comes to stir things up. The giant Golden Queen shoots a laser beam onto the arena floor every so often, so keep out of the way. Occasionally a bomb appears in the red and green targets on the ground. Stand in the target and interact with it to pick it up. Throw the bombs at the stone pillars under Cali one at a time as you fight (they will appear white when ready to hit). When all three pillars are broken, the whole thing will come tumbling down and the fight is over.

FIGURE 8.78

There are plenty of enemies to battle in the Jeweled Coliseum, including a giant Chompy head, Shielded Skeletons, Bone Chompies, and Grave Clobber.

In the meantime, Bone Chompies swarm in to nip at your heels, so this is a great opportunity for a hand-to-hand fight. If you have an adventure pack magic item to add extra damage to your attacks, this is a fun place to use it. A giant tombstone appears in the middle of the arena to release **Grave Clobber**. He's tough to take down, but he's a slow mover, so get behind him and attack as soon as he hits the ground.

When you've managed to break the stone pillars holding golden Cali, head back to Skylands to see if Mags can work her magic. Your battle with the Golden Queen (see Figure 8.79) may have hit a bump in the road, but it's definitely not over!

FIGURE 8.79

The Golden Queen is *very* unhappy that you beat her minions in the Jeweled Coliseum. Watch out!

Chapter 17: Lair of the Golden Queen

Prepare yourself for the ultimate battle, Skylander! The evil Golden Queen is out for revenge, and it's up to you to track down her lair and defeat her at her own game. Bad Juju will try to put an end to your meddling with her magical whirlwind, so you must defeat her to move onto the biggest fight so far! Claim your Legendary Hippo Head, a Soul Gem for Short Cut, and three odd-looking hats: the Crazy Light Bulb Hat, a Beetle Hat, and the Classic Pot Hat (see Figure 8.80). Watch your step, Skylander—all that glitters is not gold within this dangerous temple! (Well actually it *is* gold, but not in a pretty way—more like a *run-for-your-life* kind of way!) Ready, set, GOLD!

FIGURE 8.80

Gather these collectibles as you explore the Lair of the Golden Queen and capture Bad Juju and the Golden Queen.

> ## TIP
>
> **Be Prepared!**
>
> Have Grave Clobber (Earth) and Bad Juju (Air) in traps ready for their Villain Quests. If you haven't played before, you'll have to come back and revisit Bad Juju's quest after you capture her in this chapter.

Tomb of the Forgotten Queen

Troll Radio alert! In this first area, there are white beams surrounded by blocks near Cali. Your job is to shift the blocks so that the beams can meet the crystal on the wall. Flick a switch near the crystal (twice), and a block will drop, creating a doorway. Run through and turn left to cross the bridges.

The Halls of Treachery & Cradle of the Four Winds

Shielded Skeletons come running toward you as soon as you enter this arena. A Bad Juju comes in when they are nearly gone. Stand inside the green target on the floor to catch a bomb and then use it to throw at your enemies. Defeat them all to drop a battle gate to your right. Don't go there yet! First, stay to visit the Air Gate (Cradle of the Four Winds) on your left. Although it seems pretty straightforward, this challenge is quite tricky! Whirlwinds come along the path in groups, so you have to run through the spaces that aren't affected, as fast as you possibly can, to reach the end of the hall. If you have a Winged Boots magic item from another Skylanders game, it will come in handy to speed you up. Try moving along the outside edge of the hallway to reach the Hat Box. You'll earn a Classic Pot Hat (+30 Armor). A teleport pad will take you back to the gate entrance.

The Darkest Reach & Remote Location

Try to cross the bridge to the right of the Air Gate. Again, you have to be really fast. Wherever you see an X on the stone, jump past as fast as you can. If it breaks, you'll fall down to the creepy-crawlies of The Darkest Reach. In the sludge under the bridge is a Villain Stash to claim, but first you'll need to defend yourself from the Skeletal Dragon and his minions of flying eyeballs that attack you. Mut challenges you to a game of Skystones Smash. You'll have to defeat him to teleport back to The Halls of Treachery, where you can run through again.

Once you've made your way back to the bridge and crossed (don't fall again!), Glumshanks has a **Villain Quest** for Bad Juju called **Remote Location**. You will defeat Bad Juju later in this chapter, but if you've already been through, have a go at her quest now. Glumshanks asks Bad Juju to create a tornado in the pit to retrieve a spare remote for the Ultimate Weapon that he dropped. You don't have to do anything here, but your reward for turning up to the party is a Beetle Hat (+30 Armor) as well as an upgrade. Too easy!

There's a blue circle on the floor in the corner; if you have a *Skylanders Giants* character, swap him or her in to jump on it. Coins will fall out of the holes in the walls surrounding the blue circle.

To the left of Glumshanks is a Traptanium Crystal. Smash it to gain access to the left-side ledge; then jump down and shift the box into the middle section to use as a step to jump from the left ledge to the right, where there's a **Soul Gem** for Short Cut.

There's another bridge ahead with "X" stones on it that can fall away, but this time, there are spiked stones as well. Try to avoid the tiles with holes in them in case they spear you as you run past (see Figure 8.81). Be quick! There's a secret path in the next section (with Legendary Treasure inside), but you won't uncover it unless you step on every stone of the bridge.

FIGURE 8.81

The bridges have combinations of different stones; some with holes (spikes!), "X" marks (crumble), green pluses (restore health), gold lines (decrease health), circles (coins), and blue dots (increase XP).

The Secret Vault
On the other side of this bridge, blocks are in the way of an electric pulse. Shift the blocks so that the laser lines meet; then flick the switch in the corner of the floor (twice) to turn it off. A door will open up in the wall.

Before you enter, check the back wall for a hidden path. (This will only be accessible if you touched every stone on the last bridge.) Claim the **Legendary Hippo Head** from this area. Then, return to your new door in the wall.

There's another, larger bridge of faulty stones to cross here, with two aims. First, you need to collect the key from the back left of the area. You can use the key for only one of two nearby gates—one leads to a Winged Sapphire, and the other gate to a Treasure Chest. Each play of the chapter will allow you to use the key once, so you have to choose. If you use it to unlock the nearby gate, you'll get a **Winged Sapphire** reward. Make your way across to the other side. On your second trip through this area, grab that key again, and continue to carry it through to the door on the other side of this bridge (**Parade of Broken Soldiers**) to claim the **Treasure Chest** instead.

The Parade of Broken Soldiers

Inside this room, there are lots of blocks to push into the empty space between them. They'll form a new path that you can use to reach a high ledge that runs the back of the room. Follow it along, taking care to keep out of the spotlight shining down from the golden Spy Guys (see Figure 8.82). If you get caught, you'll begin this section again. Straight down this path is a lowered room with a Treasure Chest on a ledge at the back. Again, shift the boxes around to create a straight ramp that you can jump across to reach the ledge.

FIGURE 8.82

Don't get caught in the Spy Guys spotlight! Attack the pillars on the edge of the path to crush them.

Let's keep moving. The path to the right leads you past another couple of Spy Guys. A red and green target mark will appear on the floor every so often, stand inside to grab the bomb that drops. Blow up the stone statues beside the Spy Guys to knock them out so you can pass by.

Where Is Flynn?

Straight ahead, Cali is waiting with a Villain Quest for Grave Clobber (Where is Flynn?) Flynn has been captured by the Golden Queen's guards. You have ten minutes to run through a labyrinth (again, if you have a winged boot, use it here) to activate three blue buttons that will lower the spiked barriers in front of Flynn. In each section, all kinds of crazy villains will attack you. Don't stay to fight them unless they get in your way—just keep searching for buttons and teleport pads. Smash through rock walls if you are trapped. When you're done, teleport to Flynn and bomb the gate holding him captive.

Brilliant work, Skylander! Now, return to Cali in **The Parade of Broken Soldiers**.

Near Cali is a Traptanium Crystal with a golden key underneath. This will open one lock of the double-locked gate to its right. The first key (which you may have used on the first bridge to claim a Winged Sapphire) can only be used once for this story chapter. Next time you play this chapter, use the original key to open this gate, to score a **Treasure Chest**.

Continue down the side path, avoiding the Spy Guy's spotlight. A battle is heading your way again! Gravestones appear to release Shielded Skeletons into the room, followed by a Skeletal Dragon. If you catch a bomb, throw it at the open gravestones to stop enemies from crawling out. **Bad Juju** joins the fight. It's not too hard to take her out—just stay on her as you engage in melee combat. As soon as she's trapped, you can use her to continue the fight as the waves of enemies keep coming. As soon as you win, Nut the Mabu challenges you for a game of Skystones Smash. When you beat him, the battle gate drops.

The Seat of Flowing Gold & The Evershifting Abyss

Go through the doorway to enter The Seat of Flowing Gold. There are two paths you can choose to get to the same area. On the left path, another challenging bridge is ahead of you. If you make it across without falling, you'll earn a Highwire Act trophy. If you would rather take the right path, a Lock Puzzle awaits. Here, you'll score a Story Scroll just inside the gate.

Across the stone bridge to the left is a **Magic Gate** called **The Evershifting Abyss** (see Figure 8.83). This is another tricky bridge with the usual heart stones (which increase your health) and X stones (they will crack), but with some new helpful stones, too. The circle engraving releases coins as you step on it, and the stones with three blue dots increase your experience level. Unfortunately, the symbols change constantly, so be as fast as you can. There's a **Treasure Chest** waiting on the other side for you, and a Crazy Light Bulb Hat (+12 Speed).

FIGURE 8.83

Cross an ever-shifting bridge to reach a Magic Gate and continue your journey to the Golden Queen.

Head left from the Magic Gate to cross the bridge. There's a long staircase to the left that leads to your final battle with the Golden Queen. Don't go there yet; you'll come back. First, continue along the hallway to reach the **Story Scroll** that was on the other side of the Lock Puzzle, for those who chose the left path.

Right—it's battle time! The Golden Queen is ready to fight at the top of those stairs you passed. You will pass through the **Heart of Gold** as you climb the flight of stairs.

The Temple of the Divine Treasure

In the first part of this fight, our nasty villain sends golden shockwave rings that you can jump (or fly) over to survive. Attack the Golden Queen any which way you can, and collect the gold rings that fall off her to keep her from re-boosting her own health. When she begins to fling blades at you, dodge them! Try not to get hit while you attack the wing statues. The next phase begins when the wings are all destroyed.

Your battle field will be made smaller and smaller as more shockwaves and blades come your way (see Figure 8.84). Jump to a new square if you see a red line on yours—it's an indication that your square is about to be cut away.

FIGURE 8.84

Waves of attacks make your battle arena smaller and more dangerous. Keep at it!

A damaging golden ball will fall on any square that has a red target on it, so keep moving and watch the floor. You have more blades and wings to deal with—attack as many wings as you can. A golden globe smashes into the battle and sends a shockwave through the tiles like a wave. You need to jump over this as it passes underneath you. The faster you can destroy all the wings while avoiding damage from the blades, the sooner this fight is over. Attack the Queen while her blades are gone; this is the only time she can take one-on-one damage. As her health decreases, the Golden Queen will chase you down the stairs you arrived on (see Figure 8.85). Destroy any barriers in your way to keep ahead of the Golden Queen. If you don't make it to the bottom of the stairs, she'll destroy you—but if you do, she'll get stuck in the archway. As soon as she's stuck, destroy those arches to finish her off. For completing this quest, you've earned a **Royal Flusher** achievement.

You have epic skills, Skylander—that was the hardest battle yet, and you won! Brilliant work! Let's get back to Skylander Academy to see what Kaos is up to.

FIGURE 8.85

An enormous Golden Queen drags herself down the stairs after you! Knock the arches down on either side to trap her and bring her down to size.

Chapter 18: The Ultimate Weapon

It's Kaos time! That sneaky little Portal Master has switched sides again and now he has the Ultimate Weapon at his disposal. Keep a look-out for the Legendary Weird Robot, a Soul Gem for Ka-Boom, and the Brain and Brainiac Hats (see Figure 8.86) as you scale epic machinery in your search for Kaos. The final battle is upon you, Skylander—find and defeat him to rid Skylands of evil once and for all!

FIGURE 8.86

Gather these collectibles as you search for the Ultimate Weapon and capture Smoke Scream and Kaos.

TIP

Be Prepared!

Have the Golden Queen (Earth) and Smoke Scream (Fire) in traps ready for their Villain Quests. If you haven't played before, you'll have to come back and revisit Smoke Scream's quest after you capture him in this chapter.

Loading Zone & Bank on This   Let's get going! To the

left of your starting place, Dr. Noobry has a Villain Quest for the Golden
Queen called Bank on This (see Figure 8.87). He has a new invention, the
Piggybank-o-matic 3001, which spits out golden treasure. She doesn't have
to do anything here, but you'll get a nice golden reward when she evolves.
Another Piggybank on the right side of the platform has more treasure for
you. You'll find these Piggybanks sitting in corners throughout this chapter—
only the Golden Queen can open them to collect the treasure, so keep her
handy. Head up the steps for a warning from Kaos and then super-bounce to
the Receiving Dock.

FIGURE 8.87

There are many
Piggybank-o-matic
3001 machines
throughout this
chapter—swap in the
Golden Queen to open
them.

Receiving Dock   There's a Dark Gate here called Power Re-Router.

Inside is a path (including a few places to jump a gap). A line of snake head
statues on either side shoot electric pulses across the path, which you have
to dodge. The reward platform on the other side holds a Brain Hat (+37
Elemental Power).

Back outside at the **Receiving Dock**, Kaos sets his minions onto you, mostly
Plant Warriors, which are easy to take down. Bounce up on your right to a
higher platform and walk through the door at the back.

Relay System & Matter Refactoring Room   This floor

has a group of intersecting pulse puzzles (see Figure 8.88). Switch every lever
to flip up a bridge, except the left side closest to the bridge.

A door will open to the **Matter Refactoring Room**. Take a leap over the platform where the coins are to a short melee with a Smoke Scream and some
Grinnades. Attack them to reveal a bounce pad under a battle gate button.
If you jump over the edge of the platform here, you'll drop a level to a hidden **Winged Sapphire**. Grab it, and bounce back up to where you battled the
Grinnades; then bounce again to reach a higher platform. Follow this platform along to a **Troll Radio**. Flick the switch at the far end of the platform to
set another Pulse Puzzle straight. A big wheel will turn above you with a platform on it; jump on and ride around once to collect the floating coins, and
then jump off when you reach the highest point. There's a **Piggybank** here

(swap in the Golden Queen) and at the far left of the platform is a **Treasure Chest**. In the center of the platform is a Lock Puzzle. This one gets trickier with each stage. Once you've cleared it (of course, you can!), a big red button is revealed on the floor in front of you (see Figure 8.89). Kaos warns you *not* to hit it. So, of course, you know what to do... **HIT IT!**

FIGURE 8.88

A series of pulse puzzles will open a door at the back of the chamber.

FIGURE 8.89

Jump on the red button! Collect nine coins as you plummet down to earn a *Do a Barrel Roll* trophy.

Repair Platform H & the Balloon Return

On the left end of this platform is a purple tube that will uncover a bounce pad for you. Before you bounce, head to the right end on the platform to find a Story Scroll and a Tech Gate called The Balloon Return (see Figure 8.90). Inside this gate, jump on the balloon and ride it across to a rotating platform. Ride the platform all the way around until you get to the bottom, and then jump off onto another balloon. It will take to the Legendary Weird Robot. Ride the balloon back to the rotating platform. This time, jump off to your right onto a new balloon and ride it across to a second rotating platform. Take a ride all the way around and then jump off to a new balloon on the right to reach a Brainiac Hat (+15 Critical Hit, +6 Speed). Ride the super bounce pad back to Repair Platform H.

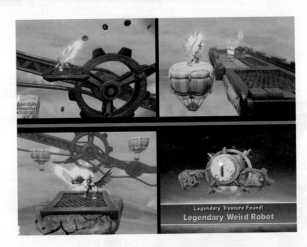

FIGURE 8.90

Jump your way to double prizes through the Tech Gate.

Okay, let's revisit the bounce pad you uncovered at the left end of the platform. You'll bounce down to a platform where another battle is brewing. Plant Warriors are the first to attack, followed by Grinnades and a Broccoli Guy. There's a door on the far end past the Broccoli Guy that will open when all enemies are defeated.

External Power Sorter & Fight Boom with Doom
Time to upgrade your Skylander? Persephone is waiting here for you on the outside ramps. To her right a little further down the ramp is a Treasure Chest. Make your way up the ramp. There are purple electric balls shooting between the mouths of snake-head statues—don't get hit! Flick the switches at the top of the ramp to connect the lasers. More ramps will fold down (Piggybank alert!), but watch out for the Raven Lobber hiding beneath a statue to the left of Buzz. Take him out and then dash over to chat with Buzz. He has a Villain Quest for Smoke Scream (Fight Doom with Boom). You haven't captured him yet in this chapter, so you'll need to replay to complete it. If you've been through before and have Smoke Scream already trapped, here's how it works: Just blow up the metal wall next to Buzz so he can get in to do some explosive circuitry and—ta-da!—you score a Treasure Chest for your efforts. Cross the new ramp to the gold and blue door.

Power Exhaust Ports
Battle time! You have lots of room to move as you fight Smoke Scream and his minion Plant Warriors. Even once Smoke Scream is captured (swap him in as your captured villain to make use of his powerful fire blast), you'll have Grinnades and a Broccoli Guy, a Hood Sickle, and lots of Raven Lobbers to contend with. A melee fight will take them down without too much trouble; just focus on the big guys first. It's one small step for Troll, one giant victory for Troll-kind! A new ramp extends to let you continue on your mission. Jump up the platforms (beware the electric balls between blocks!) to score a Soul Gem for Ka-Boom (see Figure 8.91). Continue jumping up the ramps (Piggybank alert!) until you reach a circular platform. Step on to be transported to The Grinder.

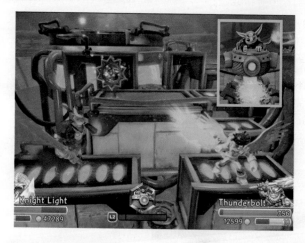

FIGURE 8.91

Battle Trolls and dodge electric balls to reach a Soul Gem for Ka-Boom.

The Grinder

Glumshanks is waiting to your left hoping to distract you with a game of Skystones Smash. There's another Laser Puzzle here (hit two switches) to raise two ramps. Follow them up to a platform with spinning electric arms across the floor. Try not to get hit by electricity as you cross to jump on the big red button on the other side (it opens an exit door). Go past the spinning arms again to reach the ramp to the left of the button. (Piggybank alert!) Walk outside to the Fly Wheels. Well done, Skylander, it's nearly Kaos time!

The Fly Wheels

There are a few enemies out here waiting for you. Switch the laser to turn on the rotating platform and then jump aboard. Ride the platform all the way around to the left and jump off onto a balloon. Super-bounce to another balloon and repeat the process—jump off the second platform to the right onto a final platform with a Villain Stash. Gather your gold and take the central path to an elevator. Ride it up to meet your destiny—Kaos (see Figure 8.92)!

FIGURE 8.92

Uh, oh! Kaos has the controller for The Ultimate Weapon. But you're *not* doomed yet.

Battle with Kaos

Kaos shoots rings of damage out from around him onto the circular platform where you begin (see Figure 8.93). If you have a fast Skylander who is great at jumping (or better yet, can fly), it will be easier to avoid the rings. Whenever Kaos floats low enough to attack, smash him to decrease his health. This one is a long fight, but every little bit counts.

Kaos sends objects flying toward you to cause damage. If you have a Skylander who is good at long-distance attacks (or a trapped villain in your portal), you can attack Kaos while keeping outside of the damage zone underneath him.

FIGURE 8.93

There are many waves of attack by Kaos. Choose a Skylander who has strong Elemental Power and great jumping skills. In fact, you might need a few!

Elemental symbols come toward you in a waves. The first set will be of the same element as your Skylander (these are good because they restore your health). The second wave will be of a different element and can harm you. You won't have time to swap Skylanders on the portal as they come, but you can switch to your villain to avoid damage when the alternate elements come through, or you can just jump over them. Keep attacking Kaos whenever you get a break from the elements; you are wearing down his health.

Doom Sharks come through next. These are hard to avoid, but do your best— fly over the top or jump to let most of them pass under you. Have a lineup of Skylanders ready to punch in, in case you take too much damage and need to swap. Kaos will keep sending out elements and rings of damage (try jumping every alternate ring to gain health but not damage). Keep attacking him.

While Kaos gains Traptanium swords to attack with, his health improves a little. He grows wings and sends laser beams across the arena floor, which you need to jump over (see Figure 8.94). More Doom Sharks and laser beams come at you. If you can go past the Doom Sharks without getting bitten, you'll score health.

FIGURE 8.94

Keep wearing Kaos down and eventually you'll have the ultimate success—trapped Kaos!

Well done, Portal Master! You've saved the day! Skylander Academy is safe from the Doom Raiders and ready to open.

Expand Your Adventure!

Four exciting Adventure Packs (sold separately) can be added to your *Skylanders Trap Team* collection: Midnight Museum, Sunscraper Spire, Nightmare Express, and the Mirror of Mystery. Within some of the Adventure Packs, you'll also receive a Magic Item that can enhance your gameplay:

- **Tiki Speaky:** Behold the mystical purple smoke of Tiki! Enemies will be struck by lightning, adding extra damage to your attacks. (Included in the Mirror of Mystery Adventure Pack.)

- **Hand of Fate:** Stun your enemies with this handy item to give you a strong arm in battle. (Included in the Nightmare Express Adventure Pack.)

- **Hog Hoarder:** Each time you attack an enemy or object, you can score a cash prize of gold coins. (Included in the Nightmare Express Adventure Pack.)

- **Ram Rocket:** Watch out! The sky is raining Rocket Rams, so enemies beware! Cause extra damage with each hit. (Included in the Mirror of Mystery Adventure Pack.)

Each Magic Item will work for a short period of time within each story chapter.

Chapter 19: Midnight Museum

The Elemental Power of the Dark Eye of Tomorrow should be used for good... but it's in danger! Your quest is to keep it safe from Nightshade, the sneakiest thief in Skylands who is set to steal it for his own *evil* plans! Seek out the Bat and Firefly Jar Hats and the majestic Eye of Kaos Hat within elemental gates (see Figure 9.1). A Soul Gem for Knight Mare and the Legendary Gargoyle are hidden somewhere on your path—but keep out of view of those pesky Spyclopters! Buckle up, Skylander! It's time to catch a thief!

FIGURE 9.1

Gather these collectibles as you explore Midnight Museum to capture Nightshade.

TIP

Be Prepared!

If you have played this Adventure Pack before, have Nightshade (Dark) in a trap ready for his Villain Quest. If not, you will capture Nightshade during this chapter.

The Night Tower
You'll begin with Buzz on the **Night Tower**, who gives you a stern warning to keep out of the spotlight of the dangerous Spyclopters zooming around platforms below you. First up, jump down onto the lower platform to your right to play the **Troll Radio**, and then follow the coins around and dive down again to the **Traptanium Crystal** on another platform below. Smash it up to score a **Treasure Chest**. Bounce back up to the middle platform with an arched door leading to the **Night Side Storeroom**.

Night Side Storeroom
Watch out! A swarm of En Fuego Chompies attack you as soon as you enter. Slay them all and then chat with terrified T-Bone the skeleton (see Figure 9.2), who is really just looking for a **Skystones Smash** partner. Play with him for a coin reward and then keep moving.

FIGURE 9.2

Follow the coins off the left side of the Night Tower to discover a Traptanium Crystal with treasure underneath; then visit T-Bone for a game of Skystones Smash.

The Prime Tower

Explore the **Night Tower** platform to the far right of the archway (sneak past the Spyclopters, keeping out of their light!) to discover the **Prime Tower**. Before you enter the arched door, take a dive over the edge opposite to a lower platform where you'll find treasure and a **Winged Sapphire**; then bounce back up. Dash inside the arched door to visit the **Bumper Range**.

TIP

Spyclopter Prison!

If you get caught in the glare of a roving Spyclopter, it's a one-way trip back to the start of your current area. Use steps, ledges, and side alcoves to dodge their spotlight as you explore Midnight Museum. They can't damage your health, but they'll slow you down.

Bumper Range

Buzz has beat you inside using his secret Ninja Commando skills! There's a glowing orb in the back-left corner that needs to be pushed onto the circular hole on the right side. First, jump up the right-side platforms, collecting coins along the way—but beware, don't get spiked over the grilled steps. Make your way across the upper-back platform to reach the glowing orb. Push the orb down into the recess near Buzz and across into the curving energy stream. Flick the central switch to zoom it through the U shape to the right side. Once you maneuver the orb onto the hole, a secret door opens at the back of the room.

Joyia's Athenaeum

Ready for a skirmish!? En Fuego Chompies attack! A melee fight will get rid of these pests, followed by the appearance of some Plant Warriors and Ooglers (those crazy little glowing guys that shoot a rope of electricity from their eyes across the floor). When all enemies are defeated, the battle gates drop and you'll find Tessa waiting with a **Villain Quest** for Nightshade. If this is your first play-through, you won't have trapped him yet—but for those who have, let's look at this quest, **Crown Without a King**, now.

Crown Without a King
The King of Woodburrow's crown was stolen a very long time ago, and Tessa thinks she knows who the culprit is... Nightshade, of course! He only has to show up for this quest, and Tessa will let him keep the stolen crown, which turns out to be the Bat Hat (+22 Critical Hit, +4 Speed).

The Night Sky Walk
Head through the dropped battle gate at the back of **Joyia's Athenaeum** into the twilight purple zone of **Night Sky Walk**. Spyclopters are on the prowl for trouble, so keep out of sight! Along the left-side path is a sparkling **Treasure Chest**. Hide from the Spyclops in the little side alcoves and smash the statues for coins as you make your way back to the right-side path. At the first intersection you come across (a path leading to the left), Plant Warriors are waiting to battle you in the **Garden Tower**. Don't go there yet—we'll come back. Continue along the right-side path to reach a **Soul Gem** for Knight Mare (The Shadow Realm) and a big, shiny pile of gold at the end. Now, backtrack to the **Garden Tower** path to battle those Plant Warriors.

The Garden Tower & Flipper Reach
Battle time! Electric Ooglers and a Raven Lobber jump into the fray but are easy to take out with a few swift close-attack moves. A battle button will be uncovered. Jump on it to bounce over to a circular platform with coins floating around the balcony. Follow them to discover the **Legendary Gargoyle**! Awesome work, Skylander! Your Legendary Treasure collection is nearly complete! At the front of the platform is a door into **Flipper Reach**.

Here waits Buzz again, with another glowing orb challenge. Boomsticks! Flick the switch on the floor to the left to lower the ball and push it off its platform onto the pink arrows. A step above on the right is another lever; switch it to launch the orb up the moving ramp onto the back platform. This is tricky—time your switch for just when the ramp is raised about halfway up. Any earlier or later, and it will hit the step and roll back down. If you launch from the ramp at just the right spot, the orb will fly straight into the back alcove full of coins, which you can collect. Knock your orb into the circle on the far left and then dash up the center ramp to the switch in the middle of the room. Flick it just as the block above it begins to descend and flash to launch it high over the left-side railing. As it rolls into the hole, another secret door at the back of the room opens into the **Hall of Trials**.

The Hall of Trials
Start by pushing the left-side switch into the first position so that it shines back on a small angle. Shift the blocks one by one from closest to furthest away (left to right) so that the light pulse can zigzag its way to the back of the room (left to right). Each block will only need to be moved once or twice to clear the space. The second switch at the back-left corner of the room needs to be flicked to the second position (directly across the hall from left to right) and a final block shifted once (see Figure 9.3). Hooray! The battle gate drops, and you're on your way to **Firefly Gardens**.

FIGURE 9.3

Are you ready for a challenging block puzzle? The beam of light must be directed across the room to get through the far-side gate.

The Firefly Gardens & The Eventide Walk
More Spyclops guards are on the lookout for trouble, so watch your step! **Persephone** is floating on the left side of the door as you leave, ready to sell you some upgrades. To your immediate right is a **Magic Gate** called **Aylis' Arcane Archive**.

Along the left-side wall of **Firefly Gardens** is a small alcove called **The Eventide Walk**. Shift the blocks to form a path to the back of the alcove where you'll earn a new **Story Scroll**.

Aylis' Arcane Archive
Inside the Magic Gate is a special **Magic Eye** (see Figure 9.4). Collect it from the central platform before you begin exploring—it will allow you to see hidden dangers in the area. Ahead of you are two side platforms, each with a golden key on the far side. Wearing the Magic Eye lets you see spinning blades as you cross the platforms, so you can retrieve the keys in safety. Use the two keys to open the golden gate and earn an Eye of Kaos Hat (+22 Elemental Power). Teleport back out to **Firefly Gardens**.

FIGURE 9.4

Without the Magic Eye, the platforms appear empty—but beware! There are spinning blades to damage your health if you touch them. Collect the Magic Eye to give you super-vision in this area.

The Firefly Gardens (Continued)

Follow the coins to the end of the platform (if you fancy a swim, some waterlogged En Fuego Chompies might be hiding in the pond near a **Traptanium Crystal**). Smash the crystal to discover a bounce pad that takes you up to **The North Side Tower** and a **Magic Gate**. Bounce up when you're ready to explore.

Straight across from the watery bounce pad, you'll see a **Light Gate** called **The Lantern Bower**. To the left of the Light Gate is a door that will take you to **Multi-Ball Expanse** and your boss fight with Nightshade. You can't come back out of there, so explore all other areas first.

The North Star Tower

You've unearthed a **Villain Stash**! Unfortunately, it's guarded by a troop of Raven Lobbers with great aim, so watch out! Avoid the red targets on the ground where their bombs will land and take them out in a quick melee. Crack the Villain Stash and then jump up the higher platform to follow a ring of coins around the balcony. When you've gathered all the gold, drop back down to **Firefly Gardens**.

The Lantern Bower

Visit that **Light Gate** across from the bounce pad. Glowing blocks need to be shifted in this area so that you can reach the back-right corner. A pile of coins is an easy reward. Move the high blocks so that they fall into the spaces below to create a single level in the back section. Climb back up the steps to the high boxes near the entrance to retrieve a Firefly Jar Hat (+35 Armor).

Multi-Ball Expanse

To the left of the **Light Gate** in **Firefly Gardens** is another door, which leads to **Multi-Ball Expanse**. Once you go through this door, you are on a one-way trip to the end of the story chapter, so don't enter until you've visited each the preceding areas. This challenge is like an epic game of pinball. There are three glowing orbs to flick into the left, right, and center holes. The two switches at the front will hit the balls as they land on the pink arrows. This can be easier to complete with two players, but you can manage on your own—just dash between the switches. One, two, three... done! Brilliant effort! Now run up the ramp into the newly opened doorway to discover the Dark Eye of Tomorrow in the **Dark Vault**. Oh, no! A masked mischief-maker has beaten you to it! Don't be fooled by his impeccable manners—he's all bad!

The Dark Vault

Nightshade loots the treasure and throws himself through the stained-glass window at the back of the room. A battle gate stops you from following him until you defeat the hordes of enemies that come streaming into the **Dark Vault**.

En Fuego Chompies and Plant Warriors begin the fight, but soon you're up against a teleporting Hood Sickle (attack while he recovers from swinging his scythe), Ooglers (jump the current line and attack them from behind), and Raven Lobbers (keep out of their red targets). Get rid of the Raven Lobbers first to stop them throwing bombs down to you; the others can all be taken out fairly quickly. This is a super-fun melee fight, but none of these guys will do too much damage to you. Never fear, the worst is yet to come—as soon as the battle gate drops, dive after Nightshade to rescue the Dark Eye of Tomorrow!

The Lower Gardens There are hazards afoot! White laser lines cross the platforms, so you need to jump over them. Spyclopters are scouting around up ahead. At the end of the platform you land on, go straight ahead and then up the stairs to jump across a series of lasers that crisscross over each other. Circle the tower to find a hidden **Treasure Chest**!

Back down the stairs, turn right to follow the platform (jump lasers and dodge Spyclopter guards). Very soon, you'll reach the final battle arena. You're battle-locked in and Nightshade is ready to rumble (see Figure 9.5)!

FIGURE 9.5

Challenge Nightshade in a daring game of chase under stone towers. Keep your eye out for the clone with the spotlight around him—he's the real deal! Take down the towers to damage his health.

In the first part of the fight there are three shady versions of Nightshade standing atop towers that spread a mist of darkness underneath. The clouds cause damage, so keep out of their way. Attack the base of the towers to bring them down.

Part 2 sees a half dozen versions of Nightshade on the battle ground, all running in different directions. Hit as many as you can to try to destroy the copies until only the real Nightshade is left standing (the real Nightshade has a slight spotlight surrounding him as he runs). As soon as the clones are destroyed, another five towers appear with Nightshade atop the center tower. As you attack each tower, cloned Nightshades creep around below. As soon as all towers are down, they'll scatter! Run and attack them all again to catch the real Nightshade, who will be throwing occasional long-distance attack moves your way.

Part 3 of the fight begins with the giant Spyclopter above, shooting purple flames down at you while you tackle six more towers. Nightshade increases his attacks as well, so this battle gets a bit tricky here. Watch out for more shady clones. Highly targeted attacks are helpful to bring down the towers and clones, so choose a Skylander with great close-contact attack moves. When the real Nightshade is the last Mabu standing, attack him directly while he recovers. All Nightshades down? You've done it, Skylander. You've reclaimed the Dark Eye of Tomorrow! Spectacular!

Chapter 20: Sunscraper Spire

A mysterious crystalline tower has appeared in Skylands full of unknown magic and, perhaps, an evil Elemental Light villain. Only the bravest Skylanders can be sent in to investigate what secrets it may hold. Do you dare? Along your way, battle blue Cyclops minions and collect the Legendary Knight Statue, a Soul Gem for Knight Light, and three new hats (the Lightbulb, Dark Helm, and Lighthouse Beacon Hats, shown in Figure 9.6). Trusty Mags will help you along the way—or will she...?

FIGURE 9.6

Gather these collectibles as you explore the Sunscraper Spire to capture Luminous.

TIP

Be Prepared!

If you have played this Adventure Pack before, have Luminous (Light) in a trap ready for his Villain Quest. If not, you will capture Luminous during this chapter.

Viewing Platform Mags leaves you here with instructions to search the Energy Pillars you see in the distance. To your right is a super bounce pad, so let's jump up, up, and away...

First Quarter Island ...to land in a battle arena full of little blue Cyclops enemies swarming toward you! They are pretty cute and don't do too much damage, but take them all out with a quick melee attack to drop the battle gates. Through the gate, a grill of spikes pops up every few seconds, so watch out! There is a **Traptanium Crystal** to the left of the path hiding a **Treasure Chest** underneath. Up the steps, a strangely glowing Mags is waiting to offer you some encouragement. Push the light block forward to let the light beam hit the crystal by the edge of the platform. A light-beam bridge will form across the gap so you can cross.

There's a switch here. Flick it to connect a new light beam to create a second bridge. Oh, no! Another swarm of little blue guys jump in to defend their territory! Take them out and dash across the bridge, but beware of the grate spikes popping up as you reach the far side.

Buzz is waiting on a little balcony on the left with a **Villain Quest** for Luminous. (If this is your first play-through, you won't have trapped him yet. Come back to visit Buzz to complete his quest **Buzz Has a Hat** when you have him.)

Keep dodging the grate spikes until you reach the end of the platform. Smash the white **Traptanium Crystal** for a coin reward. There's a door into a small house here—don't go inside yet. Let's keep exploring first. Jump off the right side of the platform to drop down to the **Hidden Path**.

Buzz Has a Hat
This area is the **Villain Quest** for Luminous, so bring him by to chat with Buzz once he is safe and sound in a trap. Luminous has magically shifted a small island out off the edge of the spire that holds Buzz's lucky hat. (Buzz is not too happy about it either!) Drag the little island back toward Buzz (Luminous will automatically do this), and you'll be rewarded with the Lighthouse Beacon Hat (+22 Armor, +4 Speed).

Hidden Path
A horned purple Cyclops is guarding a new **Story Scroll** down here. Retrieve it and bounce back up to the roof of the house on **First Quarter Island**. Another enemy is guarding an **Earth Gate** here called **Crystal Cavern**. A little Mabu called Terra is hanging around the gate to tell you how much he loves earth (who doesn't!?), with the promise of a magical hat inside. Time to explore!

Crystal Cavern
Inside the Earth Gate you'll find layers of rocky outcrops that you can bounce between. On some there are floating bombs to collect. Start on the bounce pad at the far left, which will jump you halfway up the wall to a second bounce pad that takes you to the top-right ledge. Push the rock that is in your way off the edge in front so that you can jump down to the ledge (below left) holding a second rock. Push it off to reveal a bounce pad underneath; then bounce across to the bomb on your right. Drop to the bottom level and run along to launch the bomb at the pile of rocks (tied with rope) on the far-left floor.

A single rock is left in that space, so push it to the left to reveal a new bounce pad. Jumping up to the highest level this time, you'll see another pile of rocks (tied with rope) that needs blowing up. Explosion time! Jump right to where you picked up the first bomb, drop down, and use the far-left (newest) bounce pad to deliver it to the pile of rocks. Boom! You'll need to drop back to the ground and re-bounce to the left side to reach the highest outcrop with a Hat Box on top. Awesome work, Skylander—that was hard! Your reward is a Light Bulb Hat (+17 Critical Hit, +4 Speed).

Crystal Underpass Drop down from the rooftop on the **Hidden Path** house and enter the door underneath to reach **Crystal Underpass**. The glowing purple tiles are bounce pads. Although it's tempting to jump on for a speedy trip to the other side, if you do, you'll miss the **Traptanium Crystal** four rows in. Hop from tile to tile the old-school way (with your legs!), being very careful to avoid the bounce pads in the middle. When you reach the Traptanium Crystal, smash it up to earn a **Soul Gem** for Knight Light (Brilliant Blade). Now you can bounce across to the back platform to exit this area.

First Beam Control Floor Our horned Cyclops enemy has returned with a blue Cyclops riding on his back—which looks pretty fun, actually! They'll jump off the battle platform to come after you, but are easy to defeat in close combat. Take out a second blue Cyclops to drop the battle gate. Piles of rope-tied rocks are blocking the other side of the gap so that you can't cross over. Grab the bomb that is on the left side of the battle platform and launch it at the rock pile. A laser beam will connect to one on the opposite side of the gap to make a bridge. Congratulations! You've reached the first Energy Pillar. Mags suggests you direct the energy beam toward the center tower to make something wonderful happen. (That's a pretty wild guess, Mags!) Give it a try.

First, you need to bomb the barricade blocking your way, so dash back across the light beam bridge, pick up the bomb you used before, and launch it at the rock on the barricade. You just redirected the first beam—awesome work! (Hmmm... Mags is acting a little suspiciously.)

A new light bridge has formed; dash across and grab some gold as you make your way to the super bounce pad at the end of the platform. (Grated spike alert!) Super bounce time!

Second Quarter Island, Secret Platform, & Under-Island Maintenance Area You'll land in Second Quarter Island. Under the platform you land on is a **Villain Stash**, so jump down to claim it. Climb back up the side steps to enter the door above and go into the **Under-Island Maintenance Area**.

Troll Radio alert! There's a light-beam bridge ahead with a laser beam crossing it. Be careful—if you touch the laser beam as you cross, you'll fall into the area below (see Figure 9.7). This time, that's okay, because this is a good place to look for treasure (you can climb back up to the bridge later). Drop down into the area underneath and take out a few little blue Cyclops enemies so you are free to explore. Follow the railroad tracks around to the left. There's a **Winged Sapphire** hidden under a ledge!

FIGURE 9.7

If you touch the laser beam as you cross the bridge, the connection will break and the bridge will disappear. Drop down into the Under-Island Maintenance Area to discover a Winged Sapphire and a Secret Platform with a Treasure Chest.

There are steps nearby leading up to a laser beam crystal. Flick the crystal switch once.

Drop back down off the platform and make your way to where you originally fell into this area. Halfway up the steps is a new light bridge that leads to a **Treasure Chest** on the **Secret Platform**.

Return back to the stairs leading to the laser-beam crystal in **Under-Island Maintenance Area** and flick the switch again. This time a new light bridge will appear briefly on the left side of the platform. But first, it's battle time! Watch out here—there's a Chomp Chest in the corner, pretending to be a normal treasure chest (but you're not fooled!). Defeat him to drop the battle gate behind you where Buzz wants to play **Skystones Smash**.

Cross the light bridge (jump those laser beams or you'll fall). A block puzzle needs to be solved on the next platform. Push the left-side block forward once and then the center block across toward the right-side once. Push the right-side block left once to completely block the light beam. The light bridge will turn off. Now you can drop down into the pit below the light bridge to collect some gold.

Continue across the platform to the wooden bridge and hop on the super bounce pad, which sends you up high to a gate with a **Lock Puzzle** on it. Crack the code to enter the **Second Beam Control Floor**.

Second Beam Control Floor
Mags is waiting with another barricaded Energy Pillar. You need to grab the bomb to the left side of the platform and use it to blow up the rock tied to the machine—but there's a battle gate in the way. As soon as you step down onto the platform to get the bomb, a swarm of blue Cyclops enemies attacks! Defeat them to drop the battle gate and use the bomb to blow up the barricade. The second Energy Pillar is in position (and Mags is sounding more and more like a crazy villain—eek!).

Jump on the super bounce pad (and then another) to reach the third pillar. Don't expect to land on your feet!

Oubliette & Crystal Corridors
It's a long, long way to fall into the deep, dark **Oubliette**. Try to catch coins as you fall.

Phew! That was quite a ride, but you've landed in a heap of trouble in **Crystal Corridors**. A laser fence drops to release a swarm of blue Cyclops enemies to attack you. Defeat them to drop the battle gate to your left. The laser fence rises again, so you can't access the Dark Gate behind it. Run through the battle gate to find a small platform with a simple block puzzle on it. Push the center block in the direction of the arrow (toward to laser crystals) once, and then dash back into the first area. The laser fence has dropped, so you can access the **Dark Gate**.

Chamber of Dark Energy
Inside the Dark Gate is a room called the **Chamber of Dark Energy**. Once you defeat more Cyclops buddies, climb the back platform to push a glowing orb (on the right) down a ramp. It will land in a hole, raising a step so you can reach the Hat Box on the top-left step. You have just earned the Dark Helm Hat (+35 Critical Hit). Brilliant effort!

Crystal Canyon
Run back to your block puzzle and flick the switch to create a new light bridge—remember, jump over the laser beams so you don't fall! There are a few blue Cyclopses on the other side to deal with; then push the single block once (use the arrow) to redirect the laser beam. When all of the Cyclops enemies are defeated, another battle gate will drop. Cross the new light bridge to find two new blocks. Push the block farthest away to the left once; then push the other block toward the bridge once (follow the arrows). Push the second block to the right to disrupt the laser beam.

Keep climbing higher along the platforms following the left-side wall. **Persephone** is floating in an alcove just before the next light bridge, so grab some upgrades on the go!

Continue along to cross another light beam bridge (jump the laser!), defeating Cyclopses as you move. Drop the final battle gate ahead and jump through the barrier to dash across the last light-beam bridge. Enter a door to **Crystal Chasm**.

Crystal Chasm
You'll fall onto a light-beam floor with new enemies (see Figure 9.8). Once they are defeated, push the far-left-side block to the left to disengage the laser beam. The floor will disappear from underneath your feet, and you'll fall onto another light-beam floor below. Repeat this process again to fall to the third floor. (If you don't defeat all the enemies before you fall, they will keep falling with you and you'll have a bigger fight on your hands when you reach the final level.) This time, there is treasure behind a battle gate to the left that you can reach when the enemies are defeated. Push the final light block to fall to the bottom level into a pool of water. There is a barricade here that needs to be bombed, but no bomb to use, so jump on the bounce pad—up, up, and away!

FIGURE 9.8

Enemies swarm in to attack as you battle your way down three layers of laser-beam floors.

Third Beam Control Floor You'll spring all the way to the top of the **Third Beam Control Floor**, and look—a bomb! How convenient! Grab it and run forward a few steps to fall into the gap (trip the laser beam of the light bridge so it disappears). You'll drop all the way back down to **Crystal Chasm**. Launch the bomb at the barricade. Awesome work, Skylander! You've found the **Legendary Knight Statue**! Ride the bounce pad back up to the top of the tower.

Grab that bomb again and launch it at the barricades on the opposite side of the light bridge. Run across (dodge that laser beam or you'll fall again!) to battle swarms of blue Cyclops enemies. All along this platform are spiked grates that pop up, so be careful not to damage your health (see Figure 9.9).

FIGURE 9.9

There is one last barricade to bomb—the one in front of the third Energy Pillar. Destroy it to redirect the light beam toward the center tower. You're nearly done, Skylander!

Only one more Energy Pillar to release! Pick up the bomb that is waiting next to the Energy Pillar—it's time to go for a ride!

Fourth Beam Control Floor
Take a short flight on the super bounce pad across to the **Fourth Beam Control Floor** and launch the bomb at the barricade in front of you as soon as you land. That's it! The Energy Pillar will redirect toward the center. Mags invites you to the center tower—she has something to show you....

Tricked You Tower
Whoa! You've been tricked. All along, Mags was actually none other than the evil Light Villain, **Luminous** (see Figure 9.10)! It's time to battle!

FIGURE 9.10

All is not as it seems. Defeat Luminous to win a new Skystones Smash card; then return to First Quarter Island to complete his Villain Quest and earn a Lighthouse Beacon Hat as well.

Luminous shoots three laser beams from his feet across the floor. A Skylander with a long-ranged attack move would be helpful here because you can't reach him while the lasers are up. As soon as Luminous drops the lasers, do as much damage as you can. You won't have long until he teleports away and begins another attack.

Luminous's next phase is to drop light crystals from above—keep clear of the red target marks that appear on the floor. You can attack the crystals to remove the shields surrounding Luminous, making him more vulnerable. Use every opportunity to smash this villain because he has a lot of health to get through. He'll shoot lasers and drop crystals at the same time (see Figure 9.11). This part of the fight gets trickier, as Luminous moves faster, spinning his laser beams across the floor so that you have to jump them or risk falling off the platform. Again, a long-ranged attack so you can break down his health from a distance is your best bet for making this a quick fight.

This is a tricky fight. Smash the fallen crystals to break away the shield surrounding Luminous, so you can attack him for as long as possible. Dodge the falling crystals and jump over the laser beams he is sending out from his feet. As his health bar gets low, go in for a super-heavy final attack, and you'll knock him out altogether.

FIGURE 9.11

Luminous moves onto a platform with four stone pillars that shoot lasers between them. Taking out the pillars might give you more room to move, but you'll also be more vulnerable to laser beam attacks.

Incredible effort, Skylander—you sure made light work of that! Capture Luminous and then head back to Skylander Academy to celebrate.

Chapter 21: Nightmare Express

The Trolls have stolen the Trolly Grail! Join Flynn as he heroically recovers it and records the story in his autobiography. (You might need to straighten out some of those facts, though—Flynn seems to take the credit for all of your hard work, Skylander!) While you (ahem, I mean Flynn) save the day, remember to track down the Medic, Coconut, Outback, and Cycling Hats, as well as a very handsome Legendary Statue of Awesome (see Figure 9.12). This is going to be one fast ride!

FIGURE 9.12

Gather these collectibles as you explore the Nightmare Express to capture Lob Goblin and Trolling Thunder.

> ## TIP
>
> **Be Prepared!**
>
> If you have played this Adventure Pack before, have Lob Goblin (Light) and Trolling Thunder (Tech) in traps ready for their Villain Quests. If not, you will capture both during this chapter.

Temple Ruins Approach

You are back on the ground in a very green jungle with the Mabu. A "K-Flynn" **Troll Radio** is playing requests nearby, so switch it up for some gold and dancing tunes. Da Pinchy is hoping to talk to you—he has a **Villain Quest** for Trolling Thunder called **Statue of Limitations**. You'll catch Trolling Thunder later in this chapter, so remember to come back here to evolve him when you do.

Statue of Limitations & Suspended Island Ruin

The **Villain Quest** for Trolling Thunder is an easy one. Da Pinchy has made a fantastic statue of Flynn, but someone has left a giant boulder in front of it, blocking the view (see Figure 9.13). Trolling Thunder will blow up the boulder but accidentally knock over Flynn's statue as well! Luckily, it forms a bridge over to a secret area. Roll over there to explore!

There's a Hat Box waiting for you in the new area called **Suspended Island Ruin**. Mash it up to score a Cycling Hat (+8 Speed, +7 Elemental Power). If you have a look in the distance, you'll be able to see **Cliffside Sanctuary** with a **Magic Gate** beyond the Hat Box. You will be exploring that area very soon!

After you've picked up your new hat, continue down the wooden bridge, pushing the giant bomb ahead to blow up the end gate and score a **Treasure Chest**. Okay, it's time to head back past Da Pinchy to **Temple Ruins Approach**.

Quest Discovered: Statue of Limitations

FIGURE 9.13

Brave... handsome... intelligent. They could only be talking about the legendary Captain Flynn, couldn't they? Hmmm... it seems like this autobiography might stretch the truth a little, though.

Temple Ruins Approach (continued) There is a button on the ground next to Cali that will release a giant bomb from the stone wall. You can use this bomb in **Temple Ruins Approach**. Push the bomb onto the barrier past the **Tech Gate** called **Vertical Challenge** and explore this area before you head into battle.

Vertical Challenge Inside the Tech Gate is a series of conveyer belts leading up to a Hat Box. The hat is guarded by a barricade, though, so you'll need to collect the bomb on the left-side ledge and carry it up the backward-moving conveyer belts. There isn't enough time to reach the top with a ticking bomb, so make your way up the first belt and push the gold block off the platform to create a shortcut. There is a second block on the top level to push down to create another step. Jump down and carry the bomb up your shortcut to launch it at the barricade. Hooray! The Hat Box is yours! You have earned an Outback Hat (+6 Speed).

Temple Site Overlook & Temple Ruins Approach (continued)
Back outside the gate to your right, Gobler the Mabu points out a **Treasure Chest** on a small island to the back-right portion of the **Temple Ruins Approach** area, but Flynn doesn't remember how to reach it. You'll need to complete Trolling Thunder's quest to get there. A bomb is sitting close by on the edge of the cliff, though, so grab it and run back around to the area in **Temple Ruins Approach** that you opened up past the Tech Gate, or use the giant rolling bomb you left there earlier.

Inside the battle gate, a skirmish is waiting for you. Lob Goblins and Grinnades are running around, guarding a battle gate on the far wall. Defeat the enemies and then explore the left side of the entrance to **Temple Ruins Approach** to find a platform above **Rubble Pathway**.

Rubble Pathway, Forgotten Ledge, & Hidden Cavern
Take a leap on the bounce pad up to an overhanging ledge where a **Treasure Chest** can be discovered. On the right side of the battleground there is no barrier, so drop down to the grass below to find **Forgotten Ledge**. Before you do, pick up another bomb to take with you.

Use the bomb to blow up the battle gate, revealing a small room called the **Hidden Cavern**. Inside, you'll discover treasure, another bomb, and a new **Story Scroll**. Grab the bomb and bounce back up to **Temple Ruins Approach** to blow up the remaining battle gate at the back of the area. Be prepared for an attack in **Tank Terrace Ruins**!

Tank Terrace Ruins & Underground Ruins
Wow! The Trolls really don't want you to pass through this area; they've rolled out three giant tanks to guard the main gate! You'll need three golden keys to unlock the gate, and you'll find them behind each of the stone arches (see Figure 9.14). It's time to blow up some tanks! Grab the bomb and launch it at the first tank; then collect the key behind it. Jump the red and black mines on

the grass to reach the arch to the bottom right of the path and bomb that too. Enemies will scatter, and you'll have another golden key under your belt (or floating above your head!). Backtrack a few steps to find a **Traptanium Crystal** under the first ramp with a secret door behind it.

FIGURE 9.14

Collect three golden keys from behind the Troll mega-tanks to open the locked gate.

Enter the secret door to find a dark cavern called **Underground Ruins**. In this spot, you can score a **Villain Stash** and chat with Otto, who has a side mission. He wants you to steal the nearby Legendary Treasure out of the stone cage, but you'll need a bomb to do it. There is no bomb in this room, so you'll have to duck outside again to find one. Throw it at the battle gate sign; then dash up the ledge (from front-right side and then around the back) to reach the **Legendary Statue of Awesome**. Wow, Flynn sure is remembering this mission with himself in mind—what a champion! Head back out to **Tank Terrace Ruins**.

Use the bomb to your right to blow up the tank at the top of the ramp. You'll release a swarm of smiling Grinnades who will try to return the favor. Attack them with a quick close-combat fight to clear your path. Grab the third key, but don't open the gate yet—Peebs has a **Villain Quest** for Lob Goblin. You'll battle him very soon, but if you've been through Nightmare Express before, here is a closer look at his Villain Quest.

Grand Theft Plan

Peebs needs the plans to the Trolls' latest tank, but they're locked behind a very secure gate. Lob Goblin is the lock code master (because he can count past seven!). Lob Goblin just needs to show up for this Villain Quest, and blow up the gate to receive a Coconut Hat reward (+20 Armor, +3 Speed).

Temple of Boom

Use your three golden keys to unlock the gate into the **Temple of Boom**, a treasure trove of coins and ancient face blocks. Flynn has managed to ensnare himself in a booby trap with the Trolly Grail and needs your help to escape!

There's a **Troll Radio** on the left-side wall and treasure to collect everywhere. To reach the treasure and free Flynn, you need to shift the face blocks to create a path between the left and right platforms. Start with the left block, pushing it once to the back. Next, push the front-right block to the left and then push the back-right block to the back so that it's out of the way. Move behind the small cannon between the blocks to push it forward inline with the bomb sign on the left-side wall. Interact with the cannon to blow up the wall. Done!

Gather treasure as you run up the back ramp. (Grated spike alert!) Jump across your shifted blocks to push the giant white button on the floor of the left-side platform. Instead of falling, Flynn gets hoisted even higher up! Push the block beside the white button forward off the ledge. Dash around the back of the ledge, past Flynn, to the right-side platform again. Press a second white button to finally release him. He spins around to the outside of the room, and you can follow him through the door that appears underneath.

Temple Battle Arena

It's **Trolling Thunder** time! Noodles, Trolling Thunder, Grinnades, and Trolls attack as soon as you leave the **Temple of Boom**. Follow Trolling Thunder as he spins around shooting at you, keeping out of his line of fire. It's best if you can attack him from behind, where he is more vulnerable. A long-ranged attack will really help you here. Climb the steps to jump out of reach under heavy fire. The battle gate won't drop until all of the other enemies are defeated as well.

Nasty Noodles has stolen the Trolly Grail—again! As soon as Trolling Thunder is trapped, you can exit through the gate into **Iron Tank Confrontation**. But first, take a little detour to hunt down some treasure....

Cliffside Sanctuary

There's a stone-walled path to the far left of where you fought the last battle. It leads to a narrow wooden bridge. Follow it behind the temple where you'll find a bounce pad at the very end. This is **Cliffside Sanctuary** (see Figure 9.15). If you bounce up here, you'll discover a magic gate (**Mystical Recess**). Drop down over the edge near the bounce pad to find a **Lock Puzzle** gate with a **Winged Sapphire** fluttering inside.

FIGURE 9.15

Cliffside Sanctuary is easy to miss. Explore around the left side of the battle arena after you have defeated Trolling Thunder to discover a Magic Gate (above) and Winged Sapphire (below) the path.

Mystical Recess There are four floating platforms inside the Magic Gate (**Mystical Recess**). Begin at the right and jump from one to the next as they rise to the same height, to make your way to the highest platform. Your reward is a Medic Hat (+22 Armor).

Iron Tank Confrontation & Bomb Closet
A mega-tank comes out to play (see Figure 9.16)! You'll need a giant rolling bomb to bring that one down. Run forward and smash down the wall on the right to enter an alcove called the **Bomb Closet**, where Elbow has some helpful advice. There is a small bomb you can use to blow up the barrier directly across from the **Bomb Closet**. Before you take on that challenge, though, explore toward the front of the Bomb Closet cave to drop off a ledge where you'll find a **Traptanium Crystal**. Smash it up for a **Treasure Chest** bonus and then bounce back up. Alright, it's time to bomb that gate outside! You'll enter a new area called **Lower Rolling Bomb Range**.

FIGURE 9.16

A Troll mega-tank is no match for a Skylander! Roll your giant bomb through the Lower and Upper Bomb Ranges to launch it at this troublemaker and clear your path to the Nightmare Express.

Lower Rolling Bomb Range

Musgrove informs you that the giant rolling bomb can't be pushed backward, so you'll have to push it on a detour to reach the mega-tank. Jump on the white button to release a bomb; then push it over the ledge into the field below until you reach the lift in the back-left corner. (**Persephone** is also floating here if you fancy a visit.) Jump onto the white button (back ledge) to raise the lift and drop the battle gate into **Upper Rolling Bomb Range**.

Upper Rolling Bomb Range

Battle time! **Lob Goblin** is ready to meet you with his very bad attitude and super-charged bomb-throwing skills. To the left, Da Pinchy is looking for a **Skystones Smash** game if you need a quiet break. Within this area, roll the bomb onto the center lift platforms. A horde of Grinnades and Troll Welders are itching for a fight, and Lob Goblin soon throws himself into the fray as well. Use the giant bomb to your advantage by rolling over as many enemies as you can (including Lob Goblin!). Otherwise, go hand-to-hand in a fun melee battle to bring them all down to size.

Once all enemies are defeated, roll the giant bomb onto the hole (back left) and jump on the white button to launch it over the fence. Now push the bomb into the channel, right up against the black gate. You'll get a word of encouragement from Ravenwood; then hit that button! The gate lifts and— BOOM!—the mega-tank explodes!

KABOO-oose & Box Car

Down the grassy slope to the right, Noodles is taking off on the Nightmare Express train. Jump aboard! Run from the back toward the front of the moving train, collecting the ticking bomb as you go. Launch it at the locked hatch and jump inside the **Box Car**. There is plenty to smash in here! At the far end is a movable block; shift it right, then backward to make a step into **Special Delivery**.

Special Delivery & Dining Car

Run forward along the top of the moving train again, jump down onto the second carriage, and pick up another bomb. Keep moving forward to throw it at the mega-tank in your way. You'll need to run back and grab another bomb before you can get any further; this time, climb the boxes and launch the bomb at the locked hatch on the top of the next carriage. Dive in, Skylander!

There's not much food being served in the **Dining Car**, but there are some very cranky Trolls and a Lob Goblin instead! Take them out and run through to the front of the carriage and onto the Nightmare Express platform to teach Noodles a lesson once and for all!

Noodles

Two Troll Copters are trailing the train as you battle a few of Noodles' henchman. Use a long-range attack to target the Copters before they drop off more bad guys. Noodles will keep his distance until you've battled the Trolls and Grinnades (see Figure 9.17). A few Trolling Thunders will appear (attack from behind so you avoid their blast!).

Finally, Flynn is back, just in time to take out Noodles and the credit. (Hey, that was the easy part!) So, it's back to Skylander Academy to reap the rewards of his (I mean, *your*) hard work. Well done, Skylander!

FIGURE 9.17

Oh, no! You're on your own Skylander. Poor Captain Flynn has been left behind! Make your way to the front platform of the Nightmare Express to battle Noodles' henchmen and save the Trolly Grail.

Chapter 22: Mirror of Mystery

A terrible fate has befallen Skylands! Master Eon has become Evilon, an awful villain who plans to bring an end to the heroic deeds of the Trap Team! Without your protection, the inhabitants of Skylands have no hope. Enter the topsy-turvy world of Mirror of Mysteries and defeat Evilon to restore the magic of Skylands before it's too late! As you lead the rebellion for peaceful Trolls against warrior Mabu, gather the Carnival, Cornucopia, and Gondolier Hats, as well as a very fancy Legendary Windmill contraption (see Figure 9.18). Remember Skylander—things aren't always as they seem!

FIGURE 9.18

Gather these collectibles as you explore the Mirror of Mystery to capture Mad Lobs and Chompy.

TIP

Be Prepared!

If you have played this Adventure Pack before, have Mad Lobs (Tech) and Chompy (Life) in traps ready for their Villain Quests. If not, you will capture both during this chapter.

Tubtub Hub
Can you believe it? Kaos is a good guy! In the crazy Mirror of Mysteries, good guys are bad, and bad guys are good—poor Glumshanks is very confused! Let's begin to solve this riddle....

Kaos is waiting next to the giant fish tub with a **Villain Quest** for Mad Lobs called **Fishiness Protection Program**. He needs his new fish friend to flee from the Troll attack, but doesn't want to scare him. You'll capture Mad Lobs halfway through this game, so make sure you bring him back here in a trap to complete the quest. If you've played before and already have him, we'll look at his **Villain Quest** called the **Fishiness Protection Program** next.

Fishiness Protection Program
Mad Lobs has a roaring voice and must put it to good use to assist Kaos. His enormous pet fish in the **Tubtub Hub** must be scared away before the evil Mabu attack! (Is it a bird? Is it a plane? No, it's a gigantic flying fish, of course!) Mad Lobs will evolve and be rewarded with a shiny pile of silver coins.

Troll Village
Follow the path around the fish tub into **Troll Village**. Across the bridge, Moonbeam is gathering Trolls for the peace rally. There are secret places in Troll Village where you must search out lost Mech Parts to help build a machine to fight against the Mabu invaders. Make sure you explore every area in Troll Village before you bring the three Mech parts to Moonbeam. A huge battle against Evilon and that nasty Captain Flynn awaits you. DOOM!

There is a **Villain Quest** for Chompy on the left of Moonbeam, called **Workers' Chompensation** (see Figure 9.19). Come back here after you capture Chompy in **Chomp Dude's Rest**. If you've played before, sink your teeth into his quest now.

Quest Discovered: Workers' Chompensation

FIGURE 9.19

A peace-loving Kaos?! Skylands really has gone topsy-turvy! Poor Glumshanks doesn't know what to do.

Workers' Chompensation
Ouch! Chompy needs to use his chomping teeth to wake up a sleeping Troll by giving him a bite. Just show up, and before you know it, Chompy will be sporting terrific tiger stripes!

Rainbow Harmony Farms & Rainbow Rockside
To the right of the dirt garden (behind the fence) is a glowing, magical Boingo nut. Pick it up and plant it in the hole with the sign above to grow giant purple pumpkins. Smash them up to collect extra coins! There are another three plant holes in the garden above.

Up on the left end of the verandah is the first part of the Mech machine. Follow the line of coins around the back of the house and jump over the left-side railing to claim the **Legendary Windmill**. Great detective work there, Skylander!

Sage's Stewhouse
The house to the right of **Rainbow Harmony Farms** has a pink and blue flag hanging across the open doorway. This is **Sage's Stewhouse**, where you'll find another Mech piece to collect. Unfortunately, Sage is using it as a boiling pot, so you'll need to haggle it from him for 20 gold coins. Jump up, grab it, and don't forget to play the **Troll Radio** before you leave. Outside on the hill you can leap for a coin reward on the bounce pad.

Pawn Shop
Ready for a game of **Skystones Smash**? Strawberry the Troll is waiting for you in the **Pawn Shop**, a colorful little building just below the bounce pad. You can earn a **Carnival Hat** (+10 Critical Hit, +4 Speed) here, but you'll need to win the game first!

Uncle Ziggy's Garage & Chomp Dude's Rest
Inside **Uncle Ziggy's Garage** is the third part of the Mech machine you need to collect, but you'll have to solve a block puzzle to reach it. There are four rows of

blocks. Make sure you don't push any blocks into the area where a fifth row would fit beside the barrels at the back of the room; otherwise, you'll block the path to **Chomp Dude's Rest**!

Move the left-side block in the first (closest) row to the right once, then the center block of the second row right once. Move the center block of the third row back once, and the right block of the third row to the right once. There should now be enough room for you to make it through the back door (smash the barrels in your way).

It's **CHOMPY** time! Chompy will attack you as soon as you exit the garage into his grassy backyard lair. It's fun to take him out in a hand-to-hand battle; just keep out of reach of those pointy teeth! He's a speedy little guy, so he's a bit tricky to hit long distance. A few close, strong hits should take him out easily. Make sure you go visit Butterfly near **Rainbow Harmony Farms** to complete his **Villain Quest**.

There is a **Winged Sapphire** and some coins on the roof of Uncle Ziggy's Garage. Jump across from the top of the hill near Sage's Stewhouse to reach them. Once you have collected all three parts of the broken Mech machine, take them back outside to **Troll Village**. Moonbeam will fix the machine, and you can hop in and drive it into battle against the evil Mabu. Make sure you have explored all areas here first, though, because you won't be visiting again.

Totally Trail & Lazy Lookout
Follow the Trolls in their Mech suits out of **Troll Village** to begin the next part of your quest. To the right side of the path, you'll find a **Life Gate** called **Lazy Lookout**. On the left are some more magic pumpkins to plant.

Inside the Life Gate, a swarm of Chompies are guarding a very tasty **Cornucopia Hat** (+2 Speed, +15 Elemental Power). Attack the Chompies and jump up the garden path to claim your prize.

Flower Power Fields & Paisley Perch
There are plenty of angry Mabu to keep you busy as you explore **Flower Power Fields**. Attack them to release the trapped Trolls in cages; then jump up the top of the left-side hill to play the **Troll Radio** in **Paisley Perch**. Break down the wooden fence at the top of this little hill to discover a **Story Scroll**.

A little further down the path on the right, smash the **Traptanium Crystal** for a **Treasure Chest** bonus as you and your team of peace-loving Trolls prepare to battle bad guys in mega-tanks. Before you get too far, **Mad Lobs** will track you down with his crack-shot bomb-throwing skills. He's a tricky one to catch because he is always on the move, but aim to attack him just after he has thrown his bomb while his arms are down. If you can get behind him, even better—but watch out for the tanks that join the fray. Your Troll buddies should be fighting, too, at this point, so let them take some of the heat while you focus on Mad Lobs. Trap him in a Tech trap for his **Villain Quest** at the beginning of this level the next time you play through.

Secret Stashaway

Secret Stashaway Battle your way up the path until you defeat all tanks. A handful of Mabu warriors will jump out to follow them, but with a quick melee, you can take them out and the gate in your way will fall.

Persephone is floating at the **Tree of Doom** (see Figure 9.20), but she's definitely not offering you any upgrades this time, Skylander! She is *Evil* Persephone and she *loathes* Skylanders! Oh, no! Her Mabu minions will use their bombs to keep you from getting past her house onto the next phase of the battle. Luckily for you, there's a bomb on a platform on the right side of Persephone's house. Drop down to retrieve it and then throw it at her house. Sorry, Evil Persephone, it had to be done! With her evil house gone, you can cross the mountain down into the dreadful **DoomHelm Pass**.

FIGURE 9.20

Drive a Mech Machine into battle against Persephone's Mabu soldiers to break down the gate in front of The Tree of Doom. Persephone's house is blocking your way to Evilon—tick, tick, tick, BOOM!

DoomHelm Pass & Lonely Locale

DoomHelm Pass & Lonely Locale Evil Flynn sure is angry! As he zooms off in his ship of *DOOM*, you will be faced with a new battle arena. Six metal structures along the path each have a big green button underneath. These areas will provide you with shelter as you run through (bombs ahoy!). Jump on the green buttons in each shelter to drop the laser gates that block your path. Keep clear of the red and yellow targets on the ground as the bombs will fall in these spots. I hope you have your running shoes on, Skylander!

Just through the first laser barrier, you will see a **Water Gate** called **Contemplation Cascades**. Duck into the gate for a quick time out and earn a reward for your trouble. Keep dodging bombs and disarming laser fences as you fight your way along the path of **Lonely Locale**. Just before the final laser barrier at the end of DoomHelm Pass, drop off the left-side ledge to discover a **Villain Vault**.

Contemplation Cascades
Inside the Water Gate, take an Olympic dive off the tallest platform into a series of water pools below. Jump from one to the next, but beware of the spinning water sprayers, which will damage your health. At the end of the pools, dive again to reach a third drop level, this time with a swarm of water-logged Chompies hoping to take a bite out of you. Attack them to earn a **Gondolier Hat** (+5 Armor, +10 Elemental Power). A teleporter is close by to take you back to **DoomHelm Pass.**

Peaceful Palace
If you thought evil Flynn was cranky, wait until you see **Evilon**! Prepare your turrets, Skylander! The final battle is upon you (see Figure 9.21)!

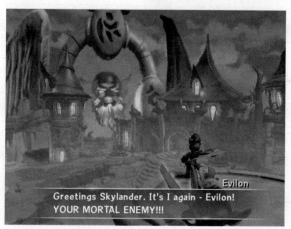

Greetings Skylander. It's I again - Evilon!
YOUR MORTAL ENEMY!!!

Evilon

FIGURE 9.21

There's a terrible surprise waiting for you in the Mirror of Mystery—the wise Portal Master Eon has become Evilon! You must battle against his evil Mabu forces to return Skylands to peace.

Legions of Mabu soldiers with cannons try to knock you out of the sky. Aim your targets at the cannons you see scattered around the palace grounds to destroy Evilon's forces. Tanks will roll out of the castle gates followed by Mabu soldiers, so hit as many of these as you can from the turret as well (see Figure 9.22).

FIGURE 9.22

Make your way through the explosive battle arena of DoomHelm Pass by seeking safety in the horned shelters. Green buttons will deactivate the laserbeam fences. Jump into a turret ship to blast the Mabu cannons into smithereens!

Knock evil Flynn's ship out of the sky, and you've won! Congratulations, Skylander!

Now to break the bad news to poor Glumshanks that it is time to return to the real Skylands, where Kaos is back to his selfish, evil ways.

Kaos Doom Challenges

Do you dare, as shown in Figure 10.1, to challenge Kaos?! Of course you do! Visit the Kaos statue outside the main entrance of Skylanders Academy or select Kaos Doom Challenges from the main menu to begin. These challenges (also called "Kaos Mode") offer a great way to fill your coffers quickly if you would like to buy upgrades for your Skylanders from Persephone. Treasure abounds for those who succeed!

FIGURE 10.1 Ready for a new challenge? That dreadful Dark Portal Master Kaos has cursed the training simulator at Skylanders Academy, creating a series of battles that get more difficult each time you play!

You have 100 waves of enemies to defeat in the Kaos Doom Challenges—but don't worry, they are broken up into bite-sized pieces! Each challenge is suited to a Skylander who has reached a certain level of difficulty, beginning with the easy challenges. Work your way through each of the Doom Challenges, unlocking more difficult battles as you progress.

Each new wave has a different villain hiding inside the Mystery Box of Doom (see Figure 10.2). Enemies will try to break open the box and release the villain to join the fight against you. You can still make it through the challenge if the Mystery Villain is released—you'll just have an extra enemy to fight along the way!

FIGURE 10.2   Your goal is to damage your enemies, protect your Elemental Towers, and try to stay alive!

TIP

Defend the Mystery Box of Doom!

A green health bar on the right side of the screen shows you how much damage your Mystery Box of Doom has taken. Try to keep it safe, or you'll have another enemy added to your troubles!

When you begin a new wave, elemental symbols will appear around the battle ground. This is the "Build Phase" of the wave. Before you begin your fight, swap in Skylander characters of different (matching) elements to build defensive towers. These towers will attack enemies on your behalf—they will help you fight back! Defend your towers and the Mystery Box of Doom to keep them from being broken. Move close to your towers as you fight to regenerate your health.

If your tower survives a wave, it will be upgraded with extra strength. After three upgrades (gold stars will appear on the bottom of the tower to indicate how many upgrades it has achieved), the surviving tower will begin to earn you bonus coins instead. These coins will be released at the end of each wave from fully upgraded towers, as well as from the Mystery Box of Doom. Level up your new Skylanders quickly through challenges, and then use them to your advantage in Story Mode.

At the end of a Kaos Challenge, Persephone will drop by to offer you upgrades. After you have completed each challenge, you'll also receive gold stars that will increase your Portal Master Rank, depending on the difficulty of the challenge.

When you have built your defensive towers and you're ready to fight, flick the wave switch to begin the "Combat Phase." Let the games begin!

So It Begins Temple (Waves 1–3)

Suggested Skylander Level 1–5

Let's go! In the first challenge, Kaos tempts you to keep the Mystery Box of Doom safe from Plant Warriors and Grinnades (see Figure 10.3). You'll learn how to build a new tower before the beginning of Wave 2. The tower will attack enemies for you, but remember to defend it as well; otherwise, the bad guys will break it down. Wave 3 gives you an opportunity to build a second tower, but watch out! Cuckoo Clocker is on a mission to destroy it. Some enemies are bigger and stronger than the others, so they take a bit more effort to defeat. When all enemies are down, you'll be rewarded with a **Treasure Chest** full of gold!

FIGURE 10.3 Swap Skylanders on your portal to interact with Elemental Symbols on the battle ground. Defensive towers will appear that have a unique elemental attack to help you fight enemies. Run past them to regenerate your health as you play.

Enfuego Rain Temple (Waves 4–10)

Suggested Skylander Level 2–6

More enemies are on the loose! There are three exits from the Enfuego Rain Temple streaming with Cuckoo Clockers, Grinnades, Bomb Shells, and Troll Warriors. Luckily, you have two new towers to help you defeat them (see Figure 10.4). Enfuego Chompies will begin falling from the sky in Wave 5, so dodge the targets on the ground before they hit! Battle your big enemies hands-on first because they'll cause the most damage to your Mystery Box of Doom and towers (see Figure 10.5).

FIGURE 10.4 Enemies will escape from one of three swirling red gates to attack your towers and the Mystery Box of Doom. Don't let them release the Super-Villain inside!

FIGURE 10.5 Focus your attacks on the biggest, strongest enemies—your towers will take out smaller villains.

Horrible Something Temple (Waves 11–20)

Suggested Skylander Level 3–8

Four towers are on your side this time (see Figure 10.6), but you'll need to smash a Traptanium Crystal to access one of them. There's a new kind of trap to watch out for that shoots fire from the perimeter of the towers. This is a big help in keeping enemies away, but be careful fighting nearby in case you get caught in the blast.

FIGURE 10.6 Uh, oh! There are five exits now that enemies can attack from—three at the front and one on each side. Keep on your toes, Skylander; this challenge is about to get tricky!

From Wave 13 onward, Flaming Chompies will fall from the sky. Dodge them by keeping clear of the red targets on the ground. They won't do much damage to the Mystery Box, but they make it more difficult to move around. You have a big battle field to play on, but that means it's hard to keep an eye on all the entrances at once. Make sure you stay close to the Mystery Box of Doom. Although they are small, a charging line of Grinnades can be a big problem for your towers, so you'll have to take them out with a long-distance attack if you have limited range.

From Wave 15 onward, you'll have to deal with the flaming towers, Chompy Rain, red hot spikes (see Figure 10.7), and big enemies all at once, including Bomb Shells, Pain-Yattas, and Cuckoo Clockers. Focus on these big guys first—they could take the towers out in no time at all.

FIGURE 10.7 Wave 12 onwards brings red hot spikes into the mix, popping up around the battle arena. They rise to ground level first, before they spike out, so you'll have time to jump out of the way.

With all dangers coming together in the final waves, your battle will get quite tricky (see Figure 10.8). It's easy to take damage with so many enemies on the loose, so dash past your towers as often as you can to regenerate your health. Good luck, Skylander!

FIGURE 10.8 A hoard of golden coins and gems await you after each wave. Swap in new Skylanders to share the wealth; then visit Persephone to upgrade your fighters for the next challenge round.

TIP

Beat Villains with Villains!

Remember, you can always swap your trapped villains in to play during heavy attack to take some of the heat. Save your Skylanders' strength at the end of a wave by giving them a rest.

Worst Nightmare Marsh (Waves 21–30)

Suggested Skylander Level 10–12

Three new enemy gates are ready to throw you into battle, but first, swap in a Trap Master to smash up the Traptanium Crystal covering one of your two tower spots.

Ooglers begin the fight by flinging damaging lines of electricity across the ground. Jump the lines and take them out quickly. Tombstones will erupt from the ground from Wave 22 onward, releasing bats that slow you down (see Figure 10.9). The bats can be attacked individually, but your efforts are better spent on bigger enemies. If you can destroy the tombstone without risking your Mystery Box or towers, you'll close their gateway so no more can appear.

FIGURE 10.9 A new trap erupts from the ground in Wave 22—a tombstone swarming with bats! They aren't too damaging to your health, but do get in your way.

Pirate Henchmen join in, but can be taken out by the towers. Save your energy for the strongest enemies—they're on their way! Eye Fives will be your first nuisance, as their strong fists are capable of bringing down a tower with just a few hits. As soon as they emerge, race over to attack them. Pain-Yattas are double-trouble as they head straight for your towers and the Mystery Box of Doom in groups of two or three, so send that confetti sky high as you show them who's boss!

As the waves continue, you'll face more enemies and stronger counterattacks to complete each wave (see Figure 10.10). Keep your towers safe, Skylander—soon you'll be swimming in gold!

FIGURE 10.10 Ooglers fling blue ropes of electricity out of their eyes and across the ground to damage your health. Jump over the ropes and knock out the Ooglers from a safe distance.

Twice Doomed Marsh (Waves 31-40)

Suggested Skylander Level 12-15

During Build Phase, you'll find a rock blocking a tower base that can only be broken by a Skylander Giant—if you have a giant, put it on the portal to create a new tower (see Figure 10.11).

During Combat Phase, strong villains head straight for your towers—you'll need to launch into heavy attack mode to get rid of them. There are more bats swarming from tombstones. Smash them up to stop the bats from escaping. The watery marsh is also full of dangerous green traps called Wicked Water. They steal your health, so keep your toes dry!

FIGURE 10.11 A new trick is thrown your way! If you have a Skylander Giant, use him or her to smash up the rock with the Giant symbol on it—an extra defensive tower will come in handy!

Grinnades come out to play in Wave 33. Individually, they aren't too damaging, but they tend to join forces to make a big hit. Watch out for Shield Shredders and their whirring blades near your towers because they make a big impact—join forces with your tower to send them spinning. Staying near your towers (see Figure 10.12) allows you to regenerate your health quickly, as well as protect the towers from bigger enemies that could destroy them in a few hits.

Your big boss fights during this challenge will come from Brawl and Chain, Pain-Yatta, Eye Fives, and Cross Crows. Ooglers will send zapping electric ropes across the ground to add to the craziness. One on its own isn't much trouble, but they are relentless with attacks, so get rid of them as soon as they appear. There are plenty of Pirate Henchmen in this challenge, but your towers will counter them well alone, unless it becomes too outnumbered. Pain-Yattas are a hard-hitting enemy and very fast on their feet, so attack them quickly when they are vulnerable—while doing their happy dance after an attack. Hop to it, Skylander!

FIGURE 10.12 Keep to the center of the towers where you can see all enemy gates. Also, be on hand to defend your Mystery Box of Doom.

Itchy Lilies Marsh (Waves 41–50)

Suggested Skylander Level 13–17

From the swirling, purple mist of the Kaos temples, enemies are preparing to swarm and traps are set underwater to slow you down (see Figure 10.13)! Swap in a Skylanders Giant to smash open one rock-covered Elemental Symbol and set up five new defensive towers. Pirate Henchmen and Eye Fives will come running out to greet you with fists flying. Focus on the Eye Fives first—they do more damage. Jump-rope the Oogler lines moving across the ground. Pain-Yattas will make a mad dash for your towers in Wave 43 onward—these guys are super-fast, so give them all your attention when they appear. After they hit something with the lollipop, they'll do a little victory dance, leaving themselves open to attack.

Brawl and Chains are a super-powerful villain that appear in Wave 43; they have a long reach and can take your towers down very quickly. Use a long-range attack to keep out of harm's way. Evilikin Cannons throw themselves into the fray after Wave 45, but keep your energy for the Eye Fives and Pain-Yattas, which can cause damage most quickly. Protect the Mystery Box of Doom and let your cannons take on the smaller foes (see Figure 10.14). Enemies will come faster and with more force as you work through the waves—this is getting pretty difficult, Skylander! Don't forget to swap in your trapped villain as backup in heavy battles and fight next to your towers to regenerate your health whenever you aren't protecting your Mystery Box.

FIGURE 10.13 Wicked Water floats in the swamp, so keep your feet dry to avoid damage if you can. If you attack these plants, they will disappear, but only bother if there are no big enemies nearby.

FIGURE 10.14 Smaller enemies such as these Grinnades can't do too much damage individually, but a line of them could take down your tower together.

Kaos Fury Docks (Waves 51–65)

Suggested Skylander Level 15–18

The pressure is really on now! Kaos has invented a new machine that builds up pressure during the fight (see Figure 10.15). Each time the trigger reaches its highest point (the red zone), Kaos Fury is unleashed upon the battleground! To ensure that you don't hit Kaos Fury mode, flick the switch on the machine to release the pressure as often as you can (see Figure 10.16). Just the same as in previous waves, you must still defend the Mystery Box of Doom and your two new towers as you battle for glory.

Cuckoo Clockers and Cross Crows begin the battle, and it only takes a couple of minutes for pressure to build up in the Kaos Fury machine. There isn't much room to move in this arena, so stick to the middle so you can reach all areas quickly (see Figure 10.17). Scrap Shooters come out to play, but are pretty slow. From Wave 53 onward, Shield Skeletons, Grinnades, and Grave Clobbers emerge from enemy gates, but again are slow to move. The Grave Clobbers, Scrap Shooters, Krankensteins, and Cross Crows have a very strong attack and can take your towers out super-fast. Attack them hands-on as soon as they appear. Let your towers help you finish the job. If you're quick with taking out the bad guys, you might get through a wave without the Kaos Fury machine hitting the high-pressure zone at all.

FIGURE 10.15 Enemies will become stronger and harder to defeat if the Kaos Pressure Meter hits the red zone.

FIGURE 10.16 Keep an eye on the Kaos Pressure Meter while you defend your towers and the Mystery Box of Doom.

FIGURE 10.17 The attacks grow faster and stronger as you progress through the waves, so take a breather between each one!

Twisted Twister Docks (Waves 66–80)

Suggested Skylander Level 17–20

Smash a Traptanium Crystal during Build Phase to set up your four new towers. In the following 15 waves, the pressure in the Kaos Fury machine builds up quickly, so stay on top of that switch! Raven Warriors and Krankensteins begin the fight. Stick to the big guys to keep your towers safe. From Wave 67 onward, you have a new trap to dodge—a Twisted Spinner (see Figure 10.18)! A whirly-tornado spins around the battle floor wreaking havoc on whatever gets in its way. If you get picked up and spun by one of these traps, you'll be sent scuttling off balance and will take a few seconds to get back on track. Little guys such as Shield Skeletons, Raven Warriors, Brawlruses, Cross Crows, and Grinnades will spread out across the battleground, but most of these can be managed by the towers. It's the giant villains you need to worry about again here—Cuckoo Clockers, Krankensteins, Grave Clobbers, and Pain-Yattas. They may be slow moving (except the Pain-Yattas—they're super-quick!), but these guys all pack a punch you'd rather avoid!

FIGURE 10.18 Beware of Kaos's new trap—the Twisted Spinner! A mini-tornado will pick you up and spin you for a few seconds, taking you out of the fight. If your Mystery Box or towers are under heavy attack, this can mean big trouble.

There are only two enemy gates on ground level, but enemies will drop down from gates on balconies above as well. Keep to the center of the arena, where you have the best view of what area needs attention the most, and remember to leave any dropped food in place at the end of each wave in case you need a quick health boost while fighting (see Figure 10.19). Remember, swap in your villain if you're under heavy fire to give your Skylander a timeout. The closer you get to the final waves, the more giant villains will attack and the faster your small villains will become. Hang in there, Skylander, you're nearly at the end and your reward is well worth the effort!

FIGURE 10.19 Food is often dropped when objects are smashed at the end of each wave. Leave them be until you need the health boost during battle.

Finally Final Docks (Waves 81–100)

Suggested Skylander Level 20

Kaos is about to inflict his worst temper tantrum yet on you—there are five towers to build at the start, and then it's straight into battle! This is a huge fight with 20 waves and a heap of big boss fights (see Figure 10.20). Enemies stream in from up to eight gates this time (eek!), and you'll feel a bit out-numbered! Pain-Yattas, Eye Fives, and Krankensteins will attack in groups of at least four, all at once, so you're likely to lose some towers along the way. Attack them all at once as they move in a line to create maximum damage with minimum effort. Once they spread out across this big battleground, they'll be harder to keep up with. Keep fighting, Skylander! Remember to bring in your trapped villain often and regenerate your health by standing near your towers.

FIGURE 10.20 Oh, no! Lord Kaos is about to throw his most unimaginable DOOM at you! Make it through the toughest challenge of all to win ten stars, a Candy Cane Hat, a treasure hoard, and ultimate glory!

The Kaos Fury Meter will build pressure much more quickly in this challenge, so watch the gauge and dash over to flick the switch as often as you can. Keeping your enemies' fury levels in check is worth losing a tower over! Steer clear of traps like Twisted-Spinners—a few seconds of distraction at a critical point might mean the difference between losing a tower and defeating a new enemy horde (see Figure 10.21). If you're playing with two Skylanders, give one player the task of watching the meter, while another keeps those towers safe. Long-range bombing and fire attacks deal a lot of damage at once and are a fantastic way to smash away the health of big villains, so keep a handy arsenal of Skylanders ready to swap in.

Shield Skeletons, Raven Warriors, Brawlruses, and Grinnades power through the battleground often. Individually, a single tower can defeat them, but they usually attack in packs of six or more, causing huge damage. Fight alongside your towers to share the load of bringing down these troublemakers. Beware of direct attacks by the villain in the Mystery Box of Doom if he is sprung loose—a single hit by this nasty surprise can take your Skylander (or tower) right out of the game.

FIGURE 10.21 Two Twisted-Spinners zoom across the ground now, whipping up a dust storm as they try to knock you off your feet.

As you progress closer to the final waves, the challenge becomes chaotic (see Figure 10.22)! Hordes of enemies charge, towers attack and explode, Twisters twist, and all the while, pressure is building up in the Kaos Fury Meter. It can be tricky knowing which area to look after first on the battle arena. Focus on the big villains and try to keep all the gates in sight so you know which villains are sneaking into the battle. There's plenty of dropped food spinning around to eat on the go to restore your health.

Keep that Mystery Box of Doom safe, and before you know it, you'll be a **Champion** of Kaos Mode, showered with golden coins, gems, and a super-awesome Candy Cane Hat (+20 Critical Hit, +20 Armor, +10 Speed) for your fantastic effort. Brilliant work, Skylander!

FIGURE 10.22 Large enemies should be your highest priority, because they can smash your towers in only a few hits. Attack them near the villain gates as they emerge together for the greatest effect.

Brock's Arena Challenges

Join Brock's Rumble Club through the game menu or by visiting Brock just inside the main door of Skylanders Academy (see Figure 11.1). You can play the arenas on easy, medium, or hard difficulty, but you'll have to make it through each level before you can move onto the next. The challenges become trickier and longer the further you progress. Food will drop from defeated enemies every so often, but leave it on the arena floor until you really need a health boost. The Arena Challenges are a great way to earn gold quickly for upgrades, to practice new attack moves, and to level up your Skylanders.

Brock

Whoa, you are one tough cookie. Er I mean, fighter. One tough fighter!

FIGURE 11.1 Brock loves to create challenges that only the bravest Skylanders would dare to fight. Visit his Rumble Club to put your skills to the test for a reward you'll treasure!

So, are you ready to rumble?

Phoenix Nest

A nest full of chirping baby birds... what could be sweeter?! It's not all sugar and spice in this challenge, as enemy hoards, raining bombs, and pecking beaks all attack you at once while you duck and weave through the Trolls, Chompies, Broccoli Guys, Cuckoo Clockers, Shrednaughts, and cold-hearted Chill Bills in the nest. Phew! Get ready, Skylander—you're about to lose feathers!

Artillery Attack

Pirates are dropping bombs on the giant nest in **Stage 1** (you'll see red targets on the ground showing where they will land). Buzzer Beaks and Tussle Sprouts begin the attack, followed by Plant Warriors. All these guys are fairly easy to defeat, but there are a lot of them. A quick melee attack will keep you safe, but very soon Chill Bills drop in for a visit. Keep your distance from them and dodge the cold air they blast at you—or you'll be put on ice. If you get frozen, mash the controller to break free. Slobber Traps and Broccoli Guys join in the fun, biting and shooting green fireballs. Your reward for getting through Stage 1 is 50 gold coins.

Stage 2 brings a horde of Lob Goblins and their flashing bombs to wreak havoc. Jump up onto the nests where enemies can't reach you and attack from above. Bruiser Cruisers will try to smash you (attack them from behind) and more Chill Bills are on the loose for a 100 gold coin reward. A handful of Chill Bills kick off **Stage 3**, closely followed by a Bruiser Cruiser and Broccoli Guys (see Figure 11.2). This is a short attack, so keep on top of the enemies as they drop in—and make sure you dodge those falling bombs. Soon you'll be another 500 gold coins richer.

Nest Ball

It's Mini-Chompy time! The nest is infiltrated by tiny biting Chompies wearing helmets as **Stage 1** begins, followed closely by Eggsecutioner Trolls. These Trolls need a few extra hits to break away their shell protection before you can bring them down as regular Trolls. There is a special new challenge here as well—a glowing purple and red football that you can pick up (see Figure 11.3). While you are carrying the ball, your Skylander will be bigger, stronger, and faster. If you get hit, the ball will drop and could be picked up by an enemy instead, giving them the advantage. Try to keep the ball for as long as you can to defeat enemies for a reward of 50 gold coins.

Stage 2 brings more of the same villains, but with Broccoli Guys as well. Bombs don't fall as often, but Lob Goblins take aim at you instead! A Shrednaught will try to finish you off at the end of this stage, so attack it from behind to clear the path for **Stage 3** and 100 gold coins. The final waves of Nest Ball introduce Trolls, Chompies, and more Broccoli Guys. Although these villains are a good hit with their green fireballs, you can also use them to your advantage by jumping into the green healing spells they cast across the nest (although enemies can receive a health boost from these, too). Focus on the more dangerous enemies first, such as Cuckoo Clockers, Lob Goblins, and Shrednaughts (from a distance!). You'll receive 600 gold coins for your valiant effort.

FIGURE 11.2 Bruiser Cruiser is the biggest enemy you face in Artillery Attack. Keep out of reach by attacking the machine from behind, but watch out for damage from falling bombs and those (super-cute) baby birds pecking from under their nest.

FIGURE 11.3   Catch that magic football and don't get hit! You'll grow bigger, faster, and stronger in your attacks while you fight with it attached—but so will enemies if they pick it up instead.

Birdy Bombs

Enfuego Chompies and Buzzer Beaks begin **Stage 1** in a fiery battle with baby birds pecking at your ankles from under the nest. In this challenge, there's a new trick to look out for—all enemies drop a bomb when they are defeated, so watch your step (see Figure 11.4)! As soon as you attack, dash away so you aren't left standing with exploding bombs a second or two later. Lob Goblins add more bombs to the mix with Chill Bills and Cross Crows joining for the big finish. Defeat them all for a 50 gold coin reward.

Stages 2 and **3** have more enemies closing in on you. Remember to use the top of the bird nests as a safe spot to stand when you use long-distance attacks. Dash away from bombs left behind when you are fighting hand-to-hand. You'll receive a 100 gold coin reward for **Stage 2** and 700 gold coins after **Stage 3**, where you may have five or six of each smaller enemy in the nest at any one time as well as a few big baddies. Use the bombs that defeated enemies drop to help you clear out crowds of bad guys left behind.

FIGURE 11.4 Every defeated enemy leaves behind a bomb that detonates seconds after they disappear. Use long-distance attacks to avoid them or run away quickly to keep safe from damage.

Perilous Perch Skirmish

There's a fancy hat on offer if you can complete this challenge! Bombs fall constantly from the sky in **Stage 1**, so watch those red targets on the ground as you move around. You'll be faced with heavy enemy attacks by all the same villains you've seen so far. **Stage 2** brings the magic ball back into play for 100 gold coins (see Figure 11.5), which will provide a strong boost to your attacks and give you a faster set of legs. Don't let one of the big guys, such as a Cuckoo Clocker or Bruiser Cruiser, get a hold of it, or you'll be up for a tough fight. **Stage 3** adds enemy bombs to the nest, which they drop as you defeat them. You still have the magic ball to carry (if you can!) but no bombs falling from the sky. The nest becomes a bit chaotic, but keep at it and you'll soon be flying high with a 1000 gold coin reward and a rather pointy Eggshell Hat (+25 Armor) to show off.

FIGURE 11.5 A magic ball, pecking birds, falling and exploding bombs, and some heavy enemies make this a very perilous perch! Use the highest nest as a long-range base and the football for extra strength.

Dream Quake

Hold on tight, the ground is shifting beneath your feet! Cobblestone blocks will break the arena apart and re-join at random intervals. Try to lead your enemies off the edge as you jump across the gaps. There are pet sheep to protect, a Cloning Circle to guard, and the chance to damage your enemies with a shockwave of red light.

Monster Multiplier

Are you seeing double? You will be soon! One of Brock's mage friends has dropped a Cloning Circle onto the arena (see Figure 11.6). If an enemy gets inside, it will replicate itself, creating two enemies to fight instead. To make matters worse, a big bomb will explode if you don't complete the challenge in time!

During **Stage 1**, enemies jump aboard from nearby shacks or float across in bubbles to pop down onto the cobblestone, ready for action. Bird Brains, Lob Goblins, Pirate Chompies, and Chill Bills launch into attack, closely followed by Brawlruses and Bruiser Cruisers. Stick close to the Cloning Circle and protect it from enemies closing in for 100 gold coins. **Stage 2** brings a

150 gold coin reward, as well as some Broccoli Guys and more of the nasty gang you've already faced. Beware of the ground rumbling and jump away as it starts to crack. If you get separated from the Cloning Circle, jump across the gap to defend it. **Stage 3** brings more enemies and faster attacks with Brawl and Chains swinging their metal fists of fury to catch you. Use a long-range attack to take them out for an 800 gold coin reward.

FIGURE 11.6 The yellow target on the arena floor is a Cloning Circle. If an enemy stands inside for a few seconds, it will split into two. Defend the area to reduce the number of villains you have to defeat.

Flag, You're It

Enfuego Chompies and Pirate Henchmen are ready to party on the cobblestone arena in **Stage 1**. There are two flagpoles, one on either end. Stand underneath them and attack enemies to raise the flag to the top. A huge green shockwave will pulse across the ground from your flag pole, damaging enemies in its path (see Figure 11.7). Unless you have two players, defend one flag pole to keep it active. Enemies may take over the other, sending red shockwaves across the ground. Jump over the outer ring as they pass to avoid damage. **Stage 3** brings stronger enemies such as Cuckoo Clockers, Brawl and Chains, and Chill Bills, so keep your distance as you attack. You'll earn 100 gold coins for **Stage 1**, 150 for **Stage 2**, and 900 gold coins for **Stage 3**. Awesome work, Skylander—you're halfway there!

FIGURE 11.7 Stand near the flagpoles to raise the flag, sending a pulse of green light across the arena to damage enemies. If the bad guys take over, the red pulse will hurt you—jump over the waves to stay safe!

Counting Sheep

Three innocent sheep need you to keep them safe. They each wear a brown jacket, which will be knocked off (leaving them white) to show that their health is low. Try to keep all three alive, but you can pass this challenge with only one sheep remaining (see Figure 11.8).

Stage 1 (100 gold coins) brings plenty of Plant Warriors and Enfuego Chompies into the fray, but the real troublemakers are those electric-eyed Ooglers that send ropes of zapping blue electricity across the ground. Jump the ropes to avoid damage and stay close to your sheep at all times. An Eye Five or two will smash their way toward your flock, so bring them down as quickly as possible. (The good news is that they will hit enemies in their way as well!) Bomb Shells explode into **Stage 2** for a 150 gold coin reward as the ground splits into smaller sections. In **Stage 3**, Plant Warriors and Chill Bills head straight for your sheep while Cuckoo Clockers and Eye Fives put up a strong fight. If you manage to keep those sheep alive, you deserve a glittering reward—1000 gold coins should do it! Brilliant work, Skylander!

FIGURE 11.8 Stay near your flock at all times, unless you have to bring down a big villain. Plant Warriors will try to throw your sheep overboard, so watch out! Only one sheep needs to survive to make it through.

Bad Dream Brawl

The final challenge of Dream Quake brings all the previous tricks into play. Get ready for some serious multitasking! **Stage 1** brings a magic ball onto the arena that you can use for extra strength and speed. Cuddles begin the attack (those floppy, long-armed clapping bad guys who want to get a little too close for comfort). They are easy to defeat with a long-range attack, which you'll need for the Bomb Shells that follow as well. Broccoli Guys drop by, but aren't too much of a problem (use their healing circles to your advantage) for 100 gold coins. Eye Scream will shoot eyeball minions across the arena in **Stage 2** (worth 150 gold coins). This time, the magic ball is gone, but you have another three flags to keep shining with green light. Defend a flag to send waves of damage to nearby Brawlrus, Cuddles, and Lob Goblin enemies. As shown in Figure 11.9, waves can cross the entire arena, so it may be a great help or a big hazard (put your jumping shoes on!). A Bruiser Cruiser and Brawl and Chains are the strongest enemies here, so focus your attention on them first. **Stage 3** brings all past villains back together with a

Cloning Circle. Defend it to keep your enemy number down and watch the bomb timer to earn your 1500 gold coins and a super-comfy **Night Cap** (+25 Critical Hit).

FIGURE 11.9   Flag poles must still be defended as the ground splits apart, but be sure to avoid those damaging red waves. If the ground rumbles, lure your enemies toward a crack and jump across as they fall behind you.

Drain of Sorrows

We're back in the Sewers of Supreme Stink for this challenge. Brock has one more trick up his sleeve—each enemy you touch can make you sick! It's impossible to fight here without receiving a counterattack, so you must collect the golden medicine bean to stay healthy. Kick up trouble with another magic ball and defend the flag poles against enemies.

Germ Wars

Enfuego Chompies jump onboard the floating arena from the pipes above for **Stage 1** (worth 100 gold coins), closely followed by Birdbrains brandishing scimitars (long curved swords). A good melee smash will take care of these guys as well as those nasty Lob Goblins that join in. Ooglers, the electric pests that fling ropes across the ground, are back—so be prepared to jump quite often. Take them out as soon as you can to save yourself trouble. Every so often, the Cyclops Slug pops his big-eyed head up, blinks, and then slimes his way across the raft (but where are his eyelashes!?). This slime trail is too wide to jump across safely, so keep away until it disappears (see Figure 11.10), because touching it will damage your health. **Stage 2** brings more of the same villains with added Broccoli Guys for a 250 gold coin bonus. Krankensteins are your main threat during **Stage 3**, with their spinning, extendable arms. If you have a strong long-range attack, this is the guy to use it on to avoid damage (and sickness!). You'll be rewarded 1100 gold coins.

FIGURE 11.10 If you get damage from touching the slime trail, pounce on a golden medicine bean whenever Brock throws one onto the arena to replenish your health.

Sheep Flush

Just like in Counting Sheep of the Dream Quake challenge, there are three hopping sheep in brown jackets to protect (see Figure 11.11). Your raft keeps rising with each wave of villains. Evilikin Cannons spit bombs at you from afar in **Stage 1** (worth 100 gold coins), but you'll have enough time to jump in close, smash them, and run away again. Trolls will try to hit your sheep with a mace. Use a long-range attack on the Bomb Shells and Shield Shredders as they drop down from the pipes, because they can do a lot of damage. **Stage 2** brings more of the same enemies with some Brawlruses shooting starfish at you. The bad guys tend to drop down one or two at a time, so it's pretty easy to keep them at bay. Your reward is another 150 gold coins. Score 1200 gold coins when you complete **Stage 3**—but beware, a Shrednaught will try to steal your sheep before the game is up! Run fast and attack him from behind before he swings his chainsaw toward your precious sheep, because if he hits it, your sheep is gone for good. Awesome work, Skylander—you did it!

FIGURE 11.11 Mary had a little lamb... but you've got three! Protect your flock to keep them safe from enemy attacks. They will change from brown jackets to white wool as their health gets dangerously low.

Sewer-Ball

The magic ball is back with a vengeance! Pick it up to boost your strength and speed. The Cloning Circle is here, too, so watch out for double-trouble! A stampede of Grinnades and Cuddles drop down to kick off **Stage 1**. A long-range attack will help you deal with this challenge. Fisticuffs join in with an extendable metal arm that shoots out, punching everything in its path. Defeat them all to win 100 gold coins and move into **Stage 2** for another 150 gold coins. The Cyclops Slug is back (he may be a toxic goo worm, but he's still pretty cute!), so you'll need to keep off the green slime trail to avoid damage as you fight (see Figure 11.12). **Stage 3** brings more of all the same bad guys and more frequent visits from the friendly slimer, so your fighting space will get smaller and smaller. Slobber Traps attack you with more Fisticuffs and Bomb Shells, so keep those long-range attacks coming. Chill Bills and Brawl and Chains show up for a final showdown worth a whopping 1300 gold coins. Remember that if you get frozen in Chill Bill's icy blast, you can mash the controller (use the same button that you would use to mash open a Treasure Chest) or swap in your trapped villain to break free. There is one more challenge to go, and this Drain of Sorrows will be all washed up!

FIGURE 11.12   The Cyclops Slug loves to pop his blinking head up, give a little wiggle, and then leave a slimy trail of toxic goo across the arena floor, leaving you stranded in small spaces. How thoughtful!

Slime Time Tournament

Keep on your toes, Skylander, because this is tricky! Pirate Henchmen leap into action in **Stage 1** of your next challenge, closely followed by Evilikin Cannons, a few Lob Goblins, and a Broccoli Guy. As you defeat each enemy, they leave behind a bomb that will explode seconds after you dash away. Use these bombs to clean up other enemies standing nearby. Eye Screams pop in for a closer look (literally!), so dodge those bouncing eyeballs. There's a 100 gold coin reward for making it through to **Stage 2**, where you can earn another 150 gold coins. In this challenge, all your enemies have suddenly come down with a sickness they'd love to share with you (oh, yuck!). Keep your eye out for that golden medicine bean that Brock throws onto the arena floor to keep you from losing health. It's time for the big guns to hit the stage! Cuckoo Clocker and Pain-Yattas jump into the fight. These guys are fast! **Stage 3** brings back the flag pole challenge (see Figure 11.13). The arena is smaller than the one in Dream Quake, so damaging pulses reach across the entire floor. There is a magic football to pick up, giving you an edge in your attacks, but you'll have to be fast as it often bounces right over the edge of the raft into toxic goo! Pain-Yattas and Eye Screams are your biggest challenge to face. They're quick to take over your flags, leaving you jumping to avoid the blast. Defeat them all for a very handsome Candle Hat (+25 Elemental Power) and 2000 gold coins!

FIGURE 11.13 Focus on defeating the largest enemies first as you defend one of the flags for your best chance of staying safe. Be prepared to leap over shockwaves in a single bound!

Exhaust Junction

The Cloning Circle is back—and this time it's even harder to defend! In the Troll Stronghold, Brock has taken charge of the stolen rocket. Powerful blasts of fire shoot from the four trapdoors at the front of the arena, filling the yellow target lanes with flames (don't stand there!).

You're MINE

Defeat the enemies, but avoid the explosive mines they leave behind. In **Stage 1**, a Cloning Circle adds an extra challenge, and it's best to keep moving. Whenever the trapdoors lift, dash away from the yellow target lanes before the heat follows (see Figure 11.14). Plant Warriors and those Ooglers (nuisance!) drop in from the gate to begin the fight, leaving bombs in their wake. Blaster-Trons march in and are quite difficult to defeat due to their strong shields. Don't let them reach the Cloning Circle! Dash around the back of them (this is easier with a speedy Skylander or a winged boot) and attack them for 150 gold coins. **Stage 2** (250 gold coins) means more Plant Warriors, Raven Lobbers, and Buzzer Beaks. Hood Sickles sneak up on you with their swinging scythes. Attack them before they do a disappearing act. Broccoli Guys can heal both you and your enemies alike, so it's best to get rid of them if you have no other threats. Use dropped food to restore your health instead. In **Stage 3**, all enemies charge into the arena, including those hard-to-kill Blaster-Trons. Defeat the final Hood Sickle for 1500 gold coins.

FIGURE 11.14 Stay off the yellow target lanes unless you're moving; rocket flames will randomly shoot from the trapdoors leaving fire damage on Skylanders and enemies alike.

Artillery 2: With a Vengeance

Cannonball! Pirate Henchmen, Shield Shredders, and bombs are falling from the sky. Just like the last challenge, random trapdoors open to let off rocket flames, creating an additional hazard. Keep moving, Skylander! Bomb Shells and Pain-Yattas are the biggest enemy you'll face in **Stage 1**, but watch out—they move fast. Earning those first 150 gold coins isn't easy. **Stage 2** has a new round of flames with Scrap Shooters added in. There are lots of projectiles to dodge in this challenge. Try to lead your enemies into the line of rocket fire and save your fighting skills for the biggest villains. A giant, silver Mega Chompy belly-flops into the action, dropping small Chompies each time it falls. As funny as it is to watch, you'll have to take it out with a quick melee or let the flames do the job for a 250 gold coin bonus. **Stage 3** speeds right up! Keep on your toes as explosions and flames limit your movement and more of the same enemies come out to play. There's a small ledge to the left of the arena where the bad guys hide, so jump up and knock them down. It's a good place to wait out the Ooglers and smaller enemies, but watch your head as villains drop down from the window above (see Figure 11.15). Defeat them all for 1500 gold coins and take a well-deserved break. The next challenge is super-hard!

FIGURE 11.15 The small ledge to the left side of the arena serves as a great hiding place, but beware of enemies falling from the open door above.

Don't Get Hit

This challenge is really tough! Brock's mage friend has reduced your health to one point—which means a single hit can end the challenge and you'll have to start all over again. There is a slight bonus—Brock will throw a power-up into the arena for you (this looks like a blue shield). The shield will hold for a single hit, then you're back to your one health point again. Essentially, it's a "two strikes and you're out" rule. In **Stage 1**, Ooglers are a real pest again, especially if you get zapped and lose your shield. Attack them from a distance and beware the rocket flames for 150 gold coins! Bomb Shells, Grinnades, and Pirate Henchmen attack you in large groups during **Stage 2**, with a couple of Pain-Yattas joining the crew (see Figure 11.16).

FIGURE 11.16 Lob Goblins, Raven Lobbers, Bomb Shells, and Grinnades all make for an explosive challenge!

If you need a quick rest, jump up on the left-side ledge and use a long-ranged attack. Once this wave is complete, you'll be rewarded with 250 gold coins and **Stage 3** begins. This is by far the hardest challenge yet, because you may have to wait a few seconds after you lose your shield before a new one appears that you can pick up. Shrednaughts and Pain-Yattas are the big enemies to watch; try to lure them across the arena to reach you so they get caught in the rocket flames for a 1900 gold coin bonus. Well done, Skylander! You're really proving your mettle now!

Flaming Flag Finale

You have your health back in **Stage 1** of this challenge (thank goodness, that last one was tricky!). A single flag appears in the center of the arena, which you must defend from enemies. Goo Chompies and Fisticuffs start the battle. Jump aside when the Fisticuffs punches their extendable metal arms. Attack them from the side before they have a chance to withdraw (see Figure 11.17). Cross Crows sneak attacks from the left-side ledge, so dash over and get rid of them to stop the arrows flying. Don't stay away from the flag pole for too long, though, because enemies will take over your post and create red shock-waves that damage your health. A 150 gold coin reward is yours when you succeed.

FIGURE 11.17   Jump aside to avoid the extendable arm on Fisticuffs; then attack them from the side before they strike again.

Stage 2 (worth 250 gold coins) switches the playing field to two new flag poles, so it's tricky to defend both. Cannonballs rain down from above, and Goo Chompies drop in from the right-side balcony. Stick to the right to ensure enemies have to cross hazardous flames to reach you, hopefully knocking some of them out along the way. You will be dropped back to one health point and a shield for **Stage 3**, which makes this challenge super-tricky! There is a single flag pole in the center of the arena, so you'll want a strong long-range attack to survive this one. Fisticuffs descend three at a time to surround your flagpole. Step back to avoid their arms and take them out from the side. Jump those red shockwaves and dodge the flames. Chompies and Cross Crows are hiding along the sides of the arena; only take them out once the big guys are all gone. For your spectacular skill, you've earned a massive 3000 gold coins and a dizzying Planet Hat (+10 Speed).

Quicksand Coliseum

The ancient coliseum of the Golden Queen is open for battle! Brock has installed a dangerous laser-eye statue at the front of the arena that zaps lines of damage onto the sand. Hordes of enemies are waiting to hit, bomb, and bite you as you battle it out on the swirling quicksand of this new arena.

MightyBall Bombardment

Stage 1 begins with falling cannonballs (look for the targets on the ground) and a horde of Plant Warriors. A magic ball is bouncing around for extra speed and strength. Remember, if you get hit, the ball will drop and an enemy could pick it up. Watch your step! An enormous Chompy mouth emerges from the swirling quicksand in the middle of the arena, dragging anyone nearby into its bite. This is great for losing a few enemies, but you'll have to run fast to escape if you're caught. Stick to the edges of the arena whenever the quicksand begins to swirl. Lob Goblins jump into the fray, but there's lots of room to move here, so you should be able to avoid them quite easily. When you see a cloud of dust rising up, it signals an emerging Tombstone (see Figure 11.18). The lid opens to throw out Tussle Sprouts. Defeat them all for 150 gold coins and progress to **Stage 2**.

FIGURE 11.18 Tombstones emerge from the sand and fling enemies into the fight. Look out for the dust clouds before the tombstone rises and smash it up to keep the bad guys from escaping.

It's laser time! The eye of Brock's statue shoots a line of fire along the sand closest to the tower. Watch the eyes of the tower—they light up before it strikes. Cannonballs and smaller enemies keep coming, but it's the giant Eye Fives that mean trouble. Take them out for 250 gold coins. **Stage 3** brings Shield Skeletons and Hood Sickles, Broccoli Guys, and more Eye Fives. Take care of the big guys and lure the little ones into the laser path for a quick reward of 2500 gold coins.

Multiplication Fever

Cloning Circles and sick enemies are back! Don't get hit, or your health will suffer. **Stage 1** begins with a ground-shattering tombstone full of Brawlruses (smash the tombstone to stop enemies from appearing). Pirate Henchmen and Broccoli Guys try to reach the Cloning Circle, so defend it as best as you can. A golden medicine bean will restore your health if you get hit. If you happen to fall into the Giant Chompy's mouth, you will take damage, but he'll disappear again before your Skylander is completely out of health. Defeat all the enemies for a reward of 150 gold coins.

Pirate Chompies, Evilikin Cannons, Slobber Traps, and Pirate Henchmen fill the arena in **Stage 2**. All enemies can be defeated with hand-to-hand attacks, so grab that magic ball and hop to it! In this final stage, a double-dose of Eye Fives leap from emerging tombstones as the lasers reach ever closer to the outer edge you are defending (see Figure 11.19). Lure the biggest enemies into the quicksand as a Giant Chompy snack—250 gold coins are waiting on the other side of this wave.

FIGURE 11.19 Brock's statue shoots a laser beam from its eyes onto the sand in front. As you pass each game in Quicksand Coliseum, the laser beam reaches further back into the arena until no area is safe.

Brawlruses and Evilikin Cannons leap into action during **Stage 3**. Eye Fives will try to get hold of that golden medicine bean to increase their health. Stick to the edge of the arena, away from the lasers and quicksand—don't worry, the enemies will come to you! Your reward is 2700 gold coins for a job very well done!

Flames and Flags Forever

Stage 1 of the Flag Defense Challenge begins with a single flag pole to defend. Sounds easy, right? Unfortunately, it is positioned straight under the laser beam! You're in the line of fire now, Skylander, so watch your back. A tombstone erupts, throwing the arena into chaos with Enfuego Chompies and Shield Skeletons. The damage they create isn't too bad, but clear the decks as quickly as possible because nastier villains (including Scrap Shooters) are on their way. A Blaster-Tron jumps in to shoot its laser gun and reclaim the flag pole. Take him out to earn a 150 gold coin bonus.

There are two flag poles to guard in **Stage 2** and a Bad Juju to distract you with wicked spells (see Figure 11.20). Blaster-Trons leap from tombstones and are difficult to defeat. A floating bomb will appear; collect and launch it toward your biggest enemies for a 250 gold coin win. **Stage 3** brings one more flag pole, so you have three flags now to raise and protect. This can get tricky—if you're having trouble, just focus on defending one and jump the red shockwaves that come from the other two. More of the same enemies come in, but faster and stronger than before. You can do this, Skylander—keep fighting; there's only one more challenge in Quicksand Coliseum.

FIGURE 11.20 Protect your flags to make damaging shockwaves against enemies, but beware of raining cannonballs and laser-beam attacks.

Scorched Sand Showdown

A giant bomb ticks down from four minutes in the centre of the arena during **Stage 1**, surrounded by enemies. Shield Skeletons, Lob Goblins, and Ooglers attack first, leaving mines in their place when defeated. Grave Clobbers leap in, so attack them as they pull up straight, before their hands smash down again—150 gold coins await you! **Stage 2** brings the Cloning Circle back and, as shown in Figure 11.21, the very toothy grin of the Giant Chompy in quicksand. (Don't smile back, he might just eat you!) Protect the Cloning Circle from quick-moving Pain-Yattas. They are large enough to escape from the Giant Chompy's bite, but if they get caught in the quicksand, their health will still deplete rapidly. At the end of **Stage 3**, Brock gives you a one-shot challenge—this means you're back down to one point of health!

FIGURE 11.21 A Giant Chompy in the center of the arena is looking for a tasty snack. Beware of the swirling quicksand that will drag you down to dinner!

Shield Skeletons and Ooglers will attack first (grab that shield for protection), so be careful of the blue ropes of electricity moving across the ground. Grave Clobbers will drop into the arena and try to clone themselves. Watch out for the laser beam as it moves further toward the back of the arena—no area is safe now! A Skylander with a strong long-range attack will come in handy here. This is a difficult fight with lots of enemies. The final Pain-Yattas to fall bring a huge reward of 5000 gold coins (you earned that!) and an all-seeing Pyramid Hat (+20 Critical Hit, +10 Armor).

Brock's Rumble Clubhouse

Brock has his very own arena! Get ready for some serious rumbling and tumbling with enemies galore, flames, lasers, and rebounding bombs.

The Flame Game

Enfuego Chompies, Birdbrains, and Evilikin Cannons begin **Stage 1**, leaping down from overhead walkways. There are eight metal grates that circle the floor of the arena, bringing new enemies from underground. Often, fire blasters will rise up on these platforms instead and shoot flames, which limit your ability to move (see Figure 11.22). Don't get caught in the cross-fire! As long as you don't damage your health in the unpredictable flames, these blasters really just serve to break up the arena floor into sections, making it difficult to reach enemies. Your reward for getting through the first wave is 200 gold coins.

FIGURE 11.22 Try to lure enemies into the path of flaming torches to reduce their health; then finish them off for a smashing good time!

For **Stage 2** (worth 300 gold coins), Threatpacks and Bombshells launch bombs—this challenge will really keep you on your toes! **Stage 3** introduces Transformed Barrels, which can bring a spot of good luck. These little blue stone barrels with fire hair stand back and throw bombs at you. A red target with a green center will appear on the ground where the bomb is going to land. Jump into the green center to catch the bombs and then throw them at your enemies instead. When all enemies are down, you'll score a whopping 4000 gold coin bonus!

Combusti-Ball

It's pinball time! For **Stage 1**, you're back in Brock's arena with some Threatpacks, Chill Bills, and Cuddles, but this time, three pinball bumpers rise up with the grated platforms, acting as a bounce pad for all the bombs and weapons flying across the room. This means you can now get hit from any direction. Stand behind the bumpers to dodge attacks if you need a time-out, but beware of big enemies such as Eye Fives, Eye Screams, and Grave Clobbers that can track you down. A Skylander (or villain) with a strong long-range attack would be handy to have up your sleeve in this challenge.

After scoring 200 gold coins, you can move on to **Stage 2** (worth another 300 gold coins), which clears the deck again and then raises four pinball bumpers to contend with. Bumpers don't prove too much of a hazard unless the projectiles are flying horizontal, from one side of the arena to another. Chompies, Raven Lobbers, and Broccoli Guys join the fight. The most difficult enemy you'll face in this challenge is the Cyclops Dragon (see Figure 11.23). It takes a lot of damage to be defeated, so focus all your attacks on bringing it down. Beware of the flying eyeball minions, too! In **Stage 3**, cannons will launch a barrage of bombs into a high arc above the arena. They crash down and explode all over the ground, so it's almost impossible not to get hit. Stick to the outside ring of the arena to stay safe; then duck into the middle to battle bad guys whenever you can. Cuckoo Clockers and Eye Fives smash into action, followed by more of the same enemies you've already fought. Two Cyclops Dragons attack in a final showdown for 4500 gold coins. That was a huge effort, Skylander. Well done!

FIGURE 11.23 The Cyclops Skeleton has a lot of health to work through and releases damaging flying eyeballs. Focus on bringing down the dragon and the eye minions will end, too.

Laser Invader

Whoa! **Stage 1** of this battle jumps straight into madness mode, with a heap of enemies dropping in for a skirmish. Buzzer Beaks, Grinnades, Cuddles, Ooglers (grrr!), and little running eyeballs hit center stage in all their glory. These guys are fairly easy to take out individually, but two damaging laser beams also zap across the floor, making the battle more difficult. Be prepared to jump! Another round of enemies brings Brawl and Chain and Tae Kwon Crow. They are tricky to beat when the battle field switches to include three new lasers for a 200 gold coin reward.

An explosive wave of Lob Goblins, Grinnades, and lasers follows in **Stage 2**. Shrednaughts follow you around the arena with whirring chainsaws. You'll need to be quick on your feet to hop over the lasers to reach behind the machine and attack it. Four lasers come up from the grates (see Figure 11.24), changing direction constantly. This battle is not for the faint-hearted! Grave Clobbers, Eye Fives, and Bomb Shells are the biggest villains in the arena, but if you can defeat them, you'll score another 300 gold coins.

FIGURE 11.24 Lasers are the most difficult weapon to avoid as they sweep across the arena quite quickly. Stick to the outer edges to avoid the cross-over beams, which make jumping difficult.

In the final waves of **Stage 3**, Cuckoo Clockers and Pain-Yattas attack you in packs. Circle around the outside of the arena, where you are safer from the lasers, and then run across the center, jumping laser beams so that the big guys follow you. They'll take damage as the lasers double-hit them. A lot of melee fighting is required in this last stage, so choose a strong, fast Skylander because you might have to jump over up to seven laser beams at a time. Take out the Cyclops Dragon in a final showdown to win 5000 gold coins.

A Fight to Remember

This arena is getting mighty crowded (see Figure 11.25)! Remember, though, there is a whopping 25,000 gold coin prize if you make it, so get those Skylanders ready! **Stage 1** will shoot Chompies from cannons and bring hordes of Shield Skeletons, Mega Chompies, Eggsecutioners, Raven Lobbers, Chomp Chests, Sheep Creep, Transformed Barrels, and Evilikin Spinners (wait until they stop spinning to attack). The grates will raise fire torches, lasers, and pinball bumpers alternately, with up to seven firing all at once. Run to the outer ring of the arena if you need a break, but stick to the areas just behind the grates to avoid more flames shooting randomly from the fence line. When big enemies such as Bruiser Cruisers and Cuckoo Clockers come to play, lure them into the fire or lasers to deplete their health before you finish them off for 200 gold coins.

FIGURE 11.25 Pinball bumpers, lasers, and flames combine to make this one very tough rumble! Watch out for random flames shooting up from the fence line.

Stage 2 is more of the same, with a barrage of smaller enemies and a faster rotation of lasers, flames, or bumpers. A Cyclops Dragon rages in last to finish the wave with another 300 gold coin bonus. The final fight (you're nearly there!) for **Stage 3** combines lasers, flames, and bumpers within each wave, with a few Scrap Shooters, Bruiser Cruisers, and Cyclops Dragons added in for good measure. There is no way of predicting which weapon will rise next, so just hang in there. The waves are longer than previous challenges. Remember to swap in your villain if your Skylander is getting low on health and save any dropped food until you really need it. The ultimate reward will soon be yours—25,000 gold coins (wow!) and a magical Wizard Hat (+10 Critical Hit, +10 Speed).

The Sky's the Limit!

Congratulations! As the newest Portal Master in Skylands, a great task was put upon your shoulders by Master Eon, and you have succeeded every step of the way! Using your magic Traptanium Portal, you have brought the Trap Team back from their earthly exile. Like a true champion, you learned to wield their powerful Traptanium weapons to end the destruction that threatened Skylands. Those evil escapees from Cloudcracker Prison have been recaptured and locked away—even the greedy Golden Queen and Dark Portal Master Kaos were no match for you!

With your guidance, courage, and skill, this brave team of heroes is now free to serve Skylands once more, protecting the innocent Mabu and other peaceful creatures. And the best news is—Skylander Academy is now open for business!

You've flown, swam, ran, jumped, bounced, and teleported all the way to the end of the game—but don't think this means it's the end! Oh, no! There's a whole lot more to discover in Skylands!

Congratulations! You defeated the horde of evil Doom Raiders that were terrorizing the inhabitants of Skylands. Not only that, but by completing their villain quests, those trapped troublemakers have turned over a new leaf!

During your Trap Team journey, you've fought hundreds of bizarre creatures, including mace-wielding Troll Warriors, eyeball-popping Cyclops Dragons, zapping Ooglers, blazing Chompies, and sword-swishing Birdbrains. There were slobbery, spikey, feathery, and freezing villains along the way. You've overcome bombs and cannons, scimitars, toxic goo, and lava balls.

But, you're not finished, Skylander! In fact, this is just the beginning!

Skylanders Trap Team offers a whole world of new adventures. By collecting your favorite characters, you can learn different tricks and master attack moves, visit Persephone to fully upgrade your abilities, and play through chapters again to triumphantly complete all the Villain Quests.

Brock is always ready to rumble in the arena, or perhaps you dare to take on Kaos in the Doom Challenges? Strap on your dancing shoes with the Skaletones gang, or put on your thinking cap for a game of Skystones Smash. Try to beat your personal best time for playing through story chapters and collect all of the magical hats, winged sapphires, and legendary treasure along the way. Battle villains together with a friend or simply explore the hidden secrets of Skylander Academy on the trail for gold and glory. There are so many magical places to discover, you'll never run out of things to do.

Keep exploring, Skylander—the sky's the limit!

Skylander Academy is officially open. Your bravery and epic skills will be renowned throughout Skylands forevermore!

Appendix

Lock Puzzle Cheats

If the Lock Puzzles are getting too tricky, take a peek at the cheat codes in this appendix. These cheat codes are just some of the many routes to escape a (single-player) Lock Puzzle. They don't include collecting coins or treasure on the way, but take you directly to the exit. Don't forget—it's always handy to buy a Lock Puzzle Key from Auric's shop at Skylander Academy, just in case you find a puzzle that is just too tricky to get past. Have fun!

Chapter 3: Chompy Mountain

Mountain Falls Lagoon

Puzzle 1: Right, up.

Puzzle 2: Right, up, left, down, down.

Undead Vista

Puzzle 1: Right, left, down, left, up, left. Right, right.

Chapter 5: Chef Zeppelin

Top Shelf

Puzzle 1: Down, up, down, right. Up, down, up, right, left, right, down, left. Up, down, up, down. Left, right, left, right, left, right, left, right, down.

Chopping Block

Puzzle 1: Left, up, right, down, left, up, left, up, right, down.

Chapter 7: Monster Marsh

Spirestone Grotto

Puzzle 1: Left, right, down, right, down, up, left, right, up, up.

The Misty Marshes

Puzzle 1: Down, right, up, down, left, up, left.

Puzzle 2: Right, down, up, right, down, up. Left, down, right, down. Right, left, down, up, down.

Smugglers Hideout

Puzzle 1: Up, right, up, right. Left, down, right, down, up, left, down, up, right, left, down, up, down, left, up.

Chapter 8: Telescope Towers

Spiral Observatory

Puzzle 1: Down, left, down, left, down, left, up. Right, down, right, down. Left, up, left, down. Left, down, left, down, right, up. Up, right, down, left, up, left. Down, left, down left, down, right. Up, right, down.

Spiral Balcony

Puzzle 1: Right, up, left, up, left, down, right, up. Right, up, left, down, left, down, right, left. Up, right, up, left, up.

Chapter 10: Secret Sewers of Supreme Stink

Outer Sewage Segue

Puzzle 1: Right, left, down, left, down.

Puzzle 2: Left, up, left, down, right, down. Right, up, left, down, right, down, left.

Puzzle 3: Up, left, up, right. Up, right, right, down, up, left.

Chapter 14: Operation: Troll Rocket Steal

Southeast Tower

Puzzle 1: Right, down, left, down. Right, down, right, down, right. Left, down, down, left, down, left. Up, down, right, down, right, up. Left, down, left, up, down, right, down, right, down, right.

Battlements 1

Puzzle 1: Down, right, down, right. Left, up, left, down. Right, up.

Puzzle 2: Down, right, left, down, left. Down, left, down, right, up. Left, down, right, down.

Puzzle 3: Up, right, down, right. Left, up, down, right, up, right, down, left, up.

Battlements 2

Puzzle 1: Left, down, up, up. Down, right, left, down, left. Right, up, left, up, up.

Puzzle 2: Up, left, down, left, down, right, up, left, up, right. Down, right, up, left, up, left, up.

Puzzle 3: Up, left, left, up. Right, right, down, left. Up, left, down. Left, up, right, left, down.

Northeast Tower

Puzzle 1: Left, up, left, down, right, down, right, right, up, up, left.

Chapter 16: The Golden Desert

Hole in the Wall

Puzzle 1: Left, down, right, down. Left, up, left, up. Down, left, up, right, up, left, up, left, down.

The Golden Springs

Puzzle 1: Left, up, right, down, left. Up, right, down, left, up. Left, up. Right, down, left, up, left, down, right.

Chapter 17: Lair of the Golden Queen

The Seat of Flowing Gold

Puzzle 1: Up, left, down, left. Down, right, down, left. Down, right, down, left. Down, right, up, right. Down, right, up, left. Up, right, up, right, up.

Chapter 18: The Ultimate Weapon

Matter Refactoring Room

Puzzle 1: Down, up, down, down. Right, down, left, up. Up, right, down. Left, right, up, left. Down, right, up, left, down.

Puzzle 2: Up, right, down. Right, left, down, right, up, left. Down, left. Right, up. Right, down, up, left, down, right, down.

Puzzle 3: Right, up, down. Down, up, down. Left, up, left. Down, right, down, right, down. Up, left, down.

Chapter 20: Sunscraper Spire

Under Island Maintenance Area

Puzzle 1: Right, up, left, down, right. Up, left, right, down, right, up. Down, left, down, right, down, left. Up, left.

Chapter 21: Nightmare Express

Cliffside Sanctuary

Puzzle 1: Right, up, down, right, up. Left, down, right, down, right. Up, left, down, left, up.

Puzzle 2: Right, down, up, down. Left, up, down, up. Left, up, left, right, up. Left, right, down, left, up, left. Left, right, left, up, left.

F

G

I

J

K

Q–R

U

X–Y–Z